PHARAOH'S DREAM

BY THE SAME AUTHOR

Deliberate Regression
Eccentric Spaces

PHARAOH'S DREAM

THE SECRET LIFE OF STORIES

ROBERT HARBISON

Secker & Warburg
London

First published in England 1988 by
Martin Secker & Warburg Limited
Michelin House
81 Fulham Road, London SW3 6RB

Copyright © 1988 by Robert Harbison

British Library Cataloguing in Publication Data

Harbison, Robert
    Pharaoh's dream: the secret life of
    stories.
    1. Imagination   2. Originality (in
    literature)
    I. Title
    801'.92   PN56.145

ISBN 0-436-19139-3

Printed in Great Britain by
Richard Clay Ltd, Bungay, Suffolk

Grateful acknowledgement is made to The Society for the Humanities at Cornell University and the Ingram Merrill Foundation for help and encouragement.

Further back, I learned the Bible stories from my grandmother and can't think of stories for long without thinking of her.

CONTENTS

FOR AARON

PROLOGUE

This book has two themes, a receding and an emergent one. It traces the decline of magical thinking and the rise of the individual. At first it seems to us that the two are contraries; by the end we are made to wonder. For it is a story which has an end, in an extended moment around the time of the First World War, when the idea of the individual loses its validity as a basis for art.

But at that point, where the human subject breaks up at the moment of intensest realization in Musil, Joyce, Proust, and Kafka, there occurs an uncanny convergence of the subtlest subjectivism with primitive modes of thought.

Perhaps it is the collision of opposites, which only looked like fusion because the collapse of the subject was so much quicker than its birth, seven centuries growing, less than one disintegrating. Perhaps Proust's sophistication and his superstition do not mix, but lie uneasily side by side. There are two main ways one could pursue the story after him, experimental fiction or prison memoirs, an exciting dead end or a bleak hole.

The book is founded on an untestable faith in a primitive stuff of narrative, from which all later stories are descended. The extreme form of this idea is an absolutely first story, the Adam of the later races of fiction. If such an ancestor cannot actually be discovered, we come nearer at some times than others to guessing what he was like.

This feeling that stories go back incalculably far into man's past has prompted me to search for narrative's pre-literary roots in religious and mythical practice. Habits which we regard as tricks of thought or poetry had their origins or have their cousins in behaviour, in a prior time in which fiction and action are not clearly separated.

Magical rituals survive in the most rationalized cultures. Christmas trees are a late rediscovery, but the lateness only proves that susceptibilities to magical thought may lie dormant for centuries, springing up again at very slight stimulus, like the larvae of certain parasites waiting between the floor-boards of an uninhabited house and awakened by a new tread.

Rituals are rarely as complete as stories, as if they were only part of a lost perfection, were misreported stories. We meet them damaged by use, like furniture carried through doorways until excrescent bits are knocked off. They wake one, though, to powers dormant in fiction because they coerce the participant in a different way. So they challenge the onlooker at narrative to work out the consequences for thought in general of the oddities of the tale.

Some of the first stories are ruined too, deformed by different processes from ritual which relies on physical transmission and preserves sometimes the letter without its meaning. Chances are better with stories that if the letter survives the meaning can be recovered, but anyone familiar with oral texts later transcribed can summon up many examples of garbling: duplications, doublings back, hiatuses.

The oldest literary artifact, *Gilgamesh*, is already the copy of a copy, having traversed a language or two and some centuries, before arriving at the form in which we read it, a microcosm of the problem of origins. We relish the glimpses, half-effaced, of earlier Sumerian forms of the epic, but must finally accept that some stages in the genesis of this organism will remain obscure. The oldest beginnings of the history of self are lost and yet even the polished *Gilgamesh* shows us individual identity in a gaseous state, before the protagonists feel the urge to define themselves. A rivalry is required in order for the story to occur. And when the opponents which the nebulous hero seeks have materialized, all remains utterly subjected to time, the dimly understood demon of the story, which is barely *seen* yet.

So the story ends with the hero's death. The novelty of Genesis is that it makes a story, and not simply a list, of the lives of successive generations and this, paradoxically, is how the individual acquires importance, by being set off against those he replaces and those who will replace him.

Doubtless there are other routes to a deeply moral point of view but in Genesis the essential constituents are kinds of division: a nature composed of foreign and native elements: though he lives here, Abraham considers that his real home is elsewhere. A sensibility whose sympathies are often divided: Isaac wins, and immediately we feel a pang for Esau. And – the most universal form of the dilemma – a belief that to find the truth, one must invert the world's judgments: success and righteousness are not friends.

The rest of mankind was a long time catching up with the complexity of this moral world. Its near contemporary, Greek myth, is more primitive, hence more lost and alluring to us. Superficially it is their violence which distinguishes the myths – dismemberment without the excuse of sacrifice, coarse transformation to beasthood, rape, infanticide. But these are only species of a ruling category: paradox or contradiction. The myths are forms of acceptance of much which is atrocious or discontinuous in man's experience. So hatred and violence are made beautiful, the alien becomes positive, and a clarity we associate with later cultural phases consorts with lack of inhibition usually reserved for those who cannot see clearly.

The oldest Norse story material seems kin to the Greek in its savagery, yet a further bifurcation appears: there are spontaneous ecstasies of bloodshed, and there is working out a method of payment afterwards, the revelry and the hangover. A new kind of protagonist is generated by this sequence, the tenacious sufferer for whom disaster is a spur to self-realization, an alternative, sometimes female, to the free but doomed hero whose fatal acts of expression are prescribed to him.

Beowulf provides a fascinating coda to this development, a softened monster story whose sensitivity to weather goes hand in hand with Christianized anxiety, which finally locates evil in the self, not in the anomalous dragons who dot the landscape and come in the end to seem no more than the exhalations of human greed. The goal is reached by a longer, more complex path, but the savage tradition has now arrived at a view like that of Genesis.

In later knightly fictions the process of internalization is carried onward. Chrêtien de Troyes is an important watershed, perhaps the greatest, in the history of European narrative, because all the constituents of future centuries of development appear there in germ: women and the peripheries of action as the foci of the story, the double plot as enforcer of relativism.

Heroes in Chrêtien are often unauthorized, setting off without telling anyone, or getting separated from the main party. A reader is liable to exaggerate the amount of space given over to women because he knows what the future of narrative holds, but they are already a subversive element, insinuating such doubts as 'What is happening behind that door?' 'What are they doing back at the castle?' It is one of those moments, which occur in any history, when the forewarned observer meets an artifact which teems with multiplied potential.

It wasn't very soon made actual. The great summarizer of the Arthurian material in English is an impossible archaist. Yet no history is free of retreats and backslidings, and in spite of himself Malory marks a stage in narrative's long descent to ordinary lives, gradually coming to match everyday experience more exactly. Malory is the Parsifal of tellers, stripping narrative of its hieratic remoteness but preserving a quotient of the old power through ignorance, in the form of questions unanswered, magic half naturalized.

The *Romance of the Rose* is an even more striking mixture of old and new, revolutionary in putting subjective matters at the centre, antiquated in the petrified form it gives them. The strange plan did not work, allegory and the amorphous interior of passion were too far apart, and the original author broke off, to be replaced by his antitype, so that the work as we have it consists of obverse and reverse, the vision and its refutation.

Better than any other writer, Dante saw the existential point of allegory and was able to naturalize it. *La Vita Nuova* awakens a hunger for allegory, which it is careful not to satisfy. This work is a moment of poise between subjective and cosmic visions, a comprehensiveness beyond the powers of its successors.

Chaucer seems more modern than Dante to us, because he comes down on the subjective side of this equilibrium. *Troilus and Criseyde* is intensely psychological – in Dantean perspective a crippling limitation: reality isn't psychological; our experience is. So Chaucer's relativist, ironic view exercises an overpowering pull on us who are still in the spiritual situation he first articulated. His other works give us pause: the marvellous armature of the *Canterbury Tales* shows that subjectivism remained for him less intoxicating than we find it, a special lesson, not the world's main truth.

English literature must be richer in unashamed archaism than any other. Sidney and some of his Elizabethan contemporaries are more medieval than Chaucer, but it is a desperate medievalism, superstition becoming rigid in apprehension of its foe. The *Arcadia* is an anti-narrative about magic on the verge of losing its faith, a last fantastic fling.

The *Faerie Queene* looks like its friend, but deep down is more like its enemy. Another endless fiction, but saddened and made responsible, not noisy clashes but slow and imperceptible healing, moving backward as much as forward, not in frivolous intricacy of mind but in the ceaseless self-inspection of a Protestant conscience in embryo.

Hamlet is a character in a play, which seems a natural place for personality to come apart into discontinuous flashes, a series of separate views it is hard to make into one, but he is the ancestor of many more creatures in fiction than drama. His creator broke open many moulds – madness as a reservoir of insights one of his best departures from common wisdom – and Shakespeare's whole career is like the history of narrative in miniature: from self-conscious artifice through naturalism to childlike resumption of the stilted equipment of primitive art, a second infancy at the other end of life.

Bunyan is not such a transcender of self, and for him the bottom has dropped out of the idea of fiction, which is tolerable only as the flimsy vehicle for an important journey. The incidents a traveller meets along the way are phantoms or thin disguises, and the story something to be put behind him.

Pilgrim's main descendants are feminine, harmless outlaws like Marivaux's Marianne threading the traps of the world, prisoners and adventurers at once. Richardson raises these contradictions to an inspired pitch: Pamela's hypocrisy is a landmark in fiction, born of the need to marry Puritan sensibility and worldly success, a conflict which continues to animate late descendants like Henry James and Proust.

Richardson's absurd yet captivating idea of truth brings us into a fevered intimacy with his herione, which becomes one of the main objects of such narratives, to feel every nameless tremor in the internal life of some timid creature. Admittedly Gothic novels are a debased genre, as is confirmed by their long afterlife as a subspecies of melodrama. But if finally exploitative they are initially profound, a Freudian revelation before its time. They are like a reconstruction of belief by a non-believer who must perforce rehouse all the antique demons in the psyche, because there's nowhere else for them to go.

Books could be written about the pseudo-scientific early-Romantic interest in superstition. Both Kleist and Hawthorne would have important places in them, the first a defiant, the second a forlorn declaimer of alienation from his chosen materials, hypnotized by evil. The end of this line is Kafka, the victim fatally attracted to power, whose greatest ingenuities are destructions, whose de-imagining of reality has all the force of magic. Transcendent visions of our century (*Finnegans Wake*, Heidegger, *The Waste Land*) swallow themselves more often than one might expect, though few are as resiliently defeatist as Kafka's.

In Stendhal it appears that rhetoric may save what metaphysics has lost, but by the end of *Chartreuse de Parme* most readers come to feel it is really ego which holds it together, in spite of archaic trappings borrowed from sixteenth-century chronicle and relocated in a tiny nonexistent state where one makes the rules, as a writer does in his lonely garret. On the page, at least, an ideal marriage is arranged between enthusiasm and irony, cynicism and simplicity, however schizoid it seems as a literal recipe.

More aggressively provincial works (Flaubert's, or Leopoldo Alas') provide more perfect instances of pervasive irony, in stories set in former capitals, whose characters get their inspiration from stories, for whom idealism becomes a definite pathology. And there are even further stages than this, more refined observers lodged in more remote backwaters, like Machado de Assis in old Brazilian society, where life fails to occur, so that all meaning inheres in unused possibility.

It has been a complaint or the proudest boast that in late Henry James one remains uncertain whether any thing has happened. The centre of *The Wings of the Dove* isn't a solid body, but a Holy-Ghost aura, a dying girl who fades while still unformed. It is hard not to take such internalization literally (and thus nihilistically) when it is presented as suppression: the main contract in the book collapses over the unread contents of a letter. In a world as ineffable as that, we find ourselves driven back surprisingly often onto the shoals of gossip.

Wherever one imagines the journey into the self (the essential story of European narrative) to have begun in earnest, with Chrêtien, Chaucer's Troilus, or with Richardson, many would agree that by the early twentieth century we are near the final limit of individual personality as a basis for fiction. Proust's work is the crowning instance of the submersion of plot in sensibility. Now events in their bareness don't really exist any more. In remembering Proust one remembers tonalities, sensations, tableaux (a child upstairs, the grownups below; the narrator spying on two girls on a sofa from his position on a grassy bank) but it would be the most unnatural feat to recite the story.

Not that there isn't one, and that we wouldn't read a summary with avid interest, but that it has been heavily disguised and deeply buried in someone's reflections and sensations. So the work is long and serendipitous, containing shreds of a system which will never coalesce, giving equal weight to mistakes and the truth, if not positively preferring the former. In fact Proust's book is the ultimate vindication of human error as a superior form of reality, because in its severance from practical attachments, error gives purer expression to the personality which produces it.

Of all books Proust's is the most deftly folded back on itself. It ends with the decision to write it, and as he has just traversed it and been overcome by it, the reader is ready to grant the momentousness of such an existence looming on the horizon. The climax of the greatest subjective work comes when the protagonist receives the call or signal that it is now time to begin pulling out the story from within, like retracing a labyrinth. The past, everything which has been told, is ratified by the decision to tell it. Literature is the confirmation of the self, but the extreme subjectivism of our approach to this goal has undermined the carefree existence of verbal art. It leads one to anticipate a breed of works in which literature is the hero, and these do in fact appear. Like English drama after Shakespeare, fiction after the development which culminates in Proust seems bereft and awash in used up possibility.

As he approaches the present, the historian becomes a special pleader, preferring one course to another because he thinks he can see where it is tending. After Proust there are two paths: the abstract and the human, the first represented by Joyce, Musil, Pynchon, and experimental fiction, where the reader is denied the old comfort of characters to hold onto. The other path starts at a different nadir, not the exhaustion of realist art, but the disgusting reversion of reality itself in the early twentieth century from hard-won civilization to primitive savagery.

Out of such artificial hells as the German and Russian prison camps comes the most hopeful twentieth-century genre. The quintessential literature of our time is the prison narrative, Primo Levi, Eugenia Ginzburg, Solzhenitsyn, Shalamov. In these places where nothing happens and everything is taken away, where human beings relearn themselves starting from zero, our faith in the person is reborn. Why these solitary voices should cause such a surge of hope remains partly mysterious, but it is a literary triumph in the widest sense, a faint song rising from a world of ash.

CHAPTER ONE

ANCESTORS OF NARRATIVE: RITUAL

The strangeness of finding such a thing indoors continues to cling to a Christmas tree throughout its life, even though it has been changed by an accumulation of offerings from wildness into art. It is constructed from the building blocks of the universe, or at least of the imagination, reduced to doll-forms accessible to a child. Like illustrations in a wordless book or examples in a grammar for foreigners, objects on a Christmas tree correspond to a simpler view than we usually take, as if the enterprise has caused us to ask, what comes first? and to answer: animals, birds, nuts, shells, stars, bells, hearts, spheres, adding a few parochial references to winter and plenty of shrunken versions of ourselves wearing wings or red caps.

From humble origins in an afternoon of glueing, tying, and stringing, these objects are raised to a consecrated state like the equipment of an Egyptian tomb, some of it usable, but not meant for our use, some of it only a replica of the usable or edible. Towards the end of the tree's life some offerings begin to look less desirable, cranberries shrivel, popcorn shrinks, oranges turn brown or even black in places. As time goes on, children, less awed by the spectacle, take bites of cookies or extract a toffee from its silver paper leaving the dented husk weightless on its string.

Like *ex voto* limbs, many of the unsightly throng on the tree commemorate specific times and persons, were made by a friend who has vanished or bought in a shop which has closed. Altogether this custom makes the most telling exposition of yearliness, of a spot returned to at unlengthy intervals to be reminded of the chain of visits stretching back into the distance. One is most lonely for the past when brought vividly into its presence like this, and the gaps between the objects only serve to heighten this private rite. They give it a kind of mosaic-glitter, jumbled syllables of lost story, like Gaudi's sinuous bench clambered over by the uncognizant.

8

A crucial difference between one's worshipful searches of a Christmas tree and the observances of primitive religion is the self-willed nature of the former, though it is true that if the tree were changed too suddenly it would lose its power like a newfangled liturgy.

However great one's allegiance, luckily it has little chance to go stale. Like an author fearful of tiring the reader, the tree-custom brings disrobing hard on the heels of dressing up. Treasured and then outcast, the tree seems an emblem of myth's current place. Myth survives in pulverized and babified form and in two weeks feels exhausted to all of us.

The more we study it, the more we *expect* to find myth garbled, and begin to suspect the hand of later restorers when its form is too satisfying or coherent. Various instances present themselves in which it appears that these constructions were ambiguous or indecipherable *from the beginning*. No one has been able to make Egyptian religious attitudes toward animals self-consistent according to any imaginable set of magic beliefs. So it proves less decisive than we might think that the Christmas tree is a product of nineteenth-century folk revival, answering a German Protestant longing for colour and shape the Reformation had taken away. For this constantly renewed reliquary cabinet is letting through very precious, very ancient echoes.

Still, no actual cult object was ever such a messy conglomerate. If the model was the Teutonic practice of bringing branches indoors to provide a refuge for wood-spirits in an inclement season, then food tied to the tree is the aboriginal decoration, but the greatest uncertainty about what wood-spirits eat couldn't account for the variety we have arrived at now. Yet the mind tolerates more easily than one might predict the coexistence of real food and models of food (and actual food formed into models of something else, to confuse the famished spirits further). Egyptian tombs contain haunches of meat, small wooden models of meat, and half-lifesize stone reliefs of meat in happy juxtaposition. But the idea of consumable things is not strictly adhered to on the Christmas tree, and food is mixed with objects of no use to the inhabitants of the tree, for whom very little room is left anyway. The original purpose of accommodation has been usurped by visible wood, straw, tinsel, and glass intruders, by lights representing souls, producing an impression of efflorescence in a dead season vigorous to the point of obscenity.

The lesson for the student of symbols is that they contain a principle of reversion, and that the line between gross, decomposing physical offerings and symbolic tokens of an intention to devote something to one's god in more enduring material, can be crossed and recrossed, that symbols can lose their value and return to earth, coming down in a different place and reascending, if they do, in a different form. When rite is as unsupervised as modern Christmas trees, it confronts us with a hubbub like the Hindu hierarchy of spiritual states, the lowest and most soiled cohabiting on the same branch with the most ethereal forms, nearing pure number or divine geometry.

Without perhaps growing more like it, aesthetic contemplation has in the past century and a half usurped the place of worship. The similarity between the two attitudes is ancient – submitting oneself to an external form of organization in the role of novice or suppliant – but for many art has been left holding the field alone. The Christmas tree, as a daimonology rescued to become a secular entertainment, is not unique; there are numerous examples from earlier epochs (in which no subtraction from the foundations of belief was underway) of the paraphernalia of devout observance turning up as the decorative embellishment of art.

So the ox-skulls which form a prominent element of the classical architectural system alternating with triglyphs as punctuation of the frieze, are a stylized rendering of the remains of a sacrifice after incineration. Of course our distinction between sacred and secular doesn't match the Greek view. At the beginning of the *Iliad* divine sacrifice and satisfaction of bodily needs are intermingled in the cooking of bulls and goats on the seashore, so that religion is a cookout and a meal a solemn rite. Nonetheless, the ability to imagine ritual leftovers in new situations cleansed of association shows a suppleness of mind growing restive in the paths of rite. One part of the event is subtracted and recombined with alien materials as if it were an independent word which could take part in different sentences.

Rite sometimes enjoys a demystified afterlife in art, and conversely trivia are occasionally remembered centuries later as tragedy. It appears that certain Greek myths arise from misinterpretation of voiceless imported images, and that the story of Theseus and the Minotaur, for example, stems from one such misreading, being the survival in art of the Cretan sport of bull-jumping, in which Athenian boys and girls are toreadors, and the Minotaur is the Cretan king in cult dress, covered with the hide and crowned with the skull of a bull.

It is supposed that painted or embossed scenes from these games were mistaken for deadly combats, an absurd raising of their temperature. Yet like other early games these may have begun as a form of worship, performed before the gods in their honour. So the dignification of the play into the familiar, momentous form only reinstills the original spirit.

Similarly, ecclesiastical garments and liturgical languages (of which Latin is by no means a unique case – besides church Slavonic there was

Sumerian as preserved in Babylonian and Assyrian religion) transport past ordinariness into a new time in which it appears freakish. Though the source of the usage is historical reverence, the effect for all but a few specialists is like anaesthesia, a dignity arising from obsolescence not antiquity. If one is faithful enough, unyielding enough, one loses touch with the old model, which becomes too remote for memory to hearken to any longer, and the way priests dress is the way they dress and always have dressed, a form now subsisting outside history and reference to late Roman ceremonial practice. All heightenings or investitures of life, of which art is one, run such risks.

To preserve something will often be to lose its meaning even if that is not one's intention. To lose its old meaning of course, and then to be free to fix a new one, one might think. But to an unforeseen degree humble things, when elevated, remain empty containers, vessels carried solemnly in a processional mood without a specific destination. Religious symbols are frequently pulled toward stratospheric vagueness, a result which is combatted by various infusions from below.

One of the most enigmatic ancient Near Eastern appliances is the cylinder seal, a little pellet of fired clay or semi-precious stone incised with a design, which repeats itself when pressed roller-fashion on the wet clay used to seal a jar or package. These seals preceded writing and represent a glimmer of it, a picture in place of the owner's name to declare his stake and at the same time to act as a primitive lock.

Such devices underwent an upward migration from commercial use like this to become certifiers of documents and finally monumental, non-accessory gifts to a god, by which time they had their own names. 'May the king in his benevolent purpose live,' one of them was called. So, as the seal was the owner in little, and often incorporated the god in its design, the name could do its designating without ceasing at the same time to pray or to wish. But extra functions cannot be tacked on indefinitely. The efficiently long winded name (perhaps only the first words the stone will think of) is really a dead end. In the temple the printing-tool's fertility comes to a halt. It will not be misplaced or chipped but, now unused, will cease to give out the message more powerful than its name, rams browsing outside the goddess's shrine, addorsed lions, or a naked figure inverting these threats to the herd. Seals come to seem fit offerings not because so precious as stuff, but because of their power to transmit images impressed in other materials. Once donated, their transmissions are over. The successful symbol, like the exhausted hero, ends by being removed from combat and established as a star in the sky, secure, far-off, and less distinctly himself than before he received this honour.

Such removal from the theatre of action is, whatever its professions, one of the motives of art; even socialist realism has its skyward tendency. Only a notion of cyclical migration from the secular to the sacred and back again, from literal to symbolic and back, a process which at no point duplicates earlier stages exactly, will make sense of certain vagaries in the history of Egyptian religion. When Egyptian power declined, magic became more prevalent, and in the late period the popularity of animal cults increased. Animals which had been symbols now became actual objects of veneration and individual members of sacred species were enthroned in temples and mummified after death, the reverse of the thought-sequence one would expect. Yet it seems likely this was a reversion to a long-forgotten stage. While Egyptian theriomorphy in its developed form is sophisticated and far from totemism, it remains possible that the origins were totemistic.

Egyptian gods as we know them are hybrids made from Hamitic animal gods of North African origin linked to localities, and anthropomorphic gods of the West Semites representing cosmic forces. The animal heads – Amon the ram, Horus the falcon, Thoth the Baboon – are not outlandish impositions on the human form, but residues of gods who had once been fully animal. Their historical development brought them closer to human civilization and mitigated the otherness they expressed originally.

In Mycenaean art the king's part is sometimes taken by a lion, a non-native species, to signify that the king is not like other inhabitants of his country, or, insofar as the king is the country, that Mycenae is not an ordinary denizen of the place it finds itself in. Depiction of animal combats, common in archaic art, may have, the more differentiated the actors, a more precise human meaning than we imagine. Lions devouring bulls are records or predictions of Mycenaean supremacy over Crete. This strange displacement contains the whole idea of literary character in embryo, one of the main ways of broadening one's field and getting outside the prison of the self. Characters are all the author's creatures, his surrogate selves, yet there is a saving difference between this relation and simply discussing oneself.

At an earlier stage Egyptian sacrifices stood for the god's enemy in diminished form, and his supposed feeding on the slaughtered flesh represented a cannibalism which, like the Mass, was theoretical from the outset. Instead of a record of primeval bloodthirstiness the usage may voice a healing wish for merger of opposing forces. Religion already inhabits the realm of the imaginary and settles conflicts by dramatizing them. The idea that gods have enemies remains a fruitful source of misinterpretation however, whose extent can never be perfectly regulated, offering a perpetual invitation to enter the fray on the god's behalf and give one's sense of beleaguerment a cosmic grandeur.

In Egyptian sacrifices the sting was at some point removed by the notion that gods needed only the essence of the animal, not the actual flesh, and that there was enough of this in a single victim to supply several god-meals, with the result that the same corpse could be offered repeatedly, until at the end of the day it furnished the priests with an ordinary worldly supper.

One sometimes sees a crevasse opening up between symbols ideally considered and symbols as palpitating flesh. Religion retains a few imperfectly combusted remnants of the time when it manipulated not dramatic entities, but living victims (at the other end we find writers like Lawrence who want to cross the boundary from the other side and to participate in living stories). Most primitive societies take an alarmed interest in the occurrence of twins, who it seems are about equally-often revered or killed, or very rarely both revered and killed, like the bear who is the central figure in Eskimo religion and is addressed lovingly as 'dear little divinity' while undergoing the cruel ordeal which finishes him off.

These opposite outcomes both produce the same kind of resolution for the tribe, if not the twins, by determining the place of a baffling exception. For the twin-ceremony in one tribe, twins and non-twins are marked respectively with red and white circles round the eyes, but when anthropologists inquire what the smears mean they get conflicting replies. Perhaps the result would not be so different if one were to poll a congregation about why the priest wore green, purple, or white, though many would have a dim sense that this meant *something* and changed with the seasons. The difference between red and white eyespots shows that a meaning is there, and perhaps the essential thing is that its place should be fixed, rather than that its content should actually be known. To us the eyespots are more vivid, and speak more insistently, than the priest's robes. But those habituated to them can doubtless take them more in stride, as if one had the A team and the B team, not that one wouldn't identify oneself fiercely with one and not the other, for reasons one didn't explore.

All of which has something to contribute to our grasp of how symbols work in art, setting up 'sides' which stay in place, leaving the user to move from one to the other. There is a strange little poem of Lermontov's telling of the passion of a cliff and a cloud for each other (together at the beginning, apart at the end of this eight-line lyric). Because of its skeletal plainness, it gives a handy demonstration of how mercurial the participant in art is frequently forced to be, assuming identities incompatible with his own and each other in quick succession. The twin-rites keep the sides straight, even if they disappoint the seeker after content, whereas the art-experience is more dislocating, and forces the participant to cede and multiply his place.

Nineteenth-century anthropologists complained that primitive religions were grotesque and largely unintelligible. That is their main beauty and function for us. Often we relish the blankness of archaic art; figures on black-figure Greek vases rarely provoke speculation about what they think or feel, which sets them apart from their nineteenth-century imitator John Flaxman. These people undergo dismemberment, religious ecstasy, or departure for battle without change of expression. A notion of individuality which regards private moments as the most real is simply not there for the Greek designers.

Even in sophisticated texts one sometimes feels a strong pull towards undifferentiated states. There are some famous examples in the book of Genesis, which level successive generations to the same bumpy outlines. Events there have a way of turning up a second time somewhat altered in detail. Even when (as in the account of creation) the second version follows on the heels of the first and contradicts it fundamentally, the text never concedes that anything like it has happened before. When Abraham presents Sara as his sister the second time, different reasons are offered for it, but it is not happening 'again'.

Various explanations of how a text gets this way suggest themselves. Frequently the materials at these points are ticklish and show the protagonist employing or falling victim to trickery. So one might suppose that these repetitions are products of anxiety like a sleeper's repeated efforts to untangle twisted bedclothes. Or perhaps adjacent stories have a tendency to become like each other, gravitating toward the form of the strongest, so that if certain motifs are missing from a marriage in one version and can be added without seriously contradicting what is already there, they will eventually creep in. Or the two incidents may represent distinct tellings, by reciters anxious to pep up discrete instalments with every available device, never meaning for them to form part of a single narration. Compilers or oral materials then need to be supposed unobservant, or so pious they feel unable to tamper with what they are transcribing. One may subversively ask, rather than why duplications weren't edited out, whether they weren't edited in, to form an overarching continuity.

More interesting still, and less debatable, are the effects of such corruptions on the reader. Far from discrediting the motif, doubling lends it authenticity. Meeting it a second time the reader feels there's a permanent truth in the event, and that present and past are more like each other than he normally allows. Yet he isn't entirely comfortable, and remains unsure whether this is a new occurrence or not. Ordinarily his confusion is subliminal enough not to send him flipping back to see if pseudo-memories are playing tricks on him.

Without giving an overtly metaphysical twist to it, the text has inserted a doubt about where the original copy of a certain perception is located, while conveying that clearheadedness about these matters is foreign to it. An answer to the question of recurrence has been offered without letting it come to consciousness as a problem. So the reader of Genesis inhabits a controlled darkness and reaps the benefits of the repeating pattern without assuming the philosophical burden of it.

Through reading inattentively one sometimes obtains chance archaic effects, losing track of persons and giving to one character feelings and behaviour meant for another, creating conundrums of motive which one accepts without understanding. Some of the most beguiling oddities in the structure of myth have been attributed to similar, if more logical errors. Perhaps Apollo is healer, hunter, and sun god not through a deep similarity in those activities, but because images of different older gods were conflated for the shallow reason that they were all shown wielding bows. The master of animals controlled them by shooting, the god of medicine pierced his enemies with diseases, and the sun god sent down powerful rays like arrows. Once the three functions were collected in a single place one had a strong but unlikely metaphor or idea of union, which abraded thought as much as it soothed it. Various ameliorations were possible and occurred: storytellers found dramatized explanations of where the union sprang from, theologians elaborated similarities, suppressed differences, and perhaps at a few points of ferocious strain institutionalized a paradox, all of which deprived the contradictions of much of their force.

In part, of course, it is a perspectival question, whether one sees Apollo as one or three, a Christmas tree as a single self or a crowd of attributes, the universe as a unity or a multitude. But it is hard not to feel that one of these perceptions is always prior. Unity may precede division, but as a mental act differentiation is first, reunification follows. Even in the wildest, like Blake, holism is a kind of return.

Many creation myths portray words as the original divisive or generative force. In an Egyptian story Amun-Re initiates creation by naming the parts of his body and in that way brings the nine gods of his immediate family into being. In another story Amun-Re gives birth to all beings by uttering them, 'Many were the creatures who came forth from my mouth.' In Egypt the word and the thing remained nearer to each other in an obvious way, because picture writing preserves a physical selfhood for every verbal object.

Though in Genesis naming is depicted as a posterior act performed by the maker's deputy, the user, ideas of creation as essentially verbal are not in the least alien to Hebrew thought. In one Talmudic rendering, as God is about to create the world through his word, the twenty-two letters of the alphabet descend from his crown, where they are engraved, and plead in turn that he create the world through *them*. The rival claims are pressed by citing valuable words which begin with the plaintiff letter, and dismissed with the counter-citation of bad words which it also initiates. However amused, we are liable to feel it is being argued on the wrong basis, with accidental features usurping the place of essential principles, but in archiac phases such distinctions are not drawn. In Egypt imperfect puns are a main means of enforcing theological dogmas.

The Jewish case only shows that efforts to think one's way back to a moment before the world existed, when there were building blocks but no buildings, soon come to grief and talk familiarly of the usual paraphernalia of life. All first stories are full of anachronism, but intermittently hint at what the world must have been like before names, and hence before the first story could be told.

Glimmerings of this world, in which to our eye things are often mistaken for other things, are fleeting. The time when names were new is characterized by a strong sense of inter-derivation among the objects of thought. Re appoints Thoth his place-taker in certain regions, not office-holder, but a translation of him nearer to earthly understandings, like the Pharaoh in place of the god, or a clarification which expresses his aspects differently, like the moon in place of the sun.

These are examples of the substitution or place-taking on which language and thought are founded, the migration through a set of terms equivalent at each step, yet remote in their destinations. This process begins hierarchically, and in Egypt much energy was devoted to maintaining strict ranking among the parts, yet one can see these changes of level as the sources above all of a certain potential energy.

One may come to feel that early stories are most important not as explanation of first things, but as themselves primal, the egg of all later talk and thought. At least in the mental realm, myth *is* the creation, positing the mind's equipment and initiating human understanding.

Much of the early energy is linguistic. One could take one's examples from many cultures and would find resemblances in the sound of words treated as occult convergences in the structure of reality. The line between pun and etymology, or false and true resemblance is overlooked, until all similarities appear to offer clues to the origins of the things denoted by words. Puns remain a kind of cement we can't take seriously, which originally crop up when divergence makes the user of language uncomfortable, so he brings it together again.

Kennings, like euphemisms, seem to reduce verbal variety by multiplying words, ploughing uniqueness back into sameness, achieving weak conflations like diffuse puns. The kennings in Norse poetry, certainly more stimulating to current readers than the first hearers, include ways of referring to characters which are characterizations rather than names. Names are the first words, so abolishing or obscuring them is a radical witticism at the expense of language.

Kennings for objects follow the same route, referring to common things by reference to less common, so that specialist knowledge is required to spot references to fire, gold, or a river, because it is named through a unique or rare instance of itself. Thus the Rhine is *Grani's road*, and gold is *Rhine fire*. Eventually the farfetched becomes habitual, yet it never functions as a name pure and simple. *Grani's road*, like a foreign word, comes from a different register than the words around it, a mock-simplicity which always fools somebody.

Norse poetry is more clearheaded than others in identifying literature as the outcome of two or more versions of the same thing. There is a poem in the *Elder Edda* like a dictionary of the languages of men, gods, elves, and further races, consisting of their respective names (actually descriptions) for heaven, earth, ocean, and the other constituents of the world. One begins to have stories when one becomes definitely conscious of more than one way of telling them; there is a story in every unfamiliar name.

The most famous Northern hero carries a name which may be that of a forgotten god or the generic term for 'hero'. Stories about Baldur are thus either god-memories coming apart, or a loose gathering of tales about a widespread type. One person, if a supernatural archetype, is not so far from an anonymous class.

Processes which we read as personifications may even be the opposite. In the *Elder Edda*, Hel is a miserable sufferer on an allegoric sickbed, in a nether region shaping up into the hell more familiar than she is. The person became her dwelling place metonymically, by a shift which seemed objectification. It was thought more accurate to identify certain feelings with inanimate surroundings than with personality, and such de-personification seemed a sign of cultural maturity.

Allegory is the same process in reverse, a re-personification which reaches back to the phase before abstractions were clearly differentiated. If only its inventors interpreted their task more often as dissolving ideas in personality, instead of giving us petrified processions like that at the beginning of the *Romance of the Rose*, where the lover walks past a series of Vices built into a wall, like a train passing through interesting countryside. Allegory would often be improved by removal of the names and the resulting absentation of meaning.

Modern fiction is full of characters denied proper names as an expression of the indeterminacy of their world. Musil's *Man Without Qualities*, one of the most hypothetical of works, withholds its hero's name 'to spare his father' (the father even more remote from actuality than the son, an even less valid excuse for decisions taken) and assigns ludicrous classical allusions to female characters in place of proper names – Diotima, Bonadea – which enhance the sense, important to Musil's wit, that everything could have been another way, and that what exists doesn't deserve the pre-eminence usually accorded it just because it is there. In this book a primitive, pre-individual state is the last refinement of scepticism.

In one of the most interesting ritualized losses of identity, the Egyptian god Osiris is cut into fourteen pieces, which are dispersed in various directions, only to come into their own as the fourteen days of the lunar cycle. We feel simultaneously the exhilaration of mental action so forceful it converts a person into time, and an underlying sadness that our world can only offer us fragments of a lost unity. Like burial it is another assimilation of human failure to more fluid vegetable cycles, but from cuttings of Osiris grow not other Osirises but quasi-metaphysical entities: the idea of an individual is both destroyed and transcended.

The Mycenaean habit of burying a sacred stone in place of a king who had died on foreign soil is a touching example of the translation of the dead, disembodied by the culture at the moment of fullest subjection to the body. A functional explanation of this custom is offered: the stone gives the king a habitation so the country can continue to reap the benefit of his presence, like the tainted idea of artist-in-residence who does what no one else can stop to do, infuses the place with a spiritual tone.

Almost opposite is the real meaning of surrogates. The stone is the king, *and* a relief from him. He has become a truly communal object, called by a human name, but without human failings, the attainment here on earth of Platonic perfection.

Most theories of kingship depend upon a certain abstractifying of the person of the ruler. Isis can be written as if it means 'throne', which was her emblem. In pictures she is shown sitting on a throne with the king sitting on her, as on a living throne, but turned toward her, to give the effect of an intimate union between the person and his power depicted as a seat pulsing with energy. The office is the wife and mother of its occupant; the power of the powerful is another person.

Most of all in picturing authority to himself and his fellows, man seems the victim of his own representations, creating puny types of human or natural eminence which then commence to awe him. Many religions besides the Egyptian have depicted the absolute precedence of the temple's inner shrine by several small steps one ascends in approaching it. Minute differences stand for larger ones, a slightly raised platform summons up the primal hill rising from the waters. Even Sumerian temple towers in the form of staircases, which sketch a route to heaven, are a faint echo of actual mountains, themselves only the intimation of a link (presently unscalable), between these two realms, and one of the sources for architecture as intimidation.

The oldest known model of the cosmic hill, the white temple and ziggurat at Warka, was accidentally preserved by being revered as a sacred hill in the entirely different cults of Hellenistic civilization 3000 years later. Yet this accident is a symbolism: a representation of a hill had in the course of time come, like other ruins, to resemble a hill more nearly, and however hazily to be regarded as a spiritual source or lost key. Sacred spots often continue to be sacred spots, succeeding cults find themselves in the shoes of old ones, like the second and third generations of gods which insensibly replace their parents in most religions; history changes but seeks to conceal it.

One consequence of the puny forms assigned to these momentous ideas of eminence (puny even when huge, because of the literalism on which they are based), is a special self-alienation peculiar to those in high positions. One might turn to Greek tragedy or Shakespeare, or to a highly developed example in a Chinese novel of the seventeenth century, an epitome of the conflict between the ideas of self and ruler: the all-powerful cannot be *him* (or her) *self*.

When the imperial concubine visits her former home in *The Dream of the Red Chamber* a separate house must be built for her even though she is not allowed to spend the night. Numerous measures are taken to distinguish her from herself and her own acts as well as from the other family members. Eunuchs precede her carrying her travelling wardrobe, her rosary, her handkerchief, her spittoon, and her fly whisk, not that some of the appliances couldn't be attached to her person, but to achieve mental distinctness for each object and take as many things as possible out of her hands.

Her first act when she arrives is to alight in a forecourt and go into a special tent to 'change her clothes', then to re-enter her palanquin and continue the journey to the Separate Dwelling. Next she is invited to proceed through its associated garden by boat, as if to stretch her arrival out to bring it closer to her departure. The family lines up to present obeisances, a duty from which each is separately excused. Then tea is offered her and three times refused; she descends from the throne and withdraws 'to change her clothes'.

Essentially these intervals are erasures wiping the slate clean, preventing the buildup of meaning by giving the protagonist a mildly irksome chore and creating a blank spot for those who must wait until she reappears. The family is tutored in relinquishment by a succession of forgone actions. Sometimes it is an honour, sometimes a rebuke to have one's proposals refused, but the burden of this protocol is that no one can think of an appropriate act, all the proposals being either humiliating or over-familiar.

In certain fictions travellers arrive at deserted inns where they 'meet no one', a more potent outcome than any imaginable encounter. Expectations are brought into higher relief when unclouded by distracting content. For all its air of renunciation, the so-called Visitation of the concubine, so continually interrupted – in the end she is summoned back to the palace before the meagre span the family were promised has elapsed – is the fullest expression in the novel of the forbidden feelings.

Similarly the Sumerian goddess Inanna's ritual of dressing for her trip to the underworld is fulfilled in enforced undressing, as the guardian of each gate requires the deposit of a piece of clothing before he will let her through. So readers will feel that certain types of narrative are unravelled rather than woven, untold rather than told, and the normal flow of time turned backward on itself.

Inanna's clothing is an additive (or subtractive) system which lends itself naturally to narrative. At the end nothing is left over or left out. There is another kind of correspondence which is often narrated, but sits awkwardly in that form. This kind of myth begins with an overall scheme and then tries to match as many features as possible without a fixed set of points to include. Constellations in the shape of animals or heroes are constructed like this, as is the Norse idea that the heavens are the head of a god from whom the universe is made (his feet the earth, his tears the ocean, and his hair all species of plants). The torso must be ignored because the distance between heaven and earth is large and expressive, but not full of anything. Hair is the right texture for what it signifies, but badly placed.

We are inclined to view this as a poetic device, an imagination running riot, but perhaps it is not a metaphor at all in our sense. Rather it speaks of a pre-metaphoric phase in which temples are not signs of some far off truth, not just *places* but *objects* of worship, and at that moment the world *is* a body in a way we can't recover.

A few strange survivors of the old view remain in our relation to the vegetable world, most evident in scientists like Ruskin, who have such powerful experience of the whole flower they can't divest themselves of a mythic approach to these objects, which are indelibly creatures to them. He was driven wild by botanists' claims that flowers were simply differentiated leaves, and repudiated the habit of seeing continuums everywhere and no real eminences. Yet to talk about plants as if the flowers came first and trailed the leaves, roots, and branches along behind is a mythic view of the subject, which still comes very naturally. Many plants are visible for twelve months and bloom for two weeks, and yet the blooms are more firmly in possession of the name and the memory than all the rest of the plant.

Even sophisticated systems of plant classification bear a kinship to myth. Our way of referring to plant 'families' is symbolic, not simply convenient. The mint-, the pea-, the rose-family, are named for members who have made the deepest impression on us and been chosen to rule over or sire the others, in the sense of giving them the model of what they should look like and the standard by which their oddity is judged.

If the basic principles have never been replaced, much old detail has been swept away, as one can measure from the late rendition of folk belief about flowers in Shakespeare, which are put in the mouths of girls gone mad or childish. In many cases there are better reasons for connecting specific flowers with certain meanings than modern readers realize, pansies and thoughts linked by a word 'pensées', rosemary and remembrance by a medical belief as well as r's and m's. Still, Shakespeare is a risky authority for what Elizabethans thought. Here, as often, he seems a resurrector of half-forgotten lore, who is able to bring it into currency by connecting it with a peculiar mental emergency. Primitive thinking enters the plays under circumstantial pressure, which shows it wasn't any longer just part of the furniture of contemporary thought.

Maybe this is only a poet playing, like the woman in Wallace Stevens's 'Sunday Morning', but it suggests that the mental integration Shakespeare produces was one of the main fruits of such belief. So whether one sees him as a heroic recoverer of long lost modes or simply as a continuer, the gulf between the processes of poetry and the earlier techniques of myth and religion becomes narrower.

Like proliferating characters in a nineteenth-century novel growing so distended it threatens to produce a confusion too nearly duplicating what we meet in reality, modern plant classification sometimes aspires to too many divisions. Another piece of classification which looks absurdly wasteful from the monotheist perspective is the Sumerian habit of assigning a different tutelary diety to each individual, as if each were a species requiring its model in heaven. But such an overview was rarely taken: the guardian spirits were never imagined in conclave, a huge population duplicating earth's exactly. Lists exist which collect the names of hundreds of Sumerian gods, but it appears that many are half-imaginary, theologians providing well established gods with belated children, servants, and hangers-on to bring them up to par with greater gods who have long-standing families. Other names are supposed obscure reference to gods already known to us.

Such proliferation and the reductionism evident in most forms of government are perhaps systole and diastole of the same movement, a tendency to individualize reality infinitely; a tendency to de-individualize it, paradoxically by fastening on a single human eminence or ruler. At first it will sound as if the first of these is a narrative and the second an anti-narrative impulse, but they are probably necessary partners instead, in narrative's ambiguous relation to the idea of the single existence, and the allied but different idea of the individual. Characters, like citizens and rulers, are pulled in these two directions, toward representing something else, toward not doing so.

The most surprising discovery to a foreigner living in the British monarchy is that the reigning monarch is never referred to by name. In all conceivable connections it is sufficient to call her 'the Queen', and her predecessor is 'the King' and not George. A personal name is gradually lost as one grows up into this post, or is half lost already when one is Prince of Wales.

This must vary from one monarchy to another, and perhaps at the beginning of their reigns monarchs are more vivid, more like persons, so the hankering for a new one, like the need felt in most religions to replace gods grown dim with time by their children, to have instead of the virtually nameless and featureless Father, the more personified Son, is a wish to see human personality reasserted. A class which has only one member at any moment presents problems of actualization, even if not, as the idea of Ruler is, almost the idea of removal or distance from all else.

The fantastic outpouring of grief which followed Stalin's death, so that one could walk through the streets in remote parts of the country, as many in their restlessness were doing, and see tearful women more shaken than at deaths which touched them more nearly, this outpouring did not show that Stalin the man was loved, any more than the seven full minutes of applause which greeted his public appearances showed he was personally respected. These practices revealed how highly symbolic the idea 'Stalin' was, how much there was of reservoir for certain human susceptibilities and how little of an individual in it.

From a very early stage in his progress the campaign was underway to bulk out Stalin's name with descriptions, Wise Helmsman, Friendly Teacher, Father of the Peoples, Patron of Linguists, many with misleading touches of whimsy. It is an ominous sign when a leader is no longer content to go by his name. In some of the worst cases the substitutes have a childish or dwarfish ring to them: how could one know the Germans' *guide* would so mislead them?

King's College Chapel is decorated with the ruler's nicknames, huge heraldic roses, portcullises, and fleurs de lys in stone, each of which is overhung by a heavy roof in the shape of a crown, keeping him before us in his absence. These emblems, known as badges, are fantasias on heraldic themes which break free from the elaborations of late medieval coats of arms and recover the totemic power at the root of heraldry. But like allegory as a belated recovery of myth, badges reanimate the world at one remove, bringing objects back to life without their settings. The result is a race of intermediate, imaginary beings, which, when big as at King's College, are creatures of nightmare, like broken bits of giants' discourse.

It has been argued that writing is divisive in a similar way, taking a unified consciousness and forcing it to perceive the world in bits. Alternatively, one could imagine the first writing as product of a hermetic overloading and crowding of images, not functional in our sense to begin with, but an occult concentration of small pictures which awe, even terrify the unwary. The massed impression is an illusion easily broken down, of course, and once a person realizes that he can *follow* the rows, that instead of a forest they are really paths, their profusion is no longer threatening.

It would be gratifying to trace the formation of writing into lines back to borders or friezes of recurrent images, but the influence probably travels in the other direction, and the Parthenon friezes are poeticized derivatives of writing, harking back to when writing *looked like* what it was saying.

It is always pleasing to hear of the rediscovery of hieroglyphs under unusual pressure, like an ingenious box of edible symbols sent to Eugenia Ginzburg detained by Soviet officials, a school sandwich to say her son was still in school, something from the hospital kitchen to say her doctor friend was still in touch, candy from the factory to say her cousin hadn't lost her job, each piece of food tied to a person and summing up his prospects. This is a marvellously indirect and vigorous statement, yet how lucky that this was what needed to be expressed. How difficult it would have been to say the opposite. Could negatives have been conveyed by bites taken out of the emblems, or grit in them, and how would she have known her friends and not her enemies meant it as part of the message? If a speaker doesn't have his hearers before him, because he is a prisoner or lives elsewhere, he will rejoice at every new flexibility in the mechanism of transmission.

The breaking of words into letters must have been fought by those who feared for the integrity of thoughts, and probably the dismemberment of scrolls into pages seemed an ugly fragmentation to subtle pagans when they first came across these new Christian codexes, which, whatever they did to apparent continuities and to the most natural ways of representing the flow of thoughts, led to a widening of man's mental field. The codex took a step beyond the scroll in severing writing from its roots in the physical world. Severing the mechanism that is, for a printed book in pages is no less immediate as an influencer of perception than a scroll recopied by a half-literate scribe.

Like a sculptor who simplifies the forms to draw less attention to the message and more to the idea of transmission, coarse Hittite pictographs give us a clearer idea than Egyptian of what is at stake in early writing. It is a codification in which some meaning is stripped away to ensure that other meanings should be more securely preserved. One may even wonder if stories couldn't be defined as that which can be passed down in a certain way. Stories are stories *so that* they will survive.

The difference between Hebrew and all other transmission of the past is enormous. In the desert they guarded most carefully the Ark containing not physical relics of their God, but His literary remains, which in their sophistication they realized was the nearest they could come to Him. Whereas Mycenaean written history had to be unearthed and decoded from administrators' memoranda, Hebrew history was formed into stories which infused themselves into the consciousness of many, as only stories can. The stories were collected and – assuring their preservation without modern intervention – deified.

All literate civilizations have cherished their accumulated verbiage, but no other has so successfully made a compendium which could be perceived by so many for so long as a single book. The Bible is set apart most tellingly from other books by the way in which its creators identified themselves with it.

That riddle which perplexed the eighteenth century: of what language a child raised without hearing speech would speak, was sometimes answered 'Hebrew' by medieval speculators. For that was the oldest language – the oldest with which they felt cultural connection, the oldest which had imposed itself on them. One of the earliest experimenters, the Emperor Frederick II, must have proceeded scrupulously, because the only result he ever got was sickly mutes who languished and died.

One of the most awful twentieth-century inventions is a kindred experiment conducted on whole nations. A printed index exists of over three hundred main banned subjects which are never to be broached in print in the Soviet Union. Descriptions of this document by former employees of the censorship have appeared in the West, but as far as I know there are no full copies of this precious, incriminating book.

Some have felt that the worst sign of the desire to prevent people from making contact with language and hence culture is the retroactive cleansing of libraries and reference works once an author formerly tolerated has joined the ranks of those who cannot be mentioned. It is difficult to read such authors in their homelands, but it is more difficult to refer to them in print. By exercising the physical means at its disposal a malevolent state can make all but the strongest thinkers wonder if there ever was such a person as the forbidden writer, who has become a mental figment. So the populace is reduced in parts of its brain to a primitive savagery like those infants raised by deafmutes in the middle of a forest. So, the richness of the present denied, much of human history is undone.

CHAPTER TWO

EARLIEST SELVES: *Gilgamesh, Genesis*

The oldest story is a recent discovery, or has, at least, a violently interrupted history. The epic of *Gilgamesh*, at this moment the oldest story, emerged from the ruins of Nineveh in the 1850s. Layard was on his way overland to Ceylon and got sidetracked by archaeological digging in the desert, a diversion which lasted years and deposited 25,000 tablets in the British Museum.

Remains are often moved before it is known what they are. A large part of the huge stocks of clay fragments divided between London, Istanbul, Baghdad, and Philadelphia have still not been put in order or completely read (not as easy as it sounds, given the obscurity of the languages and the deterioration of the written objects). So it isn't so surprising that the story of *Gilgamesh* sat in London for almost twenty years unread. Finally it was the flood-story, which now seems an interpolation, that caught people's attention. And this part of the poem was interesting because it reminded them of a Deluge they already knew, and Noah's voyage in Genesis. To this day all the literatures of the Ancient Near East are seen in relation to the Hebrew. The largest recent collection of such texts is a giant appendix to the Old Testament. Perhaps this shows that no amount of disbelief can displace our scriptures from their special pre-eminence, or that stories are always approached through other stories, so that no one can arrive early enough on a fresh enough scene to find a story without precedents.

If we manage to detach *Gilgamesh* from Genesis we will still feel there is a preparation for reading it which we lack. Genesis, with which we are more comfortable, is perhaps as late a version of the stories it collects as *Gilgamesh* is of *its* stories, and needs less explanation only because it has been enshrined so long in the place it fills. To us *Gilgamesh* will always seem a newcomer and an unexplained presence. In some way this is the source of its extreme value – a venerable artifact whose pedigree is lost, which we can therefore see as if it were new.

Before embarking on its first events – the hero's sexual abuses of his subjects' children, both sons and daughters – the poem voices a generalized paean to Gilgamesh who encompasses all human possibility, who has adventures, writes them up afterwards, and builds the commemorative walls its readers can still clamber over marvelling at how well the bricks hold up after all those centuries. A link to someone's present which leaves us out in the cold, because we came so near to *not* climbing on these imaginary monuments and decoding these inscriptions. It appeals to common experience we almost didn't have.

The opening announces Gilgamesh as the type of everything he is – actor, recorder, builder – the whole history of civilization caught in a single lifespan. He sounds more than human, an impression defined with strange exactitude: Gilgamesh is two-thirds god, one-third man. It would be difficult to work this out genetically, and his parents are undiscussed: the first hero is defined by his place in the universe rather than our limited human world.

Shorn of surrounding story, the opening of *Gilgamesh* feels dislocated and uncaused, but this is a lucky accident. The poem would not have seemed so till recently. If it gives signs of not being quite so primal for its contemporaries as it is for us, there are obscure Sumerian fragments which are more like the first, rudest materials of story.

Perhaps it is only their more ruined state which makes these fragments more mysterious. In one which its discoverer calls *Enki and Ninhursag*, someone called Father Enki (or perhaps someone else) brings water. Names in this fragment bear a family resemblance to names in *Gilgamesh*. They are an irreducible range of strangeness, yet we begin to know who Enki or Enkidu, who En or Enlil is. Characters solidify as adjacent similar actions get attributed to the same actor, so the next decipherable event in the Enki story is that someone creates marshland by a vaguely phallic act. Or perhaps it is meant as a normal bit of farming or gardening. We cannot tell whether Enki is a labourer lost in the fields or the ruler of the universe. When he has a message to send, a messenger appears. When he wants to give a gift of fruits, a servant springs up to gather them. In the meantime Enki is unencumbered by the panoply of a court.

The best moments in the poem are his repeated emergences – 'Enki in marshland looks about and looks about' – sole inhabitant of the world, who wonders each time anew, and as if uniquely, 'Shouldn't I kiss the young one, the fair' – a girl, who each time is his daughter fathered on an earlier daughter.

It is a story which learns very little from its own progress. Like this incorrigible fecundator of his own soil, the tale keeps finding itself at the

27

start all over again, in a nearly empty world where the same lonely feature catches its eye. The hero's unvarying greed for experience is eventually punished when his third wife does something with his semen which causes all the species of plants to arise. Enki is diverted into naming and tasting each of them, a procedure which enrages an earlier wife and makes him need her again. Finally he takes his seat in or near her vulva and lists his ailments, for each of which she promises a cure.

In setting and motifs this little story is like a humble creation myth. Man is outside, active at the edge, where he is able to harness the elements, and woman is inside, still at the centre, wanting to cure his unthinking excesses, a division met again in *Gilgamesh* when the harlot is sent from the city into the wilderness to tame Enkidu.

Like bringing the wild inhabitant of the grassland indoors, our description betrays as it clarifies, however, because one isn't entirely sure that Enki isn't the flood and Ninhursag the earth which soaks up its ministrations. Enki says such senseless things and seems not consistently to have the equipment of kingship because he isn't really a reasoning creature, but an ill-defined something, of which the solidest feature is that it appears to bear a name. Even this may be uniformity imposed by us. The first stories lacked names too, and swam about in a gaseous state we have trouble recognizing as an existence at all.

Gilgamesh has been told and retold, like a Greek marble known now only in numerous Roman copies. By the time a modern editor has pieced together the poem into the fullest possible form, using the best bits of all the different versions which remain, it has become a fairly rational product. Actions obscure in one version are explained in another; when one is already familiar with an anger it is a help to learn its cause from another source; or, having seen the monster Humbaba at home in the trees, to hear him called Spirit of the Forest.

The most authentic presentation might be even fuller conflation, showing the action caused and uncaused, and the monster named and unnamed with this general title. Such doubling may not be exactly what any of the old tellers planned, but the present state of Genesis shows that archaic compilers sometimes preferred to keep conflicting accounts than throw either one out.

In *Gilgamesh* Enkidu is first imagined as an answer to Gilgamesh himself, to whose strength we need a counterbalance. Gilgamesh is a denizen of and creator of cities, corrupted by power and civilization. Enkidu, covered with matted hair like long grass, lives in the mountains, eats grass, and runs with beasts. A cry now goes up against the wild man, which finally reaches the city and addresses itself to Gilgamesh.

So the tarnished hero whose misdeeds provoked the creation of the monster is asked to rid the world of him. Instead of going himself, Gilgamesh sends a temple harlot who waits by Enkidu's water-hole and corrupts him – waking up beside her, he first becomes embroiled in self-conscious reflection.

After giving vent to these primitivist sentiments – how sad to find sophisticated longings in the oldest narrative known – the story recalls Enkidu's original purpose, to go against Gilgamesh – and now the anti-hero trips the hero when he crosses the threshold with one of his stolen brides. Gilgamesh wins the ensuing fight, but a friendship between the two is sealed at once, and he stops seizing the local girls.

Like the *Iliad* it is a poem acquainted with the problems facing one who has achieved too much. Like Achilles, Gilgamesh cannot find worthy opponents and so suffers from boredom and the desire to do something, he doesn't know what. Soon after their meeting, Enkidu falls ill from inactivity, and Gilgamesh is overcome by restless desires of which he tellingly says, he wouldn't have them if they were unfulfillable, a rationality not borne out by events. He decides to go after a bigger Enkidu, Humbaba, a famous monster, or perhaps not famous because we have not heard of him till now. But Gilgamesh believes that the rumour of Humbaba's name fills the world, and is driven by a desire to leave his own in its place, stamped on bricks, erected in permanent form, an unsymmetrical opposite to the stage of being named in the first place, to *leave* one's name behind. So the ruling motive of the oldest hero in world literature is to gain entrance to literature, and preserve himself in words.

It now appears that Gilgamesh has a mother, Ninsum, a queen, because before leaving he asks her to present his case to the highest god. His troubled forecast of his ordeal turns up again in her prayer pleading that *while* (Gilgamesh's lengthy account of his trials inserted here), *the god will not forget Gilgamesh.* The hero's passionate outpouring is reused verbatim, but the second time it functions like a pro forma invoice, demoted from primary narration to a time clause naming the period she wants the god's solicitude to run.

In the Sumerian epic reiterations seem the main way of representing difficulty or protracted suffering. Later when Gilgamesh undertakes a tiring journey of twelve leagues (the length not revealed beforehand), each stage is recorded in the same words, 'After two leagues the darkness was thick and there was no light, he could see nothing ahead and nothing behind him. After three leagues the darkness was thick and there was no light, he could see nothing ahead and nothing behind him.' When this has been repeated seven times (only the number varied), a slight difference arises, and we watch the end creep slowly forward through the remaining three leagues.

The foregoing episode is a powerful expression of wonder that the same person can find himself in successive moments, and a demonstration that one cannot carry oneself over like a sum from one moment to the next. The fourth term of an identical series does not feel like the first if experienced in time rather than lined up in a visible row in front of us. The problem of how to understand progression, though less impinging on the person, is closely related to the bored anxiety over what to do next.

Gilgamesh is discovering that poems are temporal works, and so at the mercy of time themselves. It is not in their power even to refer, except at a distance, to earlier stages of their own selves. Likewise our own just finished thoughts or creations become alienated as they recede into the past, as if they were belongings carelessly left behind. The queen's repeated litany, anxiety turned into ritual supplication, shows how hard it is to outdo (or even to match) the past when one concentrates too intently on the problem, and this urges one to a less hidebound view of reality. But *Gilgamesh* finds itself on a treadmill. Civilization is largely identified with such memorializing techniques. Anxiety in all its rich variety is the form that wisdom takes. So the elders who see Gilgamesh off are full of a mechanical caution: don't stride too far ahead; let Enkidu go first. Remember this, remember that. Stopping to think means multiplying fears, and the play between Enkidu and Gilgamesh is like the psychic flux found inside single characters in later fiction.

Here at the very beginning of narrative, dramatic tension already means a confusingly rapid series of ups and downs. If Enkidu is frightened at the prospect of the projected adventure, he has good reason. He knows Humbaba. Gilgamesh on the other hand is understandably full of worries because he doesn't know him. One could invent an explanation of why it is suitable Enkidu should know Humbaba, but it is one of those pieces of information, like the fact that Gilgamesh has a mother or a wife, which is dropped like a bomb, in the sense that it would be more logical and welcome introduced earlier.

Gilgamesh is a prolific dreamer and dreams are the main injections of the unexplained in the story. There is no such thing as a non-prophetic dream, but unfortunately at first glance they usually look baleful. When the pair sets off after the giant, Enkidu's own dreams dry up, so he applies himself to interpreting his friend's. As in the Joseph story, the dreams come in duplicate pairs, for the dream mechanism realizes it will not be taken seriously unless it says everything twice.

The protagonists never tire of dreams in almost the same form bearing virtually the same message. And this glut only palls on the reader in slowed down retrospect, because he too falls victim to the suggestion that there are secrets locked in these narratives within the narrative, full of unidentified actors and impossible catastrophes – hills fall on Gilgamesh, eagles carry him off or pick his flesh, monsters attack and then bring him drinks.

Even when threatening, a dream ministers to the dreamer, cradling him in meanings. It tells him his fate matters, or it wouldn't bother to provide this key. Enkidu and Gilgamesh have such an appetite for new dreams that when the supply fails they solicit them with prayers and night-time visits to mountains, where they are more likely to strike.

The strange convention that a person's own dreams are opaque to him is finally violated in the dreams foretelling Enkidu's death, the first of which reports as clearly as a newspaper the gods' deliberations and demand that one of the two must pay for the killing of Humbaba and the bull of heaven (a second monster) sent by a goddess to punish Gilgamesh for sexual indifference. Like all other forecasts in fiction it is the story's way of enforcing its own structure, offering innocent confirmation of what the teller intends to tell. Enkidu hears his death discussed, *then* falls ill, has more dreams, disowns his achievements, above all a marvellous gate he can see from his sickbed, then curses the main events of his life, until made to retract his feelings by a god's persuasion, after which he can decently die.

The metaphysics of Gilgamesh's fall resemble those of many Greek stories. Like Achilles he is attacked through his attachments and, like its brother the grief for Patroclus, Gilgamesh's mourning over Enkidu is one of the freshest episodes in the story.

The hero's mixed nature (two-thirds god, one-third man), which seemed so droll and advantageous at the beginning, when it could blithely be said that Gilgamesh *looked like* a god, now seems a misconception put about by naïveté. Thoughtless exercise of strength, not weakness, has brought him down. An envious goddess sets a trap for him by sending an adversary (the bull of heaven) whom it is worse to win than lose against, because a feat so big is an affront to world order which will be avenged.

No one ever pretended Enkidu couldn't die, but no one had thought what this death would mean. From that point the poem turns inward, not that Gilgamesh sits inertly brooding. His grief leads him on a new adventure, a visit to the only man who has ever outwitted death, Utnapishtim, who lives at the edge of the universe. Those he meets along the way guess the new spirit in which Gilgamesh acts: despair and exhaustion show in his face. It is the poet's ingenious way of writing about ageing; the poem is older, like Gilgamesh. It is a feeling which overtakes everyone at some point in an extended work, both writer and reader: what have we got ourselves into, and how do we get out? In later stages moments always occur in which our faith fails.

Ostensibly Gilgamesh is seeking immortality, but no one who began so defeated ever won out. He is given two chances to gain eternal life, and falls down each time because he does not eat something fast enough.

After his journey if he can stay awake for seven days Gilgamesh will be immortal. But he is worn out, sleeps, and forecasts his death, most of all in the loaves he leaves untouched beside him, one for each day, like rotting corpses of unused hours (some grow hard, some soggy, some leathery and some mouldy). Utnapishtim then sees him off on the return journey, and as an afterthought confides that at the bottom of a stream is a flower, to eat which restores youth. Gilgamesh seizes it, but hasn't yet eaten it when he comes to a spring in which a snake hides, who takes the plant, which ends up at the bottom of another body of water, beyond the hero's reach.

This sequence reverses the story of the Flood, another episode which *Gilgamesh* manages to contain. Like its sister in Genesis the flood in *Gilgamesh* shows the gods both rash and indecisive, violently angry yet making one exception, plucking a single flower from the smothering excess of fluid. In both flood stories normal meanings are reversed, and moisture represents death not life, too much of something which there is rarely enough of. A flood which drowns all life is a more paradoxical conception in the Middle East than in most settings, but paradoxes are here piled high – God the creator uncreates and, in *Gilgamesh*, the gods who make the uproar are frightened by it and cower like curs.

This poem gives the mystery a profound twist when a second rescue from the waters is tried and fails. The time for magic has passed. Instead of gaping at rainbows, *Gilgamesh* allows man only the option of facing things as they are. For the poem, as perhaps for many lives, the most memorable death is someone else's. The work ends when the hero does, its span not greatly different from the operation of his consciousness. But there is almost a contradiction between the story's being told by someone else and being unable to proceed beyond the bounds of the hero's life.

All the more strange, we might think, because Gilgamesh though presented subjectively, as a rash and passionate being, is more an empty container than a character in the usual sense. He is not a recognizable type, unless 'ruler' counts as this. He is not obliged to fill any social role, is never shown as husband, father, or employer, though we know inadvertently that he is all of these. Gilgamesh is not yet a character because the world has not required him to be one.

This poem tells of someone's first steps towards individuality, or toward becoming a single person, under pressures so far non-social, love and the loved one's death, though even in a community (duality) as private as this we feel the stirrings of a society which will later lay multiple constraints upon its members.

Though it is natural to compare them, the worlds of Genesis and *Gilgamesh* are in these respects miles apart. From the beginning the Hebrew patriarchs are heads of families. We are so used to how things happen in Genesis that we cannot appreciate how strange it is at that stage in the development of narrative: Abraham and the others have their important relation to God, and their adversarial relation to the outsiders who threaten the home – a relation which may extend at times to brothers, or to servants who have borne the patriarch's child – but the core of these lives is family business.

Individuals in Genesis are more finely differentiated than we find them in earlier or contemporary stories because they are part of a larger story. The first spur for them to be distinct comes from their rivalries with a brother, followed by tacit comparisons with the father from whom they inherit the headship of the group.

Gilgamesh and stories like it, which stop short at the single span, are bound to devalue human difference. In Genesis first brothers are paired (Cain/Abel, Lot/Abraham, Isaac/Ishmael, Jacob/Esau, Joseph/the other ten), and then generations are, as every child becomes adult, mature, and finally old, so that each stage in turn begins to remind us of the previous.

In several ways this book is one of the strongest expressions of human continuity, and one may even say this is how it is spiritual. Pride of place belongs to this simple narrative fact, that ageing is repeatedly absorbed without causing the termination of the story, because there is an orderly succession of heroes who assume the coveted place one after another. How different the process is from the historical chronicle, or its rude form, the king-list, found in many ancient cultures. Genesis also includes lists of course, like the famous genealogies filling those gaps which arise when one tries to link disparate stories, which are gaps between the requirements of history and fiction. These genealogies regularly include names which someone in the present wants mentioned for a selfish reason, to lend himself retrospective dignity or to claim the same antiquity someone else has got.

There are readers who fasten on the genealogies as the firmest information Genesis provides. It is true they spawn the lengthiest commentaries, but for most people they have proved a sticking place in another sense, containing knowledge alien to the rest of the text, which we become increasingly adept at jumping over to get on with the narrative. At other times a single name is a sufficient genealogy and makes a primitive, dramatized history. We can't tell any more whether Ishmael or the Ishmaelites came first. Their characters coincide, both fierce and lonely, and the individual is said to explain the group: because their ancestor was like that, his descendants are. In fact, groups don't grow from their first members like oaks from acorns; large social realities are not magnifications of a seminal individual, and so to us it is laughable history, but a good story.

In Genesis poetry is still science, and we can deduce from the pastimes and temperaments of Jacob's sons the habits and even the geography of the twelve tribes of Israel in the writer's own time. The system works, partly because we are willing to read both backward and forward. The present confirms or lets us intuit the past, the past oppresses or exerts persuasive force on the present, and our mind is set at rest by learning how past behaviour explains privileges and penalties enjoyed and suffered by the 'descendants' of those fictional constructs today.

Seen in relation to other early works Genesis is remarkable for its interest in groups and their political relations, a far cry from the antagonisms of monsters and heroes. But for over a century stricter boundaries have been drawn between accuracy and the pleasures of narrative, with the result that the modern critical approach to these scriptures has had its fulfilment in undoing them as stories by exposing historical inconsistencies. Thus other sources have recently shown that a number of foreign kings with names confusingly like Hammurabi were conflated into an omnibus enemy of Israel spanning the centuries in a preposterous fashion. Or perhaps, Hammurabi being the equivalent of 'John' in the place it comes from, they all were called that and are thus more helplessly blended. In either case, historical sophistication destroys the possibility of a tale at all.

In fact anthropology repeatedly disintegrates the narrative by finding groups behind what appeared as individuals. The sons of Hanmor (Hanmor = ass) are not a few men with one father, but a loose confederation held together by a treaty which an ass was sacrificed to solemnize, Bathshua (= daughter of Shua) is simply 'a daughter of Shua,' hence more a random passerby than a true individual.

Remembering the origins of names is one form of historical conscious-ness. Something like it is encapsulated in the double-barrelled names for many Biblical places, which preserve the pre-Hebrew name and its successor, enshrined together like a small exhibit of historical change.

This conviction that everything was once different runs very deep in the collective mind, yet it comes as a surprise that, when Isaac is ready to seek a wife, Abraham still considers that he has a home and people somewhere else, so used have we become to the way things are now. His position is complicated because he can neither accept a local wife nor imagine retracing his steps to the origins in Ur. So he has a mixed nature, particular and universal at once, and he becomes metaphysical because in a country, but not of it. Just like any exile perhaps, yet he is different because the physical separation from the past and mental alienation from the present are both voluntary, maintained by strength of will.

Such motifs confirm Genesis as a true exemplar of narrative as mindful, not forgetful, as almost an aberration of excessive remembering. Initially we may wonder at the person who creates difficulties for himself this way, when it would be easier to lose track of the complexities of the situation. But we never really doubt it is better to remain conscious of them.

Genesis contains still more perplexing cases of divided sympathies. In the story of Hagar, a slave-woman is twice chased out by a jealous wife, and from the moment she becomes an outcast God takes an interest in her, failure being more poignant than success. One could write the history of the Old and New Testament from this point of view, and indeed this has been done. When Christ seemed to give the downtrodden a voice he was only following in the tradition of stories which are repeatedly centred on the younger son.

This motif, common in tale-material, is given special moral weight when sustained over a number of generations, and married to the historical conception of a whole people performing the role among its neighbours which Rachel, Jacob, Joseph and others fill in the family. Other nations have managed to make smallness a source of pride, but in the notion of the moral power of worldly powerlessness, the Hebrews came upon something which has had an influence out of all proportion to its apparent inability to coerce assent, far beyond anything left by the surrounding cultures which thought to overpower Israel.

The most troubling story in the book of Genesis is best read as a contribution to this theme. Of all the episodes on which we cannot look with unconditioned eyes, the binding or sacrifice of Isaac is the starkest. To this day it is called the sacrifice, not the aborted sacrifice or God's joke. The story continues to exercise an inordinate fascination, though most readers have probably wished the subject had never been broached and some boundary crossed which cannot be uncrossed.

God can say, and He does, that He never meant to let the awful event take place, that father and son were always safe in His care, but such is the power of narrative, within constraints the reader knows all the time to be artificial, that God will never look quite the same again; He has been bested by a child.

Roles are inverted, and by submitting, Isaac shines out brighter than God. How is it possible that a child should bear this weight? Partly because irony relieves him of it: at the lowest level are the servants left behind at the bottom of the mountain with the bland information that Abraham and Isaac will *worship* at the top, bland to them, convulsive of his faith to Abraham. At the next level Isaac, carrying the wood on his back for the fire in which he will be burnt, meek as the lamb he is told will appear, which materializes in his person as he carries this load. Next, Abraham shuddering with the new knowledge he can confide to no one, that what he has considered the gift of God must be returned to the giver. And last, God, whose mental state cannot be thought about, who outrages every susceptibility by His abuse of power, and who by human standards is lucky to escape retribution.

Having imagined such a conflict between earthly feelings of justice and man's bottomless obligation to God, the first teller constructed a problem which one could say the Hebrews have spent the rest of their history working their way out from under.

Isaac the victim has become the first exemplar of a condition which exercises the national imagination over and over, and of which Christ is the culminating instance. In the end, the jealous and demanding god of these early times has been unseated by a God modelled on, descended from, Isaac, and it is only an extra irony that He is always depicted as the old God's Son.

The idea of human sacrifice which was supposed to be laid definitively to rest by the Isaac story was only internalized, deepened, and set permanently in motion by it. One would never finish enumerating the descendants of this image of the child half-wittingly hoisting the weight of all trouble onto his back for the struggle up the mountain. The bundle of faggots became the cross, the climb a tour of the Purgatory of this world, and the goal relief from one's burdens through the conflagration of one's separate self, an idea with sources further east and alien to the Hebrew roots on which it is grafted.

Not many texts would have lent themselves as well as Genesis to Christian typologists looking for prefigurations of the divine hoax entering human flesh. In this book decisions are repeatedly given transcendent meanings, opposites seem to grow from each other, and uncanny patterns appear in the most mundane experience as if it strains toward redemption.

Jacob's trick in taking away Esau's blessing by dressing misleadingly is like a parody of Isaac's sacrifice and Christ's humiliation, undertaken for profit. The incident is nine parts grotesque, and one transcendent, yet there is a strange fitness in the associations with food and sacrifice. The father asks to be fed by the hunter. Rebecca prepares the food and clothes Jacob in the skins taken from the victim the father will eat. As the meal is a ritual transfer of vitality, so Jacob's impersonation is a fanciful conversion to the slaughtered victim. He submits meekly, bowing down before Isaac in his smelly bestial clothing. Esau has previously given up the ghost in his dealings with Jacob, who charges him for providing a meal. When the hunter is genuinely hungry (as Isaac later is not) he signs away his birthright to satisfy his appetite, thus relinquishing claims to be more than a beast or collection of physical needs.

But his position is complicated. Half acquiescing in the transfer he partly dematerializes it. There are too many meanings in the end. Is Esau immolated on the altar of Jacob's ambition? or of racial purity? At one point the text hints that he has alienated his father's favour by marrying a Hittite woman. Esau is another of those troubling figures, like Ishmael, whose ghost haunts the later history of his people. We may regret this guilty concern for those you have wronged (the repeated, conflicting explanations of why Esau was excluded), slightly despising those who cannot live with their crimes, but it has given this book its rich, brooding character, returning to the moral cost of success and the penalties of insensitivity paid by those who win out. For all the restless drive to preserve the nation, to keep affirming its identity in the face of difficulty, we can think of Genesis as a text which, like Lot's wife, continues to cast its eyes behind in accesses of regret.

The story of Joseph, which rounds it off, is one of the tidiest in the book, a tale of rags to riches times two. Yet perhaps it is not such a paean to success as first appears. To those who remember, as who does not, the next stage in the national history, triumph in Egypt is like eminence in Hell, more lethal the more conspicuous it is. The outcome reminds one of the odd method of solemnizing a covenant by dividing the sacrificial flesh into two piles and walking between them, or tearing a document in half (each signer to have one) to ensure observance. Division is used to express joining, as circumcision is used to signify clinging or adherence. These rituals are less disconnected than they seem, for each one threatens something: if you go back on this you will be dismembered like this token of the agreement. We can more easily portray imperfection than perfection.

Joseph's story is more contradictory than it looks. At the beginning he is the familiar figure of the child who lords it over his elders, though so far mainly in fantasy or prospect (dreams of everyone bowing before him). But when the child is thrown into the pit (a dry cistern in the desert, commentators say – he is a natural force which makes barren land bear fruit) everything falls upside down. It is a parody of the sacrifice of Isaac: an animal is killed in place of Joseph, whose blood substituted on his cloak (his badge of office, *long* not *many coloured* according to recent translations) convinces his father that the boy is dead. Later, a cloak is used to convict him a second time, when his next enemy, Potiphar's wife, grabs it and founds more false deductions upon it.

The path which has so far been thick with traps now opens out and Joseph miraculously finds himself the ruler of a foreign country. This leads to the moment when he can play the tyrant over his brothers and those old dreams come true without their guessing that anything special is happening, so benighted has privation made them.

God has disappeared as a character from the story, and at the end Joseph has taken His place, subjecting his brothers to a test like the one God devised for Abraham, with the difference that they have deserved it and he is seen weeping at the distress he causes.

Yet this triumph must have made many readers uneasy, a disquiet objectified in the bizarre note on which Genesis ends: the lengthy process of Joseph's embalming. Earlier he is shown so changed by the experience of Egypt that when he returns with Jacob's body to the land of his birth the party is mistaken for Egyptian. Joseph has succeeded too well: from *seeming* foreign to outsiders, he has gone on to be entirely wrapped in Egyptianness. At his death he is Egyptian.

Joseph's success leads directly to the most convulsive crisis of Hebrew history; his career has created the need for a different, answering figure, Moses the rebel. The pattern of Genesis is broken with Joseph, the line in some sense ends there, and the history withers away, to be regenerated *ab ovo* in the next book.

Pharaoh now hates the Israelites as one could have predicted he might; Joseph has left his family stranded as hostages in Egypt, which he thought he was only pretending to do. Reversals on an individual scale are now enlarged to national size and everyone will pay for Joseph's success.

To prevent the occurrence of more Josephs all Hebrew boy children will be thrown into the river, a command Moses' parents follow deviously, building a boat of reeds (i.e. of the river) and floating the child out in it like a Viking burial. The ritual works and the sacrifice is saved by another bather. It is a strange disruption in family history which seems to say that at times one must sever all ties in the interest of continuance.

Moses' inheritance becomes metaphysical – he has lost his parents and hence his particular nationality, but when the knowledge trickles through to him, as it inevitably does, he is a more effective representative of the whole people for having mislaid his parochial origins. Like Joseph separated from his kin, raised from an even earlier age in strange households, he is, unlike Joseph, made by this unusual process more like what he has missed than ever. Having suffered their fate first in an intense private form, he then calls the whole nation back to its true identity.

Joseph's story is not the first or the last of such detours, but viewed from far enough away it appears a narrative false dawn. When things go as smoothly as they do for him, one learns to suspect them. By equal and opposite reaction the successes of the hero become the torments of his heirs.

CHAPTER THREE

MONSTERS:
GREEK MYTH, NORSE TALES, Beowulf

Comparing the earliest literary remains of the Hebrews and almost any other people, like the Greeks, one is struck by an incongruity. Greek stories (or Norse, or Indian) are full of cannibalism, fratricide and grotesque dismemberment. Even though these events often feel foreign to the person narrating them, it is still a very different imaging of the earliest phases of human development.

Most striking is the absence of a character like God, whom it is impossible to imagine lusting after earthly women or killing those who thwart him, on a whim he regrets afterwards. None of the Greek gods is as secure in his power as Jehovah, yet none of them would hear out Abraham's long plea that the judgment against Sodom be softened. Looking at how God is imagined should tell us whether Hebrew stories represent a later historical stage, and whether that culture has failed to preserve its rude mythic origins; or whether they have been deliberately suppressed, or simply skipped.

If one collated early survivals in many different cultures, Hebrew, Greek, and Norse would form a provocative triad, which one could characterize as the civilized product of an advanced culture, primitive product of advanced culture, and primitive product of primitive culture, to match one's feeling that the Greeks are experimenting with barbarity, while the Norsemen are appalled by its hold over them. For us it is tempting to see some of the goriest stories as something other than they appear: we make them psychodrama, ritualized *depictions* of hatred like a Klimt embrace or a Japanese mask, as if these lurid motifs were the grotesque projections of desires which possess another form at a more profound level.

The Greek stories themselves frequently translate their extravagances into something else, making them socially acceptable. Thus Demeter, stopping in her long search for Persephone, finds her energy diverted into magic performed on Demophoon, her hosts' son. Every night she thrusts the child into the fire and turns him like a carcase she is cooking or curing, a process which would have converted him from human to divine, if his mother hadn't spied on the experiment and cried out in fright, supposing that Demeter intended to kill the boy.

As it happens the goddess is grieving for a lost child. So in appropriating this one, she plays the part Hades did with her, contesting the son with his mother. Hades meant to make Persephone queen in hell, an unwanted honour; Demeter assumes it will suit his family for Demophoon to become a god and attributes her own disappointment to others in the vicinity. Somehow the kinship between the young people's fates is consoling in itself. Antecedents and their echoes make a sort of company for each other; stories which follow on from older ones don't stand alone.

Against this concord are played all the contradictions in the Demophoon eposide: the goddess means well but behaves furtively. A method usually swift is here slow, the victim not consumed but preserved. In fact myth differs from ordinary life most glaringly in the leading role it gives to paradox or the meeting of opposites. How familiar is the pattern, dimly suggested by Demophoon, of salvation through suffering and finally sacrifice. Christian myth diverges from Greek in taking this as if it could be a model for daily behaviour, but the cult of Dionysus contains such translations so far unmoralized.

Yet perhaps no story is free of dubious, universalizing interpretations. Motifs larger than the characters overshadow the whole tale of Demeter and Persephone, in which Demophoon forms an unimportant digression. Persephone's mother is the goddess of fertility, her ravisher the lord of death. The girl's disappearance produces a general stoppage of growth, but in a roundabout way: the life- not the death-force gives the directive for life to stop. So the characters' actions express the contraries of the allegorical labels – Hades rude vigour, and Demeter inert grief.

When Hades comes upon Persephone, she is picking flowers, ignorantly forecasting her fall, or greedily seeking the end of inexperience. Is she a killer of innocent life, or a maiden acting maidenly, participating in the season which will be taken from her? She personifies the spring yet will miss it when it goes. By a familiar illogicality of allegory the carrier will sometimes experience what she is teaching us, like a writer undergoing what he writes.

Before long Persephone is underground, from which she may simply return to life as it was, unless she can be persuaded to *eat* in hell, after which she will be tied to it forever. Viewed narrowly, the consumption of food is part of the transposition of living to non-living, something the dead do not do, and so, anomalous in this place. Thus, the proposed abstention would come easily to the truly dead. In order to live again one must imitate the un-living.

Like Genesis, Greek myth is a world in which facts and not motives count. Persephone doesn't give in; she is tricked, and when she recognizes the trick, it is too late to undo it. 'Eating' means simply that Hades has insinuated pomegranate seeds into her mouth. She doesn't feel them going in, but can't deny they are there. Socially it is much easier to take pregnancy every time as a proof of guilt than to weigh the woman's story that she has no idea where the baby came from.

Though built on sexual differences, these stories confuse them. Hades gives her a fruit stongly suggestive of feminine anatomy. Eve eats and then makes Adam eat, two acts neither of which follows the normal logic, the first self-semination, the second fertilization of the man by the woman. In that story, to make things worse, sensuous experience has come to stand for its converse, articulate knowledge, and the moral overlay has made it one of the most blighted narratives in all of storytelling, the greatest slander of women ever devised.

At first glance these various interpretations – eating the apple = sin, Persephone's abduction = the coming of winter – might seem no more than separable elements which have attached themselves to originally simpler narrative material. Both interpretations are founded on great disparities of scale: from a small act flow vast, long-surviving consequences. From an insignificant seed grows a huge plant. Such abrupt enlargement of the material is a general resemblance which dwarfs the specific differences in the two transfers. Moving from fruit to sin one leaves the graspable for the indefinite, from abduction to the seasons one moves from the weird to the everyday. But if the two are in this way opposite mental processes, finding the complex in the simple, and the simple in the problematic, the structures by which the advance is made are the same.

At some point every story generalizes its material. The ones we call myths do this more radically and by methods which later narratives begin to find unacceptable. So it is more plausible to say that the saga of Persephone is about sexual experience mainly, but when curtailed that way, the story is no longer a myth. Without the farfetched connection to something we have known all our lives, the departure of summer, the arrival of spring, this story would never have seemed interesting enough to get itself discussed.

The mythic imagination stands forth as one unembarrassed by these huge disparities; it revels in them, multiplies them. Yawning incongruity is the main stimulant in such structures; one only experiences healing where the flesh has first been torn. The violence of myth is enlivening because it is the violence of deep mental surprise, whose consequences are not shirked but followed out with relish. The final reward is that emotional risks lead to mental discoveries.

We are sometimes encouraged to think that the profundity of myth is entirely depersonalized, but it arises instead from a balance struck between the doings of persons and supra-personal principles. The Biblical stories for all their air of coming near the first dawn of literature and thought, have grown reticent about the operation of great forces in individual lives. We could extract a Persephone pattern from the story of Joseph but only with difficulty, so recessive has the pattern become.

It is a story of burial and resurrection to a new life, but the expression of wonder is so completely suppressed that the miracle happens twice. First the boy is cast into the pit, from which he is sold into slavery, which ought to work like a kind of rationalized death, but does not. The next step in his rise is to fall and be entombed again in prison, which leads directly to a higher place than he has yet reached.

Like Persephone, Joseph is associated with vegetable growth, though of course it is a long way from the overseer of granaries to the deity of grain, from the management of famine to the metaphysics of winter. Or is it? Joseph's role is the same, with the fatal difference that the magic is made believable, or half-believable, which is perhaps worse.

For some reason we hate to see the farfetched recede, which is why we will tolerate the protracted playing with whether Joseph will punish his brothers. Speaking sensibly, Benjamin is the only one who hasn't injured him, but the flirtation with doing him harm is powerful because Benjamin is Joseph's true rival, the usurper of his old place. Benjamin has supplanted him as youngest or last, which in the Hebrew world means first, as if a folk tale responded each time it saw the youngest son go off by producing a younger and then a younger and so on. The underlying view is both realistic and uplifting, yet we occasionally hanker for a story in which all is not forgiveness and orderly replacement of goals by their legal successors. Then we return to the truly remorseless world of myths, feeling that squeamishness is a late product.

The most atrocious stories are sometimes the most humane: the same myths which pose the greatest test of one's stomach for horrors are the best demonstrations of the redemptive power of Greek stories, like the dark and gruesome tale of Tereus. This myth is a startling demonstration

of the reassuring power of pattern ingested simply for its own sake. It is
like a house made entirely of echoing corridors, so woven back on itself it
begins with a reminder: we remember Philomela as a nightingale (showing
that we know the outcome without remembering the details), and the
opening tells how Tereus, married to her sister Procne, fell in love with
Philomela's *singing*.

As a result, he hides the sister in an isolated hut and reports her death,
at which their father offers him Philomela. When Procne learns of this,
Tereus cuts out her tongue and sets her to making bridal clothes. Into
them Procne stitches the bad news, and when Philomela reads the
message she rushes into the slave quarters, where her sister runs in circles
chirping unintelligibly. Freed, Procne cooks and serves up her son to his
father; discovering this, he chases the women with an axe.

Just as the axe is about to fall the gods intervene, changing all three into
appropriate kinds of birds. Procne becomes a swallow, whose cries do not
form a connected song. Philomela becomes the sweet-tongued
nightingale, and Tereus the thuggish, bullying hoopoe.

This resolution is like one of those musical effects in a late Romantic
symphony where, after a tense struggle to articulate a theme, suddenly a
way is found to a plateau along which the melody can sail in long relaxed
glides. Yet here it doesn't seem escapist because a terrible impasse had
been reached, because bestiality is absorbed and rendered harmless by the
regression to true beast-hood, because, best of all, insuperable inequalities
in the situation vanish once the mode is changed (no kings or slaves among
the birds).

In spite of our horror the earlier exchanges are satisfying in themselves:
to get Philomela's voice, Tereus takes Procne's away. Unable to speak
easily, she talks laboriously in stitches, a message so deeply felt it is woven
into the household gear, becoming a permanent part of life. The main
thrill of the story resides in the idea that the weak cannot be completely
suppressed, and that the truth can be devious too.

At this point further murder seems gratuitous, and feeding Tereus the
child-pie is one enormity too many. But it carries further a deep
congruity: Procne gets her revenge in parodies of domestic functions,
sewing and cooking. She destroys the home, but is only doing her job.
Readers know the violence that courses under the calm surface of ordinary
life, yet if they are like us, these creatures are also refreshingly alien, and
we are avid to know more of them because they play by such different
rules.

In this kind of story the question of relevance, of whether we need to see
these events in relation to us, seems *un*-perplexed. We do not. Many of the

most potent myths are ones whose moral significance is hardest to detect, the story of another female victim, Leda for example, loaded with fatalities and grotesquerie equal to the other story about birds, yet issuing differently.

Tereus and the sisters are transposed to animals when we are worn out with bloodshed and cruelty. It is a desperate remedy, releasing us from unbearable tension. The story of Leda *begins* with transformations so rapid the eye can hardly follow them. Nemesis becomes a fast animal to get away from Zeus, who becomes a faster or fiercer one and finally catches her (a goose) when he is a swan. Or did it happen that, running up to Leda, Zeus pretended to be a swan chased by an eagle – his own bird, so he is playing Leda's part, the soft victim of the god, but as soon as she offers to shelter the swan, she finds herself ravished by it?

This flutter is only a prelude to the story's core, which takes up the consequences of the forced union. In the two versions, either Nemesis laid the egg and Leda only warmed it, only appeared to be the mother of the strange brood who emerged, or Leda was inseminated by Zeus, and bore ... eggs. The first version reads like an attempt to dissociate Leda and the strangeness, to say something was odd, but only *appeared* to belong to a human actor and was actually normal, in its own terms. That version argues backwards to make magic undisruptive without entirely relinquishing it. For it still has her hatching the eggs and children coming out of them. The second version, which seems the true one, preserving the mystery in fuller strength, accepts that a god in bird form will father on his unwilling human mate not birds, but semi-divine children who issue from eggs. Are Helen and the others part-bird? That is simply how we convey that a person is not like everyone else, or explain the havoc she spreads without knowing what she is doing. A cynical onlooker will find in this story the most alluring releases from responsibility. Whether he takes Zeus or Helen he has the spirit of mayhem in human form. As always in Greek stories, the gods are simply freer selves, but some times freed only to find out more awful things.

When the situation of the Leda story is inverted and the woman chases the man, the results are less amusing to the Greek tellers. Pasiphae is one of the most alarming figures in Greek myth. Her passion for the bull, which seems so demented, is different from Zeus' various promptings only because she is not its master. Instead of becoming a bull and trampling someone, she imagines being trampled. Strong passion is a common occurrence in the myths; seen now from the other side, it fills the imaginer with horror.

Her way of approaching the problem is devious: she has Daedalus build

45

her a cow in which she can hide and lie in wait for the bull. Like Jacob she can bring off only intricate semblances of transfiguration. The artifice fools the near-sighted bull however, and Pasiphae gets her wish, the consequence of which is an awful birth, the Minotaur, a hybrid not tinged with fatality invisible to others like Helen, but lumbered with a gross bull's head, like Bottom with an appetite for slaughter.

For obvious reasons the monster can't be killed. It is Pasiphae's offspring and the consequence of her wish. So another elaborate device is built and this time it is the Minotaur and not Pasiphae who goes inside it. Again bestiality is to be tamed by human art, but the cost is very high. It is as if the Trojan horse were permanently lodged with one, exacting periodic tribute which sapped one's enthusiasm for life.

Caging the Minotaur in the labyrinth is costly because it must be fed some of the community's normal young. It doesn't ravage the countryside indiscriminately or remind the populace in the grossest way (by appearing) of its presence, but hangs like an infernal heaviness in the air. It has been suggested that the labyrinth is an image of hell, coiled like the bowels out of sight, like them taking in things which will not be seen in recognizable form again. It has also come to seem an image of the intellect defeated by its own products. His own ingenuity is too much for man, and cultural devices can be turned on their inventor. The deviser of laws can be oppressed by them and the builder of prisons shut in them.

The Minotaur seems in the end strangely welcome in the country which possesses him, which requisitions his food from surrounding nations and resists the clearing up of the mystery. Theseus' helper in solving the labyrinth and getting out again – it is no good after all to kill its inhabitant if one ends up taking his place, perhaps maddened by that irony to become a monster oneself – is viewed as a traitor to her people, destroying a national asset.

The story becomes more and more preposterous as succeeding stages are reached. The root-improbability is the Minotaur's ability to demand submission if he is really unable to get out. Thus myth has become central to us *because* of its devilish intricacy, because it manages to implicate a whole world in the fruit of Pasiphae's flash of unspeakable desire. Or maybe it was unravelled in reverse: the prompting to the storyteller was the existence of human sacrifice and the desire to explain it. Where could it have come from? Intolerable to imagine it truly gratuitous, so he must tie it to a human act, the strange but fitting consequence of a very strange one.

Pasiphae's madness resembles states associated with Dionysus, the Zeus of women, dark side of the god and tutelary spirit of the irrational.

Women who have failed to sacrifice to Dionysus become possessed of his energy in an uncomfortable degree, roaming waste places believing themselves to be cows and lending themselves to wanton practices which would shock their former, frigid selves. Before setting out on their wild chase they sever normal ties, rejecting husbands and killing children. Other Dionysian celebrants mistake themselves for hounds, and the god's enemy for their quarry, and before anyone can stop them have ripped him limb from limb.

One of Dionysus' most effective opponents, Lycourgos the wolf of Thrace, chases the god's women into the sea and then turns to exterminate the god in the form of the vine. He prunes the nose, ears, and limbs from his young son, believing that he is destroying Dionysus' plant. The child god's agony produces wine, or wine produces these errors of perception in them and later in us. Rather, wine stands for a heightened range in which everyday truths are swallowed up.

Under Dionysus' influence, worshipping him or punished by him, ordinary mortals participate in magical transformations. It is a sophisticated idea of the miraculous, to see it as perspectival – while the practitioner is under a certain influence, the impossible is true.

As a spawner of tales the idea of Dionysus is a strange juncture of the primitive and the decadent, and brings into later stages of society promptings for which there is no rational accounting. The primitive is not a historical stage which we have passed, but a faculty or susceptibility which will have its due, which we can grant willingly, or which we will suffer, watching it pass over us like a battle leaving awesome destruction in its wake.

However disorderly the Greek tales appear on the surface, however abandoned to the irrational, by contrast with Norse they seem engines of clarity, imposing symmetrical patterns on experience.

Greek stories end; Norse ones don't, but continue to unfurl in neverending consequences instead of stopping after a few turns of the wheel. The tales are boisterous like their inhabitants, founded on verbal conceits, carried away in floods of insults or other mental acrobatics. If not a more violent world than the Greek, theirs seems more unsettled, with swings from bloody revenge to negotiating the prices of things. Even gods will engage to pay a certain amount for their crimes, as if one can find rational equivalences for and therefore convert to commerce the wildest unleashings of instinct.

Of course this belief frequently turns out to be wishful thinking, and the arrangement breaks down. But the play in Norse stories continues to veer between extremes of rationality and irrationality, a span too great for any bridge. When Norse stories double back, instead of the clear repeating structure of the Greek, they produce a kind of tangle or interlace.

One of the tales begins by casting back to a fish in a stream, who is a dwarf in disguise, a disguise quick and passing like a metaphor. The teller's brother comes to the stream in the likeness of an otter, and catches the fish. Next the gods' jester Loki appears and catches Otter. When he stops for the night Loki begins to brag, displaying the pelt of the beast he has caught. But he is staying with Otter's father, who fixes the condition that his son's skin, turned into a sack, must be filled with gold.

To say that reality keeps disguising itself is simply to objectify one's own propensity for making mistakes. Such a method means responsibility is late catching up with one, but is on the way. No event is really decisive for long: we try to leave no loose ends from which trouble could spring, yet as soon as an action is complete we notice consequences which will spawn further change. Treasure, transferred, needs to be distributed or guarded. As it always does, the proximity of treasure calls out new qualities in its owners. It was paid in compensation to the family, which it disrupts more completely than the death of Otter.

The father won't give the sons shares, so one of them kills him in his sleep, and another one ends up with the loot. Which is where the story began. Its protagonist is the dispossessed brother looking for a path back to the gold, who adopts a promising orphan, an act with a concealed motive. Regin is making Sigurd a good warrior in order to regain the treasure.

Urged to go after the dragon – guilt has turned Regin's brother Fafnir into a dragon and the storage-sack into a deep and sinister lair – Sigurd decides to avenge his own father instead. Once this is accomplished, Regin prevails and Sigurd goes against Fafnir, whom he easily defeats. Now the warrior has a long conversation with the dying dragon, who warns him against his employer.

A dispute arises over shares in the victory, for Regin assumes Fafnir's blood (which he drinks) and heart (which he will cook while Sigurd sleeps) belong to him. The next thing we know Sigurd is roasting Fafnir's heart on a twig. He burns his finger, and licking the hurt, accidentally tastes the dragon's blood. At once he understands the speech of birds, who warn him to kill Regin so Regin can't kill him. Without stopping to wonder if all advice is good which arrives by wonderful means, Sigurd chops off Regin's head, eats Fafnir's heart, and drinks the dragon's and dead man's blood.

Like many stories this one lives by overturning its own first principles, now seen as obstacles to its further development. The moral justification for whisking Regin from the stage so the more attractive Sigurd can have his place in our minds, is that deviousness, which makes a good story (makes a story at all), must be squashed, and the killer himself is the right one to eat the corpse. Like other simplifications this one is more gratifying because it wasn't obvious – it replaced complexity, which has been given its due, but is not around any longer to confuse us.

All this is only a prelude to the hero's real task, winning a maiden asleep in a hall full of gold, no more than a beautified analogue of the dragon in his lair. As usual, the gold is surrounded by flames – metal like red embers, fire like burnished helms – what ought to be pleasure and help is the chief source of harm.

Here the story forks to run in two separate streamlets. In one version Sigurd comes upon the flamelike glitter from a wall of shields around a figure asleep in fire. Or the fire is simply the fierceness of these weapons. When he removes the sleeper's helmet he sees she is a woman and learns her name is Sigdrifa, a mutation of his own, as if he is peering into a special kind of mirror.

After receiving magic charms Sigurd says goodbye and wanders on, arriving at a court where he takes the owner's daughter as his wife and simultaneously leaves on a bride-fetching expedition with the host's sons, the object of which is Brunhild. Before leaving her father's house Brunhild sleeps with Sigurd, innocently, with a sword between them. Sigurd feels that he has chosen badly, and would rather have her than his host's daughter, but suppressing this feeling he returns to the court, where Brunhild, married to Gunnar, is now queen. She, too, gradually realizes she wants Sigurd, and in lonely walks over the ice hits on a solution to her dilemma: to incite her husband to kill Sigurd for fear the young hero may supplant him.

This Gunnar does with reluctance, stabbing Sigurd in his bed. His thrashing awakens the dead man's wife, whose cries and movements rattle the cups and provoke answering calls from the geese in the yard. Brunhild overhears and rejoices, but later in the same night announces her intention to die with Sigurd. Her pyre is set up next to his and the flames of the two mingle.

In the other version of the story, related by Brunhild from beyond the grave, she is tricked at an early age into an unwanted marriage (like Persephone), and soon dispatches her old husband Gunnar, for which the gods' punishment is a prick with the magic thorn and a long sleep in the ring of fire from which Sigurd wakes her.

Earlier the warrior rides through flames in search of Fafnir's hoard. Is Brunhild a replacement for the hoard, part of it, or simply the sharer of its

place? Women and treasure are two kinds of luck which easily shift from
happy to baleful. Like other Norse heroes Sigurd dies at night in bed with
his wife. Beds are more treacherous than fields of battle, and human
entanglements end in trouble.

The lives of the survivors become so perplexed one sometimes can't tell
if a relation is enmity or alliance. Sigurd's wife mourns by fleeing and then
by working the story therapeutically into embroidery. Soon her brothers
are pushing her into marriage with the enemy. Since she has lived away
from them, a wish to be rid of the expense of keeping her cannot be their
motive. It is one of many instances where characters' calculations are a
closed book to us. Their acts detached from motives acquire a free-
standing vigour like monoliths on some ritual site.

When Gudrun has lived at his court some time her new husband tries
to make her brothers visit him. Norse stories brood continually on this
question: can one safely venture into a strange hall? Are the fire-dreams
which erupt then, intimations of gold and success, or forecasts of war and
destruction? It seems a point of honour with male dreamers to ride into
the flames, casting forebodings aside. They feel an urge to accept
conflagration calmly, or something more: a fascination with gruesome-
ness, which desires to know the worst and to experience it. Atli is warned,
Gunnar and his brother Hogni are warned, and all of them sail on.

Atli's invitation contains lures of gold, which rouse the reader's
suspicions, but not the victims'. In one version Gudrun sends her
brothers a ring with a wolf's hair threaded through it, first interpreted by
them to mean treachery, and then triumph. In another she devises a
message in runes, subtly altered by the carrier, hung up in the hall, and
pieced together by Hogni's wife in the firelight, while the hubbub of
carousing echoes round her. Either her literacy is shaky, or expression and
penmanship are obscure, because though alarmed she lacks conviction
cautioning Hogni, who discredits the notion of omens.

The brothers' capture is elided. When Atli's revenge of Brunhild is
over, Gudrun dispatches him, and then wants to die, but fails to drown
herself and ends up married to the king of the coast she floats to.

The last turn in the tale is still connected with an offshoot of Sigurd: his
daughter by Gudrun, like her mother the unwilling wife of a neighbour-
ing king. Rumours arise that she will run away with his son, which prompt
the king her husband to have her killed. Hearing this, Gudrun cannot rest
until she has sent off her sons by the new marriage to take vengeance. As
long as there is anyone who can go to even the score, he must be sent.

On the way to the old king's hall the boys meet a mysterious figure who
taunts them until they kill him and are at once overcome by a sense of

doom. He was their half brother Erp who meant to help them. They ride on to the king's hall, and the story ends in one of those bloodbaths which interrupt feasting. Gudrun's sons die deep in enemy territory, having pulled another rich and well-equipped house down around their ears.

The reader is left to imagine how Gudrun gets through the rest of life, shorn of the means of making others feel her power. In spite of their laments, one feels that disaster is gratifying to these actors, for it has become a means of self-realization. Gudrun complains she has been bedded three times and had three homes, and we recognize it as boasting. Who would have guessed when Sigurd blundered into marrying her that she would so successfully outlast him?

Sigurd and Gudrun correspond to two models of the exposed and prominent life: the hero whose greatness makes him a target, who will not last long because he towers over others and attracts resentment. And the tenacious sufferer, enduring horrors which would finish most of us, able to adjust to change and start over. Rigid characters aren't always noble, adaptable ones aren't always base, and luck doesn't always follow as smoothly according to pattern as it does with these two, but the story seems at war with its own perception of what assures life's continuance.

The most reliable principle in the Norse world is that when a person achieves something strongly desired, he discovers he was wrong to want it. The stories show human desires out of tune with the forces which rule the world. Their tone is pessimistic because it is clear nothing can be done about this: people cannot and should not adjust to how things are, for it would remove what we admire in them. They will go on applying rules clearer than reality can ever be. They will think one step ahead, and the next twist of events or the emotions of others will take them by surprise or leave them undefended. Honourable behaviour could almost be defined as rushing in without thinking more than one step ahead.

The interesting heroes here do not last long, but in flexible, long-lived characters like Gudrun appear the first signs of a new view of life's and narrative's possibilities. One can imagine a new ideal springing up – not triumph or exploit as the measure of success, but the amount one has been through, a person to be judged as an old tree is, by the signs of buffeting and passage counted up at the end of long years.

In his retellings of Norse stories William Morris treated the old texts as if they were remnants of something fuller, which needed elaborating to be intelligible. Perhaps it is impossible to read anything without supplying our own running commentary, on themes thrown up by the old imaginer. Anyway, by now Morris' versions are interesting to students of Morris, and only in a circuitous way to students of the poetic Eddas and prose sagas. Comparing them with the originals we get an outline like a negative of the original, as Morris reminds us what the old tellers have not thought of saying. His justification for supplying atmosphere, trappings, and interstices that they leave out is that we know such fringes and depths existed and that for a full entry into old minds we need to have it reimagined for us.

Morris' approach is materialist: he wants to live in a Viking hall, to climb the stairs, wake in the night, or simply to let his eye stray over hangings, rafters, landscape. Where is the reader who hasn't clutched at the scanty suggestions of empty heaths, black forests, and biting winds, which make one feel that Northern literatures are more deeply infused with a sense of place? For just a few seconds in Gudrun's boys' last ride we get an intoxicating sense of wanderers in unfriendly expanses, a rootless band of fighters who take bleak wastes for granted.

So Morris' warrant for his melancholy additions is several-fold. The landscapes in which the stories occur are inhospitable, and by Romantic theories of man and nature this must have its effect on the actors, predisposing them to the fondness for trouble they do in fact display. And then of course Morris was excited by the visual survivals from those centuries and hoped to reconstruct the man-made environment in its original completeness and splendour. So he gives us an *illustrated* Edda, all realized in words it is true, yet entangling the reader with the subject in a whole register missing from the original. Next to Morris the Eddas themselves look like stripped Platonic forms, and he seems deliciously mired, lost in elaborations which speak to us of all the intervening time since this happened, as if old events would naturally slow to a lugubrious pace, or seem to occur under a great weight of sea-water. Norse halls are dim, Norse skies lour, Norse wives lie sleepless through unmeasured hours to express *our* relation to them: we are far away and don't see them clearly. Most of Morris' tonal effects are brooding tones, not because these works are so prone to reflection themselves, but because they inspire it in us.

Morris' most traitorous improvement, however, is to impose moral sense on the actions in the Sigurd story, not by altering the course of events but by making characters unhappy at what they are about to do, or vaguely uneasy about relations we find ambiguous: he changes the kind of responsibility they feel. Of course it is an interesting experiment, and he is far from the only one to have tried it, to put a nineteenth-century sensibility in rude conditions which would in fact not tolerate one for ten seconds. The idea is impossible, yet everyone approaching outmoded fictions does something like it. We accommodate their strangeness by going partway toward them, while at the same time coercing them into greater nearness to ourselves.

So Gudrun becomes a modern divorcee in search of peace and quiet, and her sons become modern teenagers. No one could now look at Brunhild without Freudianizing her and applying our ideas of what contradictory desires mean. Similarly, it may be impossible to look at a Cubist painting without trying to read its strange shapes as familiar objects. Depending on how hesitantly it is done, this can propel the viewer deep inside the painting, instead of flattening it to a predictable form. He doesn't solve it, which would leave it discardable like a completed crossword, but discovers step by step, by a more complicated route perhaps than its genesis required, how it got the way it is.

The 'missing' feelings and interior views in Norse tales provoke a similar effort of reconstruction, whose goal isn't to supply the parts lacking, but to measure what their absence means. As the comparison suggests, we can't help assuming that the starkness of Norse tales is deliberate like Mondrian, and that certain patterns in behaviour have been consciously abstracted from the original welter to be displayed more sharply.

Even so, we are far from Nietzsche's envy of primitive amorality. One does not learn how to behave Romanesquely from studying eleventh-century carvings. One may study them because one is tired of certain kinds of precision, not in hope of refounding the old civilization (wonderful recreations like Lethaby's folk church at Brockhampton notwithstanding), but in pursuit of formal purity with later ornament scraped away. So one seeks a certain escape from complexity within the confines of art.

It sounds wrong to call early Cubism and Scandinavian interlace, or these stories with their confused chains of responsibility and reprisal, simple. Yet all three stand out in the history of art because their complexity is immediately declared. They are like unashamed machinery or diagrams which thrust forward a hidden circuitry for analysis or absorption. The lack of disguise feels cold blooded to some. To plunge right in by stating essential truths is not polite or respectful of our mental distance from the work, welcoming us by stages into the strange hall.

A work exists which occupies an intermediate position, because it is an uneasy hybrid of Christian and pre-Christian materials, an old monster story which has been incompletely moralized and softened to modern uses. It almost seems that the teller of *Beowulf* is becoming a moralist in the course of telling it. The hero's final exploit is more heavily interpreted to provide a lesson afterwards than his first one, but perhaps defeats naturally give rise to soul-searching, which fits more with the end of life than the beginning.

Mercifully, in the episodes for which this poem is remembered, the pattern of events is left to act on us without much discussion. We perceive a connection between the magnificence of the ruler's hall and the depth of his trouble, a link which escapes him. Feasting by day and despair at night are two parts of a single whole which never gets a name. When Beowulf prepares to meet Grendel (news of whom reached him in his far off land via poems, which in the twelve years of this monster's crimes have found a worldwide audience), he knows instinctively how to behave. He hands over his weapons and removes helmet and mailcoat, made by the greatest of smiths, Wayland. Then he lies down in bed, as if to sleep. Here is a mystery for which no explanation is supplied, except Beowulf's remark that Grendel is reputed contemptuous of weapons, especially blades. Is the idea that the monster will be lulled to inattention by seeing victims lying ready like food on the plate? In fact relations with evil are occult, and one defeats it by indirection, by displays, like Christ's, of fictitious weakness. In the event everyone but Beowulf has fallen asleep, unlikely given their fears, lying down, that they would not leave the hall alive, apt in some allegory of the sleepiness of the average Christian's soul.

Grendel carries a Biblical pedigree, but Beowulf possesses nothing equivalent. The monster is said to be one of the descendants of Cain, banished from centres of civilization to barren heaths and marshy fens, and condemned to wander around the edges of the human world.

So he is a vessel of an unredeemable wickedness God gave up on centuries ago and ordered removed to a distance, a condition which makes the poet strangely tolerant of him: no matter what he did he could never come any nearer to God, and he acts under a different compulsion from ours when we will evil. He approaches the hall as an outsider who *must* hate it because he is permanently excluded. It is only an inkling, but how far from rigid morality is this idea that evil is an alien world of feeling.

Grendel is passionately propelled to destruction, but Beowulf isn't really a matching or answering force of light, who trusts in God and goodness, his pure heart, etc. He is simply *strong* (Hrothgar has heard that he has the strength of thirty in his hand, the exact number of Grendel's first batch of victims). Brought before Hrothgar he breaks instantly into indelicate boasting, has exterminated whole families of giants single-handedly, and so on. By contrast, Hrothgar is the tedious (and ineffectual, as we recall when he is named 'shield of the Danes') voice of wisdom. Improving anecdotes are the province of the old; Beowulf hasn't yet had time to draw the morals of things.

But if the actors are sometimes petty, this is a poem which, from the first, cultivates its pockets of mystery or evocation, like fog patches in the fens. It begins with a castaway picked out of the sea who sires someone named Beowulf (not our Beowulf, but Hrothgar's great-grandfather) who is then shown setting out to sea alone, as the corpse in a lavish funeral boat. It is a lonely beginning and prepares one for the troubles in Hrothgar's hall. No sooner is the greatest building in the world completed than Grendel's incursions begin, as if the noise of the feasters' rejoicing had called him out of the depths of the country, the answer or dark echo of joy.

So happiness divides the world with sadness, and there are two regimes at Hrothgar's. By day life proceeds as before, but nights are unlivable, and the hall stands empty. This continues for twelve years, but is practically intolerable, not really life. The picture of power which deserts one and then returns is not a happy balance, but a world more and more eaten up by shadow. One only wonders how long before they give up and move away, ending the suspension between life and death, and leaving Heorot to fall.

It is a romantic picture, which heightens the contrast between life inside and outside the hall by imagining the safest place become most dangerous (inside become outside), polarities reversed as by a change of current. The situation could be moralized as a story of God's grace, but it isn't, and feels suspiciously tainted with older beliefs in the sun's power. Christianity hasn't impinged much on the fear of the dark which lies at the root of it, which we originally shared and only laid aside because it was inconvenient.

Settled pessimism is one way of dealing with such perceived contradiction; wit is another. Grendel's ravages call out a special kind of joking: the survivors could tell they'd had a visitor. Before long it wasn't hard to find men who wanted to sleep away from the hall. They didn't expect rich compensation from this 'ruler' (who doesn't observe the normal code of service). There would be no funeral expenses if Grendel got Beowulf, because there were no leftovers from his meals. Such jokes show a fascination with, even a participation in, the horror, as if it were needed as an antidote to success.

The poem admits this perversity when describing what makes a good poet. As Hrothgar's men return happily from the terrible lake which is Grendel's home, now first revealed to them because he has returned to it leaving a trail of blood, one of them puts the monster's defeat into a poem, but obliquely. Nothing could be fresher – he doesn't even wait till they are back in the hall, but composes and recites it as they ride along. The key part of his task is finding the right parallels in pre-existing stories. This singer hits on one he thinks suits Beowulf, and then the momentum of his telling leads him on to a counter-example. Beowulf is *not* like X who became proud, hated by his people, an unhappy exile. Back in the hall, there is rejoicing for 'the Danes have *not yet* begun to plot against one another'. A poet entertains the revellers, and tells a tale full of treachery: large armies reduced to tiny bands watching their comrades consumed on pyres before winter descends. If anyone still is listening, it should give him pause.

Stories always have a warning function in *Beowulf*. People tell them when they carouse together (it is the only way for warriors to distinguish one night of drinking from another), yet they take a far from lulling form. Light is followed by darkness, and after the good prince comes the selfish tyrant. After the construction of Heorot, the visits of Grendel; after relief at Grendel's death, the surprising discovery that he has a mother, not much less awful than he. Heroism isn't simple; victory has an aftermath. So the valiant band must pay another visit to the boiling lake. Instead of gloating over it, Beowulf must give himself up to it.

The second fight has a similar shape to the first: before he meets the enemy the hero exposes himself passively to the alien world: it takes Beowulf almost a day of sinking to reach the bottom of the snake-infested tarn, where he is whisked by the lady monster ('hungry and sad') to her gloomy hall in which luckily he finds air instead of water to breathe. Grendel's mother wields a dagger, which suggests she possesses quasi-human form; probably she is more like Heathcliff than a dragon.

After the fight Beowulf dutifully ignores the system of underwater caverns full of glittering treasure. There is only one thing he wants here, Grendel's head, which is brought back to Heorot and sobers the drinkers when dragged through their midst by the hair.

Objects suggest anecdotes; possessions have become historical; an outsider realizes on entering someone else's dwelling (even Hrothgar's, not to speak of Grendel's) that it has a history, that another life has taken place there, and a thoughtful warrior is semi-paralyzed in the presence of this buried experience. Like any comprehensive moral view, Christian doctrine seems to offer a frame which accounts for this divergence; otherness is often evil, but sometimes not. Yet although there is a certain congruence between older Romantic pessimism and Biblical chastenings of man's pride, they are distinct in the poem, the second an awkward overlay.

Beowulf is earlier than the Norse texts we have, but seems to have brooded longer on a similar sense that things will go wrong for human beings, and to have made itself at home in a landscape deeply, beautifully coloured by despair, which Christian doctrine glosses but can neither digest nor argue away.

The poem jumps over the bulk of Beowulf's life with sketchy recapitulations. It consists of two parts, the young warrior proving himself and the old warrior stirring himself for a final effort. The poem savours this idea of the *last*: the treasure which the final dragon guards was first hidden in the tumulus by the lone survivor of an ancient race, who took his revenge on the world which mistreated him by removing this wealth from use.

Feelings about the hoard are ambivalent: it is a waste to have it tied up, inert; yet men do well to skirt it widely, because it carries obscure possibilities of harm. The dragon who guards it is a malicious being, for gold is useless to dragons, but he reinforces the quasi-pious purpose of the original possessor. So when Beowulf sets out to recover the hoard he embarks on a dubious errand: now a grave robber as well as the saviour of his people.

Rich meanings attach to tumuli: they are untenanted spots, which of course no one would live on, yet desirable, attracting the unsavoury interest of dragons who fly over the earth looking for these eminences and then claiming them. These beasts are the embodied power of superstition to draw an uncrossable line around such humps: if you meddle there you are doomed.

This particular mound has smouldered harmlessly for centuries and now erupts through the agency of an outcast serf, ransoming himself back into favour with a bit of loot he has stumbled on unwittingly. Finally the stolen cup comes into Beowulf's hands, and when they set out for the hoard, the serf (their guide) makes the thirteenth of the party. Far beneath the surface is a hint of Judas' enticement of Christ, a miserable traitor half-conscious of his act, a predestined bitter drink.

At the crucial moment Beowulf is deserted by his companions who run into the woods. He bears the intolerable force of the dragon's flames and is fatally infected. When it is too late, a young fighter helps him kill the dragon, but now the king can only haul himself to a good point for surveying the hummock and hope that his man can bring tokens of the treasure before he expires.

It is one of the least Christian parts of the poem, yet obscurely moral. The youth, entering the grave, is appalled and thrilled by the rusty magnificence of so much useless stuff hanging from the walls or tumbled on the ground. Beowulf's melancholy directives, those last glimmers of the waning light of the folk sinking beneath the hill, are a far cry from the smug pronouncements which capped the Grendel affair.

He thinks he has bought the treasure with his life and tries to present this as an expensive but worthwhile trade. His people know that without him they will be overrun, and they foresee an era of trouble. Finally Beowulf is entombed on a headland as he has asked to be, his importance visible from afar, and a help to sea travellers, but a large treasure is buried with him. Freeing one hoard, he has called into being another, to be discovered and corrupted by another dragon, and centuries hence to bring another Beowulf to grief. Thus, in a way that reduces human moralizing to rubble, all eminence is levelled. Thus the corruption which overtakes heroes is embodied: virtue decays like the flesh.

CHAPTER FOUR

SECOND THOUGHTS:
CHRÊTIEN DE TROYES, MALORY

Between Beowulf and Chrêtien de Troyes occurs the most momentous shift in the whole history of narrative. It is a shift away from the centre to the edge, from a single to a double strand. Instead of one hero we find a troop, across which the poet's gaze plays in turn, producing a cycle of adventures which skirt a central inviolable space, the Grail, or true knighthood, a perfection to which all stories aspire without real hope of occupying it.

Arthur's court is larger and more highly developed than Hrothgar's but no longer the focus of such boastful claims. Characters are more like individuals and less like figureheads, and they are at the same time only one of a possible many. Always we remember the other warriors waiting for their time at the centre of our mental space, which even so may not come, but is not ruled out by a rigid preselection as in *Beowulf*. Chrêtien has discovered the interest of subcentres and seems almost to prefer leaving the beaten track and avoiding the announced destinations. This knotting of the thread is an outward sign of scaled down claims for the protagonists: the world is larger, and the self smaller, than in earlier stories.

Chrêtien's *Erec and Enide* begins with a laboratory demonstration of this shift, inconceivable in any earlier writer. He loses his way ostentatiously, in order to follow an interesting side path. First, Arthur announces a hunt and departs, then Guinevere follows after a short interval. Further back still is Erec, and by the time the knight catches up with the ladies Arthur has disappeared in the distance. At this point the adventure comes forward out of the trees. It appears as a matching party of three, and the upshot of a calculated rudeness on the strangers' part is that Erec would like to challenge the offending knight, but can't, for an interesting reason.

What was planned as a hunt needs to become a fight, but Erec's armour is back at the castle. So as not to lose the knight Erec shadows him, hoping his path will intersect at some point with armour he can borrow. So the story begins with a series of deflections, and diversion seems to offer a fresher significance than one finds in old narratives following well-paved roads.

From the beginning Chrêtien's story goes forward in two places at once and the backwater is the real focus. One can hazard that double plots, diagrams of divided consciousness, arise from a simple frustration – the world is full of unsynchronized schedules, and when you try to harmonize any two of them, one of the parties endures boring delays.

Thus the problem of Erec's armour looms larger and larger as an index of Chrêtien's concerns. Like *Beowulf* this poem glories in wealth and enumerating the details of rich clothing. But unlike *Beowulf* it remembers that even gorgeous armour would be an encumbrance if you didn't need it. It is so impressed by this particular irony that it generates the story from a problem like wondering whether to take an umbrella and deciding not to.

When Erec, armed at last, defeats the discourteous knight the crowd's reaction is tabulated: though some rejoiced, many were sad because they took the knight's side against the stranger. Without adopting a thorough relativism, Chrêtien deprives us of the feeling that there is a single way of understanding what we see. If he took fully to heart his depiction of human behaviour, philosophical relativism is what he'd be driven to, but as yet these perceptions are only dawning, and he draws back from the shattered vision his best dramatic insights suppose.

It was probably a fatal concession to allow perspectivism any sort of foothold, but whatever the final destination of this train of thought, its tendency immediately, and for centuries to come, was clearly humanizing. It has been usual to trace the softening effects of these doubts of any single perspective to the new importance given to women by the chivalric code, and many signs in the romances confirm this.

People in other rooms, people with other feelings – there begins to be covert empathy with alien sensibilities almost for the sake of their alienness. When Erec arrives at the vavasour's where he is to spend the night, he is met by the host, who calls out the ladyfolk. Instead of materializing from nowhere as would have happened in *Beowulf*, the women enter from a workroom, shutting its door behind them. Chrêtien says mock-ingenuously, 'I don't know what they were doing there,' like trying to catch a glimpse of their privacy before the door closes on it. Other people are more themselves *when they are not with you*, but you are barred from knowing them that way. Once he takes the woman's feelings seriously the man finds himself an outsider.

Pausing later, during their fight, the knights glance toward the watching women and see that they are both weeping, both praying. There are various perspectives on the battle: each man has his female supporter, but the women are separate from and almost pitted against the men. War is alien; men who wage it are alien. Conversely, struggles alienate one from those outside them, an effect which almost, but not quite, ends when the struggle ends: the men look at the ladies and think, my enemy is more like me than my ally.

Chrêtien's story is obsessed with a class of twilight-occurrence where further uncertainties appear – departures, leavetakings, arrivals, and most surprising of all, expectation of arrival. Underlings at Arthur's notice a certain young knight at a distance, and run to tell the queen ('Why have you mentioned him? Is there word of him?' she says), whereupon she hurries to a place from which she can examine the approaching semi-stranger.

Beowulf is not a complicated enough web that one strand of it could forget about another and need to be reminded. When it occurs in Chrêtien, this splicing is a luxury, not a nuisance as is briefly pretended, providing you with so many links that you can lose track of some of them, like the owner of two houses. It is almost a dynamic law of complex narratives that the parts cannot stay together long, and joining only sets the scene for splitting. Erec hasn't been back at Arthur's more than a page or two when he asks permission to visit his father. The court is always there: a knight goes off on adventures, and at any time Arthur will have a certain number of adventurers out, like a fisherman's lures.

Narrative singleness comes apart, and great changes are taking place in the hierarchy of values as well. Vaguer, more passive activities, weakened derivatives of anticipation, like waiting, begin to seem mysterious and thus more profound than action itself, but are basically feminine, and hence not available to men. So when Erec is swallowed up by the life of the castle, staying indoors near his new bride Enide, he provokes a universal murmur of disapproval.

Chrêtien's greatest discovery is a kind of psychological impasse which is the negative form of noting differences between sensibilities. When life slows to a standstill among those unsure of their functions, a troubling sense of individual differences emerges. Enide watches the sleeping Erec (alertness and oblivion having switched sexual places), and reproaches him wistfully with inaction. He overhears her, and now begins an alarming concealment of one person's purposes from another, Chrêtien's dark vision of the will to self-destruction. Erec orders Enide to dress for travelling and her horse is brought. She thinks she is being sent into solitary exile, but to everyone's surprise, Erec also dresses and arms, and they leave together.

As punishment for having spoken, Enide is enjoined never to speak, and so, by laborious artifice, the benefit of solitary imprisonment is obtained. In some way it is a deepener of their relation: nothing trivial can remain. Enide will brood on this proximity and Erec hope to control her thought with no gauge of his success. But it is less stable than Erec imagines, because it proves impossible to prevent impingements from outside. Now Enide sees dangers which Erec does not. If she didn't warn him, he wouldn't survive to punish her. If a knight requires a woman's help how secure are his triumphs? Erec is humiliated to realize that his need of Enide is not a courtly figure of speech, and his cure for this distress is to link the two of them more excruciatingly than ever.

It is a bleak portrait of marriage taken seriously instead of casually, and one of Chrêtien's profoundest ideas – that in exclusive relationships lies hidden the deepest loneliness. Yet, one would think, for all the sense of minutes which last years and an empty landscape stretching endlessly, it is a self-imposed ordeal and Erec has only to say the word and it will disappear.

But this is not so. The faulty premise leads to a true conclusion, and Erec's arbitrary psychological experiment brings an authentic revelation. Chrêtien's are the first characters in fiction so unsure of what they want, hemmed in by perversities of will, maiming their own desires. He gets further into his characters than was customary and finds deep within, as if the root-principle of the organism, ambivalence, and the uncertainty which flows from granting its central place.

Erec's penitential purpose is not directly expressed, except that when events try to go smoothly he repels reality's favours, refusing food, lodging, and comfort. He finally relents when he has convinced Enide of his death, and overheard from his bier that, even then, she will repulse the advances of another rich Count, refusing food for her husband's sake to be dead like him.

It is a sinister way round the divergence of individuals to hear what they say of you when they believe you asleep or dead. In Erec's defence one would say that he too thought himself dead: it was a real wound, not shamming, which kept him unconscious while the funeral display was set up and the funeral feast consumed. From the beginning, Erec had no reason to suspect Enide's faithfulness, except that she was sometimes awake when he was asleep, and that she might outlive him, which is to say, that they could diverge in some literal sense absolutely. His mistrust was a thorough rupture with all of reality outside himself, like losing faith in the external world.

'Events' and even an agreed external reality are devalued by Chrêtien's discoveries about personality. If he acted consistently he would replace adventures with something else, but he's not fully conscious how subversive of the old story some of his ideas are, and so falls back on the ability of the world to spawn adventures no matter what. Whenever Erec appears to reach the end, another knight rides in from somewhere looking for a fight. Half these fights are fictitious, depending on artificial concealment. Erec's armour is so battered his insignias have been obliterated, so his friend attacks not knowing it is he; or, even worse, someone coming to rescue his corpse can't imagine he is still alive, or see in the dark, and so attacks.

Mental confusion or mistakes, regarded by Chrêtien as positive sources of interest, are further signs of the internalization of perception. Erec has concealed more than his identity. It turns out when he is undressed that he has been bleeding profusely inside his armour, stoically ignoring many wounds. Running on such suppressed force as this, stories become more devious. Counter-impulses to the whole idea of adventures as the basis of a story emerge in abortive form, and incommunicable inner reality begins to exercise a fascination which has as yet no satisfying literary outcome.

After the moonlit fight with his most devoted vassal, which like all Chrêtien's fights ends with the combatants in a state of grotesque exhaustion, they decide to spend the night right where they are, among the bushes. Tents are erected, flints struck, and tapers lit until it begins to feel civilized. Erec's friend orders a bed to be built and then tempts him with meat patties he takes from a box.

It all began as an unmeaningful delay and has become more interesting than the fight itself. Ancillary or under-activities usurp the centre of the stage; a servant's eye view appears truer. Earlier when parties are rushing to Arthur's court the order of their arrival is described: first the cooks, butlers, and squires enter and begin to set up lodgings; only later the knights appear. The question of how things work begins to interest Chrêtien, and he wants to know what precedes or lies behind sleeping or eating.

At the same time, adventure is becoming more and more ritualized. It is a motif, not a primary reality, hence vulnerable to parodic exaggeration. In a later romance, *Yvain*, the story is *portrayed* as something to be told over and over. It begins with the king turning away from a feast. He gets up before it is over, closets himself and falls asleep talking to the queen.

63

She detects the murmur of a story teller outside the door, steals up on the group, and makes them start over from the beginning. The king wakes as it ends, and it is now re-repeated for him. Apparently it is just what he is looking for, a dangerous adventure: he plans to leave the following day to see for himself.

Yvain is more taken with it still, makes secret preparations, and departs then and there. Everything goes as we have seen it before, in recountings outside the king's door, until he defeats a strange knight and chases him to a city, where Yvain gets trapped between portcullises like a rat. This tiny space is apparently adjoined by rooms from which ladies can issue, for one does, to whom Yvain did a kindness many years before.

When the city dwellers recover from the grief his opponent's death has thrown them in, they will tear Yvain to pieces. In the meantime the lady offers him a ring which will make him invisible. So the adventure which began as illegitimate or stolen (Yvain slipping away from court unde- tected) has ended with the knight squeezed out of existence entirely. Even so, the inhabitants of the castle know he must be there, for the two halves of his horse on which the portcullis fell are still visible. Now the citizens conduct a search with clubs, banging at the walls and furniture, while Yvain reposes on a couch they don't molest.

That test passed, he is threatened by the funeral procession. His victim's body is set down between the portcullises and all its wounds commence bleeding vigorously, which sets the entourage off on a fresh rain of blows. This time Yvain is plentifully hit and the widow's taunts tempt him toward discovery – only a coward could stay hidden etc.

All this luridness turns into an intricate psychological knot: Yvain's captivity has been sealed by the grief of his victim's wife. Now he wants nothing but to be locked up near her. Again the knight has been defeated by the woman, strength overcome by weakness, an inversion of *Erec and Enide*, where physical impasse corresponded to an impasse of feeling.

Meanings finally come round to their opposites and the enemies end as lovers. The ring-lender is the agent, making the lady think of Yvain, at first with horror, then in revulsion from the strength of this emotion. She is told it will be hard to produce him quickly – he must be located in his own country. All the while he is being washed and groomed nearby, and will surprise the lady who expects him hot, tired, unkempt. Meanwhile he is told the lady has learned his hiding place and insists on total power over his person. So he creeps terrified into her presence, who waits in a fever of anticipation.

Other romances pay lip service to the idea of subjection to the lady. Here it is presented with utter inward conviction. The obverse of the warrior ideal is its truest completion; now a way is found to be both victor and victim. The last twist in the inversion is that she marries her husband's killer because she needs to defend the magic spring, where the story began, and which Arthur will soon attack. So Yvain first asserts his new allegiance against his former friends.

From this point on, the story never approaches its earlier intensity, though it contains some noisy adventures. The presence of a long aftermath proves once more that Chrêtien didn't know where his inspiration was leading. He shows us lives with downhill portions for their second halves, as if like the fickle reader, the active knight at some point laid himself open to boredom, both promising and discouraging as a route for further fictions. That ungraspable suggestion may be the most exciting of all. Chrêtien trembles on the brink of a key Romantic discovery, the abyss of personality, which a hero first falls into when he has lots of time on his hands.

It is a nice question to decide between Chrêtien de Troyes and Sir Thomas Malory which of them undercuts the heroic ideal more thoroughly, Chrêtien who recognized a good deal of the mocker in himself, or Malory who imagined himself a true believer. As a narrator and a thinker, Malory is a regressive character, aiming to go back to a clearer outline of action than his French sources provide. But it is the appearance of clarity, not clarity itself. The reader is carried along at the strangely rapid pace, watching things happen which raise many questions, none of which are answered. Malory seems incapable of surprise, so enchantments and other improbabilities are assimilated to the flat world of fact. There is a lady who has been sitting in a hot bath in an iron room for years; she cannot get out. Lancelot comes, hears the story, opens the door, and frees her. Tristram's father goes hunting and is captured by a witch. When he does not return, his wife runs into the woods (where he hunts? a different one?), gives birth to Tristram and dies. Malory is under a spell: he must repeat what he has heard, knowing there is a magic cure in it, but not sure where it resides.

What makes him rush on? Is it a profound superficiality, which fears the least inkling of what it is *like* to be trapped in a burning fire, or lost in the forest, or suffering *anything* prolonged? Is he the Malory of Warwickshire imprisoned for murder and rape, an unsavoury character? When he calls himself *knight-prisoner*, does he mean as is often thought that his book is the product of all those hours in prison?

So a man of action was forced to sit still, and produced not a work of introspection or a serene narrative, which has all the time it needs to explore byways and lose itself in eddies, but a narrative which presses forward constantly as if chased. It is a telling which while its eye is fixed on its single goal – of keeping its personages in constant motion as if in a ball game where one can't let the rallying stop – allows other things to get in desperately contradictory states.

For all his allegiance to a knightly code, in which responsibilities are clear and heavy, he has a knack for creating moral tangles, like the question of who is responsible for rescuing the abduced lady, wife of Segwarides, whom Tristram is caught in bed with. This recurring sense of adult existence as intolerably messy, especially in the sexual triangles it throws up, fits with the idea of Malory the rapist, liable to fall under the delusion his characters do. Right will win; if one wins, one is justified.

But the entire story of Arthur's court says just the opposite. Lancelot, 'the best knight in the world,' betrays his master. His strength is made to serve a lie, defending Guinevere's purity, but remains undiminished: he causes many deaths in the bad cause. Malory is the perfect teller for this tale, because he is so reluctant to see a moral in it. His hero is right in detail and wrong overall, but Malory has almost no sense of the tragic.

It should be a doomladen story but it conveys a sense of bewilderment, much lighter in tone than Tennyson, and than earlier tellers too. Do these disasters need to happen? Can't people be sensible? we hear Malory ask, as if he would be content for his story to be less momentous, less awe-creating. It is in that way that one can regard him as an innocent teller (in so many ways an impure man and imaginer), because his own conception of the story leads him toward milder endings.

Malory's passing over marvels as if they weren't there, as if we had the option of taking them at face value, has the effect of enhancing them. So the strangeness is multiplied: what is its meaning? and is it there at all? Like one who stands in the door of a room without letting us see fully into it, Malory makes readers feel it would probably help to know more than this narrator tells them.

Malory does not exploit his opportunities, as the person standing in the doorway does not fully employ the space beyond. Not by elaboration or embroidery, but by a sense of things unsaid he creates his effects. Thus when Tristram's first fight takes place on an island, with spectators ranged on the two riverbanks, Malory occupies himself with getting his fighters out to the middle in boats. It is left for us to pick up the strange dissociation the episode conveys, which inheres in the spaces round the participants. They are like characters in Henry James, who exist in a private fog so extensive that other passers-by seem continents away. Not that one finds Jamesian richness of reverie in Malory, but the barrenness which that richness tries to clothe, as it were the skeleton of a truely subjective fiction.

The loneliness of this island battle is felt internally, as if Malory's knights were widely spaced lights in a dark landscape – the modern reader cannot avoid such allegorizing – so the events described become a model of looking from the inside out. Malory is describing how a self perceives the world, a lonely self and an unreliable world.

Many of the motifs which most engage his imagination are pictures of dissociation, like the empty Siege Perilous, waiting on and on for the right person to sit in it, or the two pieces of Tristram's sword, united again in a series of fantastic accidents. A small portion of this found lodged in Mordred's head is preserved by his sister, who, prowling in Tristram's chamber while he is in the bath (having come here to be cured of the wound Mordred gave him), notices a gap in the knight's idle sword, into which her fragment fits, one of those reunions which provokes worse disjunctions.

All these people shut in small spaces, baths or bedrooms, hearing each other through the walls, jumping out the windows to evade pursuers or the horror of their position, are the involuntary nightmares of a prisoner. Lancelot has no sooner rescued the woman cooped in the bath than he finds himself shut by enchantment in a room with no chinks to let through the light which would reveal that it is Elaine and not Guinevere he has spent the night with.

Malory's boldness in making intricate drama of the unmentionable happenings of the night can hardly be exaggerated. At first the approach seems sordid (what the intriguer wears, his cold bed), yet these mean details loom up like objects in fog, with a curious grandeur born of their isolation.

In another intrigue of the same sort, Tristram comes to his lady fresh from a scuffle along the highway and bleeds on both top and bottom sheets, leaving her to explain to her husband. Elsewhere he is surprised naked with the king's wife, bound, and carted to the vicinity of a chapel, which he defends like a fort until, abruptly shamed by his nudity, he jumps from its narrow window onto the sea-rocks beneath, off which he is later hoisted with towels.

Lancelot gets caught in similar traps. A large party yells insults outside the queen's door, behind which he is shut. Failing to disperse them by persuasion, he holds the door open a little, lets in a knight, slaughters him, and donning the armour thus captured, sallies forth to decorate the queen's threshold with twelve of the remaining thirteen.

Malory's view of these squalid happenings must be different from ours.

Repeatedly he shows the cuckold-king opining that he can't accuse the guilty knight and hoping no envious bystander will make his shame so public that he is forced to salvage his honour. Malory won't allow that the herioc ideal is seriously undermined when calculation is admitted as the basis of the warriors' league. The most sordid moment arrives when Tristram, confronted by Mark accusing him, ducks the king's sword, waits to see if anyone comes to Mark's defence, and then chases him ignominiously, slapping him with the flat of his sword until the king falls on his nose. Soon after occurs the reconciliation dictated by prudence.

Ludicrous possibilities in all these situations are lost on Malory, as if he cannot perceive incongruity and, for all his fascination with points of chivalric procedure, has little sense of decorum. The pure knight Galahad is conceived by trickery. And only when Tristram is in bed with the second Isolde does he remember the first, developments Malory presents innocently, which is to say phlegmatically.

He renders romantic events without their aura or afterglow, and closes the hazy distance between the heroes and us with such gross literalism as the claim that Gawain's skull can be inspected today in Dover Castle, where one can touch the gash left by Lancelot's sword. At this point the story offers the wrong kind of proof, and misunderstands the class of event it is dealing with. Philosophers would extract general ideas from Malory's account which never occur to him, conclusions about human behaviour, speculation about other ways people might have acted. Instead of this he gives us the hard central kernel, the story as a compact physical object.

At one point Isolde sends a letter to Guinevere saying there are only four great lovers in the world, the writer and Tristram, the addressee and Lancelot. It is what Malory does least well, commenting on the wider reverberations of his story. His personages are the greatest, the Grail is the richest in the world, so we are told. Yet events as Malory perceives them are not so much amazing as they are solid. Kings can fall on their noses and heroes come crashing into the shrubbery after a leap. Which is not to say that Malory is a debunker, because he does not seem to feel that his characters are lowered by such vulnerabilities.

Yet realism is not by any means his ruling principle. The great battle at the end of the *Morte D'Arthur* may read to us like a political struggle rather than the ideal confrontation of romance, nearer to Shakespeare's histories than miracles in the world of faerie, yet when he wrote it, filled with nostalgia for an outmoded heroism, Malory intended to hark back to a different age. He is that rare phenomenon, sceptical in small things, pious in great. Or perhaps he can see it both ways at once: he remembers the past, *and* he realizes Lancelot is lying, no matter how good the knight sounds. Yet he shows all Lancelot's hearers except a single enemy reduced to tears by the hypocrite's recital.

One can't even be sure that Malory wishes the best knight in the world were a little better. Perhaps the world is wrong to demand more of strong men than they can deliver. But this writer is so acquiescent that one does not feel strong kicks against the traces. True knights accept outcomes with minimal comment. It is another way in which he reapproximates a primitive narrator, welcoming events rather than interpretations.

The high claims made for the old knights are stated so flatly that we have no choice but to accept them, yet matching them against the occasional bits of tawdry behaviour seen in all alike, we may feel them to be words of which the meaning has been lost. Malory repeats something which we can no longer understand and so must take on trust.

When he comes to present the times of Christ he imagines them knightly: that 'good knight' Joseph of Aramathy preserves the Grail and some scraps of divinely effective armour in his spiritual-military progress from Palestine to Britain. Biblical times are medieval, medieval times are sordid like the present. In both cases the anachronism is Malory's way of bridging a large gap, a deliberately awkward metaphor which lets one make contact with the unknown.

At the end of the *Morte D'Arthur* the king finds out that it is time to go by asking an unwilling knight to throw a valuable sword into a lake. A hand appears to catch and brandish it, then vanishes. That seems to be a signal to Arthur, or perhaps returning the sword was his way of saying he wanted to leave. He rides to the lakeside where a boat is waiting for him, very sumptuous and gay, containing three queens who welcome him magnificently. The entertaining ceremony is spoiled by two things: at some point the women who have rejoiced at their reunion with Arthur begin to wail, which jars with the general air of magnificence. Also one wonders where a boat on a *lake* could come from or go, because they evidently regard Arthur's action as a final departure from these shores, not the start of a short jaunt.

So one has the perplexing junction of festivity and mourning, and an eerie resemblance between setting off without an announced destination and ancient methods of burial which trusted the body to the current in a hopeless attempt to say that the dead person was leaving here, but would arrive somewhere else.

Malory handles Arthur's departure with unusual tact, so that it feels both momentous and unmomentous. How does one know it was decisive? Only because nothing follows it, Arthur is not seen again. Or at least one cannot be sure. Bedevere travels on and arrives at a hermitage where there are sounds of weeping. Who is the departed? he asks, and is told that a corpse arrived mysteriously in the night escorted by three ladies. Is it Arthur? Why can't we know one way or the other? He hasn't ascended into heaven after all, but come to earth at a point very near his leavetaking. We aren't left wondering where he will reappear, yet are deprived of a secure final glimpse.

A more numinous instance than usual, essentially it is congruent with Malory's attitude to events throughout. A prosaic explanation comes within inches of accounting for everything but somehow fails to cover what we have seen, making us feel there is more. Without saying what it is, Malory gives a powerful sense that something has escaped.

Unlike any other early narrator I know, he is content to leave it at that: when Lancelot visits the Castle of Case, twenty-two knights are listed with semi-descriptive names in garbled French which who knows how they came by. Malory's world is like the map dotted with the names of English villages, wonderful relics preserved for no clearly-seen reason by semi-reverent and uncomprehending hands.

He is able to restore the data to a purer state than his sources through qualities which sound negative, like indifference or lack of curiosity. Undoubtedly much was lost when Malory was turned loose on the French romances, for many meanings passed him by, yet something more important was recaptured, dumbness in the face of things, or undemonstrative awe at how the world works.

Yet Malory is an inappropriate teller for the story of the Grail, at least. A spiritual quest is shown undoing the earthly community. It isn't a spectacle Malory can enjoy; we feel him sitting glumly by while everything he values falls to pieces. Religious houses now clog the landscape, and knights are frequently racked by dreams which push them toward monasteries or hermits' huts in search of explanation. To Malory such seriousness seems a flight toward unreality. He is profoundly out of sympathy with the subjectivizing tendency of spiritual experience. Some would find the prospect of 150 knights, formerly connected with the Round Table, each setting off in his own direction to seek the Grail, exhilarating. What possibilities of story seem to open before one. Yet for Malory from this moment everything becomes increasingly ghostly and insubstantial. For him the introspective tendencies of the very romances he devoted himself to retelling in an older, less cluttered form, spell the end of narrative.

CHAPTER FIVE

SUBJECTIVE ALLEGORIES:
Roman de la Rose, La Vita Nuova

We can't easily comprehend the medieval popularity of love-visions like the *Romance of the Rose*. Still, something remains vivid for us, if not the poem, perhaps the idea of it. The title alone seems immense: this Rose is more than a lady – it is a world, or a series of corridors extending from outermost petals to rich core, like a feminized version of a concentric universe.

Could the medieval reader have yielded himself up to such parodies of religious ecstasy, as he brooded on the name of Guillaume de Lorris' poem? Or would the work have seemed the illegitimate offspring of an older, more serious dream-literature whose otherworldliness was genuine, not merely a more nebulous form of subjectivity?

Perhaps the poem's hold on readers stems from a convergence of other-worldliness and subjectivity: we leave reality behind in order to explore the self. But to see the *Romance* this way one has to cast off much of its bulk as useless ballast, and could almost stop reading after 4000 lines where Jean de Meun takes over from Guillaume de Lorris. Such pruning is too radical to preserve whatever medieval readers valued, but the arid schoolmen's debates may be in part a disguise, holding the lover's agonies at one remove.

Disentangling the 'story' proves unexpectedly difficult. For that, we need to hear the dream told without the informative labels which instruct us that the girl approaching is called *Idleness*, distracting us from anything else about her. At parties one misses the names: at allegories the names oppress one so powerfully one can't attend to much besides. A perverse effort to ignore the labels in the *Romance of the Rose* would produce a cloudy story like this:

A young man goes to bed and dreams he wakes on a May morn to go into the woods to hear bird songs. He follows a brook which leads to a wall with a row of unpleasant ladies painted on it, like sculptures in niches. Walking round its circumference the youth finds only a single tiny gate. He bangs on this and is answered by a polite woman, who after a long explanation lets him in.

Once inside, the youth follows an overgrown path, which leads to a group of dancing couples whom he is invited to join.

After this dance ends and the couples disperse, the youth is pursued by an archer, carrying two bows each with five arrows (subheadings in the allegory, further qualities within the shooter's Quality). Fleeing, the youth comes to a well, whose surface is a mirror which shows him a rose-bush. While he pauses to study this vision he is hit by the arrows, and removes each in the same way, leaving behind the head.

Now he hears a long definition of love from his attacker (wordless before), who at the victim's instigation turns a key in his heart (where the arrows, which went in at the eye, ended up), locking it. After this interlocutor vanishes the youth tries to breach the hedge separating him from the rose, of which he is now enamoured. Abruptly the Rose appears nearby and he kisses it, but finds he has acquired a new enemy through the kiss, who orders the construction of a fortress round the rose-bush, incorporating a prison in which the youth's helper will be shut.

At this point Guillaume left the poem unfinished, and forty years later another author undertook its completion, reversing the polarities to make qualities (like Love) which were positive, negative, and ones which were negative (like Reason), positive.

In *Romance of the Rose* the wall, painted with emblematic ladies, turns out to be a formal procession like the dance, which has an impersonal firmness like the wall. Many experiences in the poem partake of this ritual flatness, and depictions of the 'natural' are only used to set off the artificial in an alternating structure of concentric layers. So the lover leaves the town for the country, washing himself and then becoming fixated on flowing water like a soporific cleanser or amniotic regress. But the water leads him to ... civilization again, or a sin-encrusted building. Inside it, however, is nature once more, giving an intensified echo of the lure which summoned him from the original town – birdsong, which stands for the voice of thoughtless passion, or the first stirrings of the poet to convert seasonal urges into permanent, transcribable shapes. Kisses turn into or provoke stone walls. Fleeting fears appear rock-hard obstructions. When Jealousy builds the fort to keep the rose away from its would-be ravisher, everyone forgets this will make a fort within a fort.

Desire and the defensive reaction it calls out continue to form a receding series of barriers and assaults upon them, like one of Kafka's infinite recessions, or like a rose of which one can't count the petals or reach the centre, which can only be earned by study of the outlying parts.

Guillaume has taken the essential step toward the endless see-saw of subjective narrative by identifying ambivalence as the ruling principle. He still perceives subjectivity as such a strange condition that he dramatizes entering it over and over again. In fact the poem's chief message is that we all contain a bizarre terrain where logic is defeated and where the same battle is refought as soon as the previous meeting of the warring forces is resolved. The recurrent images in the *Romance,* of which the most powerful is a fort surrounded by a meadow and containing a garden, are images of this central truth: that we don't really know what we want, and that gratification always opens a new chapter in a search which keeps returning to the feeling of lack, attaining fulness, starting over again, and so on endlessly, because unlike a story, consciousness doesn't end, so a conclusion which has receded into the past has lost its force as a silencer of thought. Only Kafka and Dante try to match such pulsation to some consistent and buildable construction, an effort of objectification which defeats both of them.

In *Romance of the Rose* the lover's object is called a rose, but it has no colour or smell, except the most perfunctory – it is simply red and sweet. Perhaps Guillaume feels botanical data would cloud the allegory. There is at least one moment in the description of the rose when he has his eye on the human analogue – the lover prefers buds to fully opened blooms, because they last longer. The lover prefers young unformed girls to mature women because ... one can say certain things in the allegory which would be tasteless if stated directly.

The lover first sees the rose-bush in water, reflected in the magical well which mirrors everything in the garden. As Guillaume approaches the most intimate experience through the protective filter of the dream, so the lover first perceives the object of his quest refracted in art. Yet the magic gives him only the general idea of such experience, he isn't able yet, in this vision, to distinguish individual buds.

It is a strange account of his pursuit of a woman. Narcissus is there at the well-side, tempting one to think that, like the earlier stream, it is a journey inward, to primitive or abandoned stages of the self. But aside from the rose-bush inside its circle of hedge (both of them contained inside the circle of the well) the vision has no content. Everything is there, we are told, and everyone will find that love has managed to trap him with what he is shown. Love is the same experience for all, though what is required to produce it will be different in each case.

Immediately after the double sight of his object the Rose, the lover is assailed by the arrows, one of the story's most explicit motifs. It is a glaring breakdown in the imagining to suggest names for the arrows which have already been allotted to dancers cavorting with the controller of the arrows.

Finding these names used twice, one wonders if it matters *what* things are called, as long as one calls them something. Naming in allegory needn't be a way of explaining – it can be a method of alienating one's meaning or putting things outside the pale of sense. So to name the arrows Beauty, Simplicity, Fair-seeming, etc. which will be fired by someone called Sweet-Looking only tells us that we are far from knowing what is happening. Meaning arrives in horrid families of like-tending events; ten Vices, eight Companions, five Arrows, which are signs advertising and restating the difficulty without truly naming it.

Allegory gives rigid form to the most amorphous moments of existence, and as the root-experience is indefinable, the carapace is alienated from it. Looking at any allegory closely one senses that the genre can never achieve consistency in the transfer of its materials to the special allegorical register. Meanings travel on the surface, go underground when convenient (i.e. become conceptual), and emerge again in full physicality without notice. So arrows penetrate the eye, make their way to the heart and can then be yanked out as if shot straight into the breast. One sees what incompatible systems jostle here, and why it was not acceptable to give any of them up. A small physical cause produces a large effect somewhere else. Longing is like a bodily wound. Each of these two perceptions can be translated by the same metaphor, but not successively without strain.

More involving than these discrete arrows or bursts of meaning is the main system of the allegory. All the persons in the story except the lover (for 'Lover' is not an idea in the same way) represent ideas: Danger, Reason, Love, Friendship, Jealousy. The only other person in the landscape (unless the confidant is counted) is rendered by the Rose. So we have the lover represented as himself, qualities and notions crucial to him represented as other selves, and the only other being who matters to him represented as a semi-animate object. The human is botanized, the conceptual personalized, around a centre which stays more or less as in waking life.

One result of such standing-things-on-their-heads is that the lover has a more human relationship with Danger and various similar abstractions than with the beloved, who seems an idea he has had. In reality, danger is usually a negative quantity one would not overcome by treating as if it were a petty official and offering it homage. That is the recipe followed in the poem, and it works, a clear case of ideas giving way to dramatic exigencies.

Likewise the absence of interesting encounters between the lover and beloved is an outcome of the initial decision to show her as a Rose. What stories can one imagine of a man and a rose? The narrator's task comes down to keeping them plausibly apart. This seems the most likely reason for his abandoning the poem: that the initial configuration was so extravagant (a rose being so unlike a person) it proved dramatically impractical. One could write a very intense lyric in which the limits of the comparison remained unsuspected. But the longer the idea is continued the more purely outlandish it seems.

Romance of the Rose is the only narrative we have met which lacks renowned, quasi-historical characters. Tellers of Arthurian stories are bringing us news of the famous, and thus increasing our stock of knowledge under a previously inaugurated heading. It is a momentous step to proceed without this warrant, which was like a base one could periodically retreat to.

The romances contain a great deal of concealed subjectivity or seem about to erupt in it. It is lurking there all the time in the role accorded to women, yet remains unrealized. So the romances are remembered as adventure stories, centred on idealized rivalries and quests. It is said that women are the prompting force behind most action yet they remain a distant goal.

Allegory cuts us off from the prompting experience in *Romance of the Rose*. At this point in the development of narrative, a writer can confess that a fiction is based entirely on his own reverses and successes in love, but he still dignifies or fortifies this by building it into a wider moral or philosophical discourse. So lonely torments become a course of lectures on the forces at work in the lovesick soul.

More accurately, allegory or allegorical narrative is a third thing, neither passional outpouring nor abstract dance of qualities. It will occasionally tip in one direction or the other (more often abstract in *Romance of the Rose*), but even in cases where one is pulled first this way and then that, one inhabits a calm transcendent place where troubles are assuaged by having people play roles not quite their own. Displacement by itself is a means of release; seen this way allegories are not barren or constricting, though evidently remote from what they are supposed to be about, any more than plays performed by children are worthless because the parts and the actors fail to match. Though not many allegories are deliberately amateurish like that, they accept a more imperfect union between meaning and vehicle than we suppose, not wanting to decide whether story or debate will finally rule the stage. They are hybrids occasionally giving painful jerks to whichever member of the pair is perceived as racing ahead too quickly.

Trying to see all later psychological novels in embryo in *Romance of the Rose* one keeps running against the distortion of its presumed source in personal experience. Sometimes one wonders if Guillaume has taken one step forward and several steps back. Yet the decision to admit one's own inner life, in however veiled and dislocated form, as the base of an ambitious extended narrative is an innovation which once ventured isn't fully retractable. However much one flees from these bottomless depths, before long one will be back looking into what would lie ahead if one decided to go further.

The *Vita Nuova* isn't strictly speaking an allegory, and *Romance of the Rose* is perhaps not an obvious ancestor for it. Dante's story seems to be told from the state in which allegory is perceived to be desirable or necessary, before the step of actually devising it has been taken. His work pretends that certain kinds of meaning are needed but not yet discovered. Of course this is the most elaborate contrivance. To produce a work whose intense presentation of psychological truth urges one toward a certain art form is the extremest subtlety of self-conscious planning.

The magnitude and privacy of his material lead Dante to the brink of a transcendent disguise for it. It is earthly experience in the last semi-comprehensible moment before it ascends to the heavens and becomes untellable. Ordinary earthly shyness and Divine protectiveness of Its favourite truths are at this point hard to tell apart. Dante the jealous lover and Dante the scrupulous metaphysician take each other's part to our delicious confusion. It could be a treacherous game, but in this writer's hands, control is assured. Although one of the cleverest books ever constructed, it does not feel like idle play, for the subtleties are not ends in themselves, but emblems of the indirection which the mind's limits impose on all its travel towards the truth. Art is seen as an *obstacle*, which is necessary and good, like exercises that strengthen a body while tiring it.

Romance of the Rose could not avoid an impression of superfluity, many pictures (in the wall), one gate; many windows, one door; many obstacles, one route which one took in a lamely inflexible order. Why should there not be nine Vices (instead of ten), six companions (instead of eight), three arrows (not five)? Dante's way out of this impasse, that details of the narrative are arbitrarily arrived at, but then treated as if they meant something (weakened by the feeling the story might just as easily have meant something else), is twofold.

As readers will remember, the *Vita Nuova* doesn't begin at the beginning. It begins with the writer trying to decide what will go into the book, whose source is ... another book, his memory, in which he finds certain pages of which he will now copy out the major part.

This state of consciousness is pre-allegorical, hovering on an indistinct border, because the objectification is not sweeping enough for full fledged allegory. Dante is only making a small technical point about the pedigree of what we were reading this minute past, as if one had suddenly become sharply conscious of watermarks and bindings. Yet with a slight adjustment of perspective it seems the most involving possible view, calling in question the fundamental ground of what is happening to us, as if the writer had appeared and threatened to take the book away. Such disruption has been tried many times since of course, seldom so successfully, because usually writers think it will be sufficiently discon-certing simply to mention the book we are reading. Dante instead constructs a little regress. This is a book, and where does it come from? a book. And that? we can't pin it down, and the work's derivativeness paradoxically increases its actuality.

All books come from other books more than they care to say, which in Dante's case has the unexpected effect of increasing the exquisiteness of this slim volume, slimness an appropriate quality in something which is only an extract, a quality one can read various ways – is it slight or concentrated?

One of the most beautiful and foolproof of this book's devices is that pages or large tracts in the source book are being, at this point or that, skipped. Because we would not believe them, is one explanation. If we were on the verge of not believing, which is to say if our attention slackened, this pulls us back and exerts a pressure toward self-reform.

Without quite seeming to, it also calls attention to Dante's shaping skill – *this* narrative isn't left to see to itself, with happenings stuck in just because they happened: everything which is put there deserves to be pondered. Maybe it has the effect of making us wish there were more. In any case the events which *remain* (one feels that Dante's revising is covertly referred to in the image of skipping over tracts of old memory) have that enviable heightened quality which constructors of allegories and visions seek after. These are transfigured events of more than ordinary import, and he has achieved the distance from ordinariness by more prosaic, hence less fallible means.

Events in this narrative become sacramental without being fictional-ized. Coming from a very different direction he manages to impart an abstract grandeur to events, like that which allegory achieves by making persons into things and concepts into people. Beatrice is nearing nine when Dante sees her first. In fact she is at the beginning of her ninth year, while he is near the end of his, as if to summarize all passage on a miniature scale. Skipping over, we see her nine years later when at the ninth hour she speaks the first words meant for Dante, who, overwhelmed, retires, and in his room pondering this, falls into a sleep or vision from which he returns in the fourth hour, which he chooses to describe as first of the last *nine* hours of darkness.

With this one exception, the world strews the nines at the poet's feet, so that meaning is reached in an inverse way to that in *Romance of the Rose*. One has a glimpse of its undiscovered state, when it lies there like any other accident. In fact we do not, even now, know how to interpret this pattern, or cannot be sure we are right, because Dante, who seems sure (otherwise why such careful notation?), does not divulge the meaning. Our main clue is the way the subject is introduced:

> Nine times the heaven of the light had revolved in its own movement since my birth and had almost returned to the same point when the woman whom my mind beholds in glory first appeared before my eyes. She was called Beatrice by many who did not know what it meant to call her this. She had lived in this world for the length of time in which the heaven of the fixed stars had circled one twelfth of a degree towards the East. Thus she had not long passed the beginning of her ninth year when she appeared to me and I was almost at the end of mine when I beheld her.

which suggests that numbers are not artificial human manipulations, but signs of our connection to the universe. In some way not fully clear to us, the nines tell of Beatrice's kinship with the stars. Which does not prevent us from feeling that Dante sometimes strains after meanings (when converting four to nine for example), but he does this not as an author beautifying his work but as a man seeking the truth, so flaws like this have the lucky side effect of consolidating the circumstantial base of the story. When he fails to achieve his meaning, that is because the reality he has convinced us of won't entirely cooperate.

Meaning is a secret which doesn't declare itself too readily. Beatrice's name is used by many who don't understand it. Dante's dream-vision after the second meeting is correctly interpreted by no one at the time, though evident now even to the simplest.

This vision begins as a fiery cloud, in which a figure is concealed, who says three Latin words which indirectly identify him. Then our attention turns to a figure asleep in his arms. The inhabitant of the fiery cloud holds a fiery object in his other hand, identified in three more Latin words, and after she is roused, fed to the reluctant sleeper. Upon which the mood suddenly changes; the frightening figure is now abashed and ascends rapidly out of sight.

In Dante, as not in *Romance of the Rose*, the miraculous is a well-defined interlude. Key events are just as opaque, but scattered more thinly, focusing our puzzlement like a burning glass. We're told that this, though understood by none at first, is now clear to all, another of those goads which draws an outline round our ignorance. Is meaning in Dante as absolute as he seems to imply, so that you understand it or you don't and one can miss it utterly? If one were challenged here what would one answer? That the dissociation interests us most: Dante sees his heart (the sleeper's food) held up at a distance, as if Christ were a spectator at the elevation of the Host? That much of its power flows from the union of decorous ritual with Aztec savagery? That Dante is dismembered, but Beatrice is now more deeply implicated, the drama having solidified their relation as more than his lonely fantasy?

Strangely, our outsiderdom does not tempt us to give up in disgust, or even make us wish Dante were less grudging with his insights. Perhaps there is an inconsistency in the idea of feeding learners with something they can't possibly digest, perhaps a kind of flattery in allowing amateurs to see something beyond them. But Dante really seems to believe reality is constructed this way, its inner nature hiding behind misleading veils. And we are not denied meaning altogether, only refused complete access. As a result, though not a story at all in the way the works of Chaucer or Boccaccio are, the *Vita Nuova* is intensely dramatic, like a mental thriller, and part of its secret is that the mysteries to be solved are so clearly stated. Costumes do not consist of a hundred chattering details (like the Vices in the rose-fort wall) but one: Beatrice appears first in crimson, then in white, and the only clue within the story is that it is called a noble colour in the first case and set off by two older companions in the second. These are nagging gaps in our knowledge: we collect the evidence of Beatrice's clothes and wait for the next time to see if the further colour will complete or extend the pattern.

The structure of the puzzle includes the commentary which regularly follows each incident in the story. Dante of the *Vita Nuova* is a poet who copes with large occurrences in his life by making poems from them. He presents himself deciding whether to compose, whom to address, how much to tell. Eating the Heart is told to other poets, asking them to reply in explanatory poems. It is our first encounter with a process which will become familiar.

From what I just told you, Dante says, I made this poem, which consists of two parts, the first addresses ... and the second concludes with ... This all sounds logical, except that the poem and the description of it don't match, not that there are glaring inaccuracies, but that the diagram gives a specious clarity. And it is a ludicrous technique to present the poems as if they were legal exhibits which will prove or confirm various things. Though placed afterwards, they were written before the main narrative of the *Vita Nuova*, as perhaps we can find outside confirmation of. We might try, also, to imagine the situation of readers already familiar with the poems who now find them encased in the cheaper? more expensive? setting of the surrounding prose. Has Dante, by stealing their thunder in the lengthy, factual accounts which precede them, really reduced his lyrics to boring exhibits, for which the right probe is the dissecting tool he pretends to wield? There are those who have held that the *Vita Nuova*, never mind its enticing title, is a technical treatise primarily interested in certain professional questions about the functioning of the poetic line.

But that is to mistake one of its disguises for the truth itself. At the point we have reached, after Dante becomes known around Florence as a lover in general, the mystery remains who he specifically loves, which is 'solved' in an astonishing way. One day in a place where Beatrice also is, listening to praise of the Queen of Heaven (presumably church), another lady along the line of sight between Dante and Beatrice thinks he is looking at her. Observers then notice her looking at him and decide they have discovered Dante's object. Seeing this, he hits on the idea of using the other lady as a screen for the truth of his love for Beatrice, making a solid fiction of the perceptual mistake. To carry out the idea more fully, he addresses poems to the intervening lady, some of which have secret references to Beatrice which only he can detect.

The almost geometrical expression of the relation between the two participating bodies seems infallible, but along the space intervening between the lover and the loved are many inessential points which could be stopping places. If one perceives only half or the first stages of the truth, one may land in a more erroneous condition than if one had never tried to find out anything in the first place. This geometrical expression gives some elementary facts about love in depersonalized form which resembles allegory. Here the natural impulse of all lovers and Dante's instinct as a writer, to come at reality obliquely, converge.

Before long the screen-lady leaves Florence, and Dante is terribly cast down at the loss of his beautiful pretext. He feels genuine pangs and moves quickly to turn them into a lament. He has suffered something like the pain lovers actually feel, through his fiction. Modern readers may question the singleness of his passion, seeing what they suppose is the diversion of his feeling onto the secondary object. But the interpolated stage clarifies the complete hierarchy: reality presents us with a series of reflectors or mediators through which great meanings are filtered. Beatrice too is one of these. If Dante were ready to take the next step, it is there waiting to be taken. As the screen-lady to Beatrice, Beatrice to the Queen of Heaven. But unlike the overweening allegorist, Dante suggests a series ascending out of sight, like hills which are always one range ahead of one, without shoving us on before we are ready. He starts us off on a longer quest for a more unreachable goal, and gives at the same time a more consuming sense of the particular stage we are in, than the allegorist who, impressed by the beauty of his system, forgets how he came upon it, and forgets that outsiders will participate more willingly if allowed to follow a similarly gentle route.

Dante now finds himself travelling *toward* the screen-lady, though not headed as far from Florence as she is, and *away* from Beatrice. This makes him sad and he has his second vision of Love, who appears as a traveller. The activity one presently pursues (travel, in this case) takes on an explanatory function for large tracts of human existence – there is a legitimate self-reference even in one's grandest symbols.

Dante has been feeling travel negatively – for the moment it consists of getting further from his true centre and goal, and now he sees this feeling carried out: Love is going the other way, and carries poor Dante's heart back from the screen to Florence, not to cancel the journey, but to show the mess the poet has got himself in with his ruse. Dante's primary and secondary objects haven't stayed in their original relation to each other, and so a new screen has been chosen by Love. When Dante turns back on the road of sighs (not a special realm as in *Romance of the Rose*, but a confusion of realms, mundane and symbolic), he returns to undertake a new deception, and this time he fools Beatrice as well, who behaves very coolly after hearing the rumours of his new diversionary love.

There is a penetration in that twist which reminds one of Henry James – an actor cannot reserve the effect of actions for those he intends them to influence. One's method of slowing one's approach to a goal may actually keep one from reaching it, though if rightly understood it was only an expression of reverence and diffidence, the very opposite of the coolness it wanted and succeeded too well in being taken for. Passionate devotion to a human object cannot be maintained in a steady state as if at a shrine built into a wall.

Experiences call up their opposites – not being greeted makes him dwell on what greetings were like, an intensely literary rhapsody, cloudy like alabaster, which has the name of Love dropped frequently into it to form a design. Beatrice fails to greet him, and he retires to his room (later to be known as the Room of Tears), sleeps, dreams, and sees Love in his dream, with whom he holds one of those dialogues in which his questions in Italian are answered by Love in Latin, lapidary like inscriptions rather than speech. He teases Dante with the idea that love is the centre of a circle, to which all parts of the circumference bear a constant relation, except Dante, who is told he does not. An encompassing spiritual structure exists but this seeker is not part of it. Hardly ever has a literary work shown a stronger desire to uncover an order in the world like the coherence of art, and now it is tormented by new certainty that such a thing exists and it cannot partake of it.

Love's practical advice is that now it is time to discard intermediaries and admit one's true object. Yet of course he means dropping one sort of intermediary and adopting another. There will be no more screen-ladies, but Dante's poems will become protective screens between himself and the brightness of Beatrice. And, further, he will not address her directly in them, and will send Love with them to soften their reception, so that she will receive them kindly (i.e. will bother to read them?).

The first poem becomes a masterpiece of indirection: it *consists* of an address by Dante to the poem, instructing it how to behave, how to *sound* (it has been sounding like this before it is told to), what speech it should make when it gets to Beatrice (but it has not left yet), how to rely on Love, what Love will say to it (another hypothetical address *within* the impossible discourse of Dante speaking to his own words as if they could hear, then digest and act on what they've heard). The poem ends with permission for the poem to leave when it feels ready. To leave the pen? To leave Dante's house on a journey through the streets of Florence? To end? It feels odd, for the previous lines have been considering when it would be time for Love and the poem to leave Beatrice's in order to avoid wearing out her patience.

After this a series of encounters begins with shadowy groups of women, into the first of which Dante is led by a well-meaning friend, so that he doesn't really know where he is when he feels strange symptoms overtaking him, a throbbing which makes him lean for support against a fresco running around the room. Only then he raises his eyes and sees that Beatrice is among the company and has caused his ludicrous weakness. All his spirits are chased away by love, and he can hear them lamenting at a distance like a crowd of tiny creatures or petulant children. He is gently mocked by the ladies and taken away by his friend. To the friend he speaks cloudily of treading near the verge of death.

Home again his thoughts talk to each other like characters, asking each other what they would say to Beatrice, assuming (an impossible assumption) they were capable of speech in those circumstances. He writes a sonnet to show how complicated it is to be tongue-tied in his case, and finishing the poem, is moved by a desire to write another, which will include what the previous leaves out. More and more the book is the drama of the writer writing, and exists to say where Dante's poems come from, explaining their personal base. Instead of autobiography for its own sake, it is autobiography in the service of an earlier, more lapidary version of the same material. Dante is again saying to his words (as when sending the poem-messenger to Beatrice), 'Go and explain to the reader what my words have meant.' The present book is seen as subservient to the earlier words, which in turn profess their devotion to another purpose higher than they.

But having circled himself with justifications as thoroughly as that, Dante is still unhappy to rely for too long on the same pretext. He has exhausted the subject of his distresses, and vows to be silent, as he now devotes a short section to saying. No more poems, unless he can find a new and greater subject.

Two things help him on his way to the new theme. Once again he is among a crowd of ladies who tease him with the absurdity of a love so timid it can't endure the presence of its object (we know and the ladies don't that Dante carefully scanned them before approaching, to make sure Beatrice wasn't there). What is it that he likes? Hearing her praised. Then his poems should be different (less about him). He feels rebuked, but has been inspired by the ladies' chatter, which forms a blur of words and sighs, like rain falling mixed with snow.

Next he is walking by a stream and a line comes into his head, which he puts away to be the first line of a new kind of poem. The ladies' murmur and the stream's motion have brought him to the point of writing again, in emulation of their various progress. The result is the central poem of the book, which connects Beatrice strongly to life in Heaven. Though much less tinged with sadness than most of the laments which come before, it is an oblique forecast of her death, and cuts her ties with earth.

In retrospect one can see how carefully Dante has prepared for Beatrice's death, but coming on these markers one by one, the reader is lulled by screens so remote from and so fancifully tied to the event they portend. First Beatrice's father dies, and Dante feels the city convulsed, as he watches women walking the darkened streets talking of Beatrice's distress. He is so moved by reports of her sorrow he wants to hide, but also wants to listen, and staying, attracts attention by his collapse at the wayside.

He falls ill for nine days and has a terrible dream, in which the city is dark, birds fall from the sky, and Beatrice has died. As usual reality and the way it appears are reversed: those by Dante's bedside fear for his life: ill, he imagines her illness; speaking her name, he is thought to give vent to the disease. When he recovers he recounts this experience extensively in verse. Her imaginary death is the great crisis of the book, a convulsion in Florence for which he seeks parallels in the pages of Hebrew prophets.

His next vision is a relaxation. Primavera, the beloved of his best friend, appears, and behind her Beatrice (whom a voice now tells Dante to call Love); they seem to pass him in the street and the idea enters his head that as spring precedes full bloom, so his friend's passion announced his own, as the Baptist announced Christ. At moments like this the incongruity of Dante's ideas takes one's breath away. Later Florence deprived of Beatrice will be likened to Jerusalem widowed by God's withdrawal, in the words of Jeremiah. The idea of foretastes or lower orders which accurately mirror higher ones in construction, if not in magnitude, gives the warrant for concocting these schemes in which superficial discord (the sexes reversed, Beatrice the husband not the wife of Florence) makes the undermeaning more achingly necessary, whips one onward in the search, and gives a more stringent kind of illumination at its end.

Right after his boldest bit of allegory, Dante introduces an objecter to the idea of personification altogether. But he chooses as his test case the treatment of Love as a person, not the more startling personifications of poems within the body of their own selves, or these daring thefts of parables of religion to give permanence to the personal passion of the poet.

Raising it as late as this in the work, Dante runs no risk of undercutting the technique of personification, so deeply and attractively imbedded has it become in the reader's sense of the story. At this point it only adds another range of discourse to pretend to divest oneself of the capacity for allegory altogether. When something's reality is long accepted, to shake it sets our circulation moving faster rather than bringing the motion to a stop.

The unstated under-principle of Dante's most inclusive justification of his work, which he slides into at this point before the final crisis, is the idea of bridging the widest possible mental and emotional distances, between earthly and heavenly, vernacular and Divine. He writes in Italian because it gives a longer dramatic space to traverse before he comes to the empyrean. Digressing on the origins of literature in the vernacular he claims that poems were first written in it because a poet wanted to be intelligible to a lady who didn't understand Latin easily.

Much flows from that: subjects other than love don't have the same secure warrant, and the original disparity in learning is an allegory of what we know here (in Italy) and what we hope to know at the finish (in the world to come). Poems in the vernacular are miraculously capable of foreseeing states we haven't reached yet and can only guess at as long as we inhabit our Italian bodies.

His little book enlarges the terms of discourse in a vertiginous series of stages. People in the streets of Florence rush to see Beatrice, who diffuses blessings through the whole city. Dante's poems aspire to imitate this process and spread this influence to those who can't run after her gaping.

The book is moving most confidently, germinating one poem about her from another, when it receives what appears to be a very rude check. Our first clue is that a poem described as a canzone (a long form) turns out to have only fourteen lines. In the next section we find out why. The poet was stopped in his course by news of Beatrice's death. In a further stage we deduce that the intended canzone was never taken up again; its broken edge is permanent testimony to the disruption of Dante's thoughts, and the hiatus in reality left forever by this event.

It comes without warning. The poet's spirits wander forlornly like a crowd of lost souls, like a complete underworld in themselves, yet he will not dwell on or even describe the death, for three reasons. One, that it doesn't belong in the book, as reference to the preface will remind the reader. Because returning to the start gives only an indistinct answer – the book is a book of new *life* and therefore couldn't dwell on death – critics have imagined another preface, now lost, which would have made all clear. But we know he is a writer who might send one on a very specific-sounding errand which grew into something else or raised further questions not soon answered.

This is the least of his three reasons, which interlock instead of just lying in a row, and which end in protestations of inadequacy and hatred of self-reference. Readers could object that this is already a work so deeply self-centred that such avoidance coming now is highly arbitrary. There is truth in this, yet Dante's scheme does not require that he be capable of self-transcendence in order to point our way to the most important, most transcendent truths.

His motives for leaving a gaping hole at this critical point are undoubtedly mixed, as he knew. It is too pleasing to the aesthete in us that her death, seen so vividly in the feverish dream when Dante and not she was ill, has been so powerfully told before it happens, that to retell it as a fact could only be a dreadful anticlimax. Yet the poet's discretion and superhuman power over where the emphasis shall fall (on the real, or the phantasmal) is neither the final cause nor the greatest subject of these sections.

Dante, in the unnerving treatment of her death, shows himself half weaned of the corporeal Beatrice before she goes. She is seen already as a route or a conveyance to realities beyond her. He will not describe the death: he will elucidate an aspect of her reality, the way in which she became entwined with a particular number until one could say she *was* nine.

The conscientious reader will scour the text gathering up the many nines left lying about in it, and will add them to four more associated with her death. In order to find these four, three calendars must be consulted: the Arabian, according to which she died in the ninth hour of the ninth day of the month; the Syrian, in which it was the ninth month; and finally the Christian, in which the year 1290 (not named, but inferred) contains not just a nine, but nine of the perfect number, ten, since the century's start. To Dante this exotic variety is a convergence, not the cacophony it appears to us; not a ragbag of civilizations, but an orderly progress from darkness to light.

What do all the nines mean? That Beatrice and the nine spheres of Ptolemy have a deep affinity with one another, and more important that Beatrice is a miracle like the Trinity, or like the Trinity multiplied by itself (three being the only factor of nine).

So her death is not the interruption it seemed but a completion, and the broken poem fits perfectly into the pattern of the whole. Dante may have thought he was writing a canzone; what was needed at that point was a sonnet (which it is) and so it takes its place in the series: ten sonnets, one canzone, four sonnets, one canzone, four sonnets (it is the last of these), one canzone, ten sonnets (including a double one after the first), or 10+1+9+1+10. The implication along the way is that he doesn't know such an order is being composed. Each act of composition has its local cause which seems sufficient at the time: someone asks for a poem and Dante is about to dispatch an old one when he decides it will be more courteous to throw in a fresh one as well; he writes two, whose loose ends or unused matter will furnish a third.

Some orders only exist, or are only perceptible, when one reaches the position of looking back. But which is truer (the higher truth), the poet's intense propulsion to say what he says, or the overarching consistency of all these utterances? Dante's reader need not decide, or can have it both ways: in youth, passion; in maturity, reflection; as an apprentice he has been entertained with the one, as the wiser person the reading has made him he is informed by the other.

Events are shown deranging the fiction in order to perfect it. Dante wants a way to exhibit, in the work's own shape, the effects of Beatrice's death. His poems are now more widowed, as he will make us feel by putting the commentary in front of, instead of after them, as if the book had turned its gaze from looking ahead to looking back toward Beatrice. So after each poem comes an absence.

Near the end, apropos something quite trivial, Dante first mentions the book's dedication and a requirement the dedicatee placed him under *before he began.* One of the last things he sees is large numbers of pilgrims in the streets of Florence, *setting off* toward something. So the end of the book is flavoured with beginnings.

The most startling and touching of these is abortive. Long after Beatrice's death, after poems written for others about other dead ladies who turn out to be Beatrice after all, Dante notices a compassionate look on the face of another lady. She understands his sorrow for Beatrice and becomes a special bearer of it, a place he can commune with it.

Before long he misses her when he doesn't see her, and feels himself transferring desire from Beatrice, of whom the other lady only existed to make him think, to the lady herself. He is horrified when he realizes what has happened, and once again gives up earthly mediators between himself and his beloved. It is a final sign of human weakness and the most beautiful confession of the poet's individuality.

In the poem which turns away from this interlude the poet's soul is a pilgrim, like those he has seen in the streets, journeying to Heaven in pursuit of Beatrice. Now the transformation is complete, and we are shown how love for a woman can lead one to God. His book is the ultimate metamorphosis of the courtly ideal and, one might have claimed, the crowning document in that tradition. Although the poet doesn't say so, his Beatrice is commonly identified with Beatrice dei Portinari, born in 1266, married to Simone dei Bardi, and dying in the year we have seen her die in Dante's book. One might have concluded it is the most grandiose and complete etherealization of a passion which fits perfectly the courtly guidelines, except that one knows it is a forecast of a greater journey and more encompassing narrative of which Beatrice is culmination if not sole instigator.

Of this the *Vita Nuova* raises only a tantalizing suspicion. After the last rhapsodic sonnet a vision appears which is so powerful it makes him determine to write no more ... until (and then what we recognize as the *Divine Comedy* is referred to as if it were the ultimate love poetry). Once again the generation of the book is dramatized, and its end *happens* as an event in the story.

Dante is again silenced, as he has been before, a longer silence this time which precedes a more powerful utterance. So the book ends, after these unintelligible hints, with a triple benediction, the last word of which is the Latin form of Beatrice's name. Thus in small compass is concluded the grandest task of any storyteller, to bring the most fleeting sensations into the presence of the eternal.

CHAPTER SIX

RELATIVISM IN CHAUCER

It always feels trivial to praise old works for their modernity. In an early Soviet play a postman comes forward to say it is time for writers to turn out plays about postmen; seekers after patches of modernity in the past are like that, and want to hear what they know repeated. Nothing is cheaper now than up-to-the-minuteness, so medieval works without medieval flavour lack what would make them rare and special. But push this far enough, and we end by claiming that we're only truly in touch with the past when not understanding it. The best historians strive for maximum incomprehension.

However absurd that sounds, some of the greatest inhabiters of the past, like Nietzsche, stand out partly for their delicacy in not presuming to know about it, for not ruthlessly shrinking the distance between us and it. Even so, who is so scrupulous he hasn't caught himself thinking that Chaucer's *Troilus* is a startlingly modern work? First and most important, it is so thoroughly *private*. Processions and ceremonies are present only as foils and spurs to unspoken thoughts. An exchange of hostages between two warring sides is seen as it affects the passional life of one of the hostages and a person she leaves behind.

The ingredients are the same as the medieval romances, with the important proviso that here there are no adventures, and the capable hero is immobilized as effectively as Bartleby the scrivener. Similar ingredients, but the way of regarding them is drastically different.

In the Arthurian stories we found incursions of domestic intrigue colonizing the life of warriors. In Chaucer's *Troilus* the centre of gravity has so shifted that we get only distant rumours of warfare. Troilus has a great *reputation* as a fighter, not that we are meant to disbelieve it, but in the poem it is something people talk about rather than know firsthand. The nearest Criseyde gets to Troilus the warrior is watching him ride through the streets of Troy. Seeing him mounted and armed, she probably imagines more easily what his valour is like, but still imperfectly.

The streets of Troy are crucial to the story in a funny way. Not that the drama takes place there: Troilus first sees Criseyde in church (or rather in a pagan temple, Chaucer's concession to the deforming power of the distant historical moment, like making the talking chickens in 'The Nun's Priest's Tale' spend the night on perches instead of beds), a sanctified start with venerable antecedents – both Dante and Petrarch first encounter the beloved there – but pagan tones undercut the religious hush in *Troilus*. The other scenes are feminized interiors, the women's quarters at Criseyde's house, or Troilus' bedroom at night when he mopes instead of sleeping. The streets become important because the motive force at this stage is provided by the go-between Pandarus, who shuttles back and forth from Troilus to Criseyde in a circuit which seems not to repeat itself though his motion is constant.

This character is the poet's most startling innovation. One could draw a line from Boccaccio's relatively innocent Pandaro, a friend facilitating an affair in hopes the favour will be returned, through Chaucer's Pandarus, to Shakespeare's. The third member is all prurience and voyeurism, an imagination diseased, far more lurid than Chaucer's Pandarus.

Chaucer's contribution is to make him a generation older (in Boccaccio he is Troilus' own age) and more instrumental in the lovers' union. Pandarus is the only conscious practitioner of the revolutionary principle on which the story turns: human imagination remakes reality, or in the poem's terms: love is largely a mental fiction, a hoax played by lovers on themselves.

One can easily make *Troilus* sound more simply sceptical than it is. Though Chaucer's main source, *Il Filostrato*, is based on Boccaccio's own infatuation and contains appeals to the beloved to lighten his misery, and though *Troilus* clearly bears no such immediate relation to the poet's own distresses, the later work is more engrossing. Mainly because Chaucer imagines the preyed upon as fully as the predator, and dramatizes the preying of each on each, until all three principals have implicated the others, if not equally, at least substantially.

The difference between *Troilus* and later Romantic works is that *Troilus* remains an *analysis* of subjectivity, more like a stage play than an autobiographical meditation. Readers of fiction always bear something like Pandarus' relation to events, not in having caused them, but in standing off to the side curious about which turn events will take. The presence of Pandarus keeps us from becoming self-conscious; a deceiver on the scene licenses our reading of characters' thoughts.

But before long we are wondering what propels the go-between so furiously. He is called a disappointed lover, and shown once thrashing in his bed with unsatisfied longing, references which are just enough to remind us that Pandarus has an inner life too, which he suppresses in the interest of something else. Like many people in Henry James and many novelists, Pandarus lives through the lives of others.

Our interest in the outcomes of his plots makes us less inquisitive about why he hatches them. It is one of the greatest mysteries of narrative that, knowing from the start the unhappy result of an episode, we can be so eager to reach each successive stage of its unfolding. A reader falls easily into taking stories one step at a time. He knows *what* the present must eventually connect up with, but doesn't yet know the route across that distance, and most of the time finds getting there more interesting than the destination. We should no more expect that readers will lose interest in stories of which they know the outcome in a general way, than that we will stop caring what happens to us because we know we will die.

Seducing Criseyde, Pandarus introduces momentous plans inconspicuously, so that we have listened for a while before we realize what he's driving at and have thus already colluded in the plan at the moment of first detecting it. By the time we've caught up with him, his innovation has become part of the landscape.

There is a similar obliquity in the story's direction, and its bending of ordinary reality to unexpected ends. Both Troilus and Criseyde see each other first without the other's knowing, with the important difference that he is on display, riding in triumph through the streets, so that she views largely his reputation.

The approach never ceases to be roundabout, and the deviousness of Pandarus's character echoes a larger truth about the human mind, which is that things happen sideways, or that, insinuated into them imperceptibly, people will accept outcomes they would reject if clearly offered them.

Before venturing to bring the lovers into one another's undiluted presence, Pandarus stages a few practice runs. He puts Troilus up to riding by Criseyde's window at a certain hour (after dinner when those inside sit talking in a desultory way), and so achieves one of those irruptions of a subject more powerful for being unrehearsed (only seemingly here of course). Then before the meeting he has Troilus approach her by letter, which the go-between only gives Criseyde after he has lured her *down* a flight of stairs into the garden.

She makes a show of refusing, so Pandarus drops the letter down the front of her dress, a symbolic violation – now she has let Troilus touch her – with the practical advantage that she will be alone when she fishes it out, and will imagine no one knows whether she reads it or not. She absorbs the letter in solitude, and rejoins Pandarus afterwards, both of them conscious she has read it.

The poem is profusely dotted with such lonely interludes; life's deepest currents are invisbile except to the experiencer, yet this is still a strongly unromantic view of subjectivity. Much of Criseyde's unvoiced thought is ignoble calculation about whether giving in to Troilus will leave her worse off than before. Will her reputation suffer? Can she stay in control after conceding what he wants?

In truly romantic consummations, between Wagner's Tristan and Isolde, for example, both parties have lost track equally of ordinary priorities and personal advantages. It is heresy in that world to suggest that lovers' views of their union always differ, so that it is more likely that one of them will be entirely beside himself than that both will. In Chaucer, Criseyde's passion is real but her absorption in it is never as complete as Troilus'.

Thus the necessity for Pandarus to go on pretending to act for other reasons, even after she provisionally accepts Troilus' love, an indirection which parallels Troilus' concealment of his passion from the world. Pandarus is moved by an appetite for deception and an understanding that Criseyde wants to be relieved of responsibility for deciding to sleep with Troilus. The resulting convoluted progress produces a stronger outburst of pleasure than occurs in Boccaccio, where both lovers are conscious participants meeting furtively without needing a go-between on the premises.

Pandarus' plan in Chaucer is a wonderfully mixed concoction. He waits for moonless nights when the weather is unsettled, and invites Criseyde to dinner. At the end of the evening it is raining heavily, and Pandarus suggests she stay over. Crouching in a latrine Troilus watches her through a peephole. As the storm gets louder Pandarus explains that no one knows Troilus is there, so that they are entirely secure (he is not reminded by his victim that she only came because he assured her Troilus was out of town). Also, Pandarus says, the lover is near the verge of madness because he's heard she loves another. The go-between never stops at one lie, but attacks from several sides. Criseyde feels safe, flattered, and sorry for Troilus at once, and when she wonders whether Pandarus is setting her up, she has only to remember the thunder which no one could accuse him of causing. So various things beyond human control conspire to bring them to bed together. Finally Troilus' involuntary swoon turns the tide, and as usual Pandarus is there to take advantage of it. Seeing Criseyde's tears, her timid lover has misunderstood and thinks she is cross with him, so he faints. At this, Pandarus quickly heaves him into bed next to her, distracting Criseyde by shredding his own shirt and predicting Troilus' death unless she is nicer to him in a hurry. Criseyde misunderstands the crisis in turn, and is so conscientious bringing him out of the swoon that when he emerges they are safely glued together.

Chaucer continues to individualize a scene on which we expect the curtain of conventionality to fall. So after the ecstasy come calm stretches of talk and trivial acts like Criseyde's pinning a brooch on Troilus' shirt.

In fact the flavour of these moments comes from giving inconsequence free play: Criseyde's resistance finally collapses for no particular reason. What writer before Chaucer and how many after could admit that people sometimes take the most momentous steps because their attention fails and they can't think what else to do? Pandarus' purposiveness (what is *its* source?) is placed in a random, aimless world.

The triad makes for strangeness and withholds the satisfaction of the ideal. Even Boccaccio's jokiest stories are self-gratifying fantasies, while Chaucer never lets one feel 'Isn't this perfect?' Pandarus breaks the spell of the lovers' union, bringing a cushion so that Troilus will be comfortable kneeling on the floor, taking himself off with his candle to read a romance by the fire, so that they are left in romantic semi-darkness. His final disappearance from the chamber passes unremarked, but the canker of his presence has been sufficiently felt.

His comings and goings are ludicrous deflations, yet we feel Pandarus' interference with our contented enjoyment to be a profound reminder of the manysidedness of reality. Chaucer is an intellectual poet in a more pervasive way than fixing on his interest in the conundrums of scholastic philosophy would ever allow one to think. He probes the construction of consciousness with a tenacity that makes Boccaccio look simple-minded.

There is an irony in the fact that this poem, more undermining of all certainty about human motives than any work which preceded it, should have been thought determinist. It is an unresolvable question in what ways we are justified in applying any story to the world outside it. There are so many ways of being exemplary that to assert (as who denies?) that all stories are, doesn't take us far. Examples too awful can be viewed as delicious (and unnecessary) warnings that if one does something which one wouldn't dream of, dire consequences will follow. In fact, writers who imagine they issue apt warnings underestimate readers' tendency to see fictional dangers as someone else's and not their own. An amusing confirmation is the difficulty which real life models of unattractive characters have in recognizing themselves on the page.

One has only to listen to perceptive readers trying to make the right application of a story to realize that such relatedness isn't a primary function of stories, though many readers will feel it as the last and highest stage of their work, to locate the story they've been presented with, philosophically, or in relation to the universe.

How common it is to think an author means by his single or small number of cases, that life is always like that. The more individual the presentation, the more sweeping the application to experience outside is likely to be. By its self-contained power, fiction acquires a wide influence which there is almost no way of laying rational claim to.

So in the case of *Troilus* readers draw the conclusion that Chaucer means that men are pawns, and human hopes are doomed, the second of these dicta following from the first for the unstated reason that human wishes tolerate no imposed necessities, and we cannot imagine anyone's enjoying his buffeting by large waves of circumstance. Western stories don't even *hypothesize* Eastern sages.

Perhaps, contrarily, the true application of this story as Chaucer tells it is not that the world invariably conspires against human beings (i.e. a tragic view – Chaucer repeatedly calls his work a tragedy), but that men are so constituted that one shouldn't rashly depend on them, or rather that the reasons for behaving consistently lose their force when circumstances change, so that there is less permanence in emotional reality than practically any coherent statement about it implies.

Troilus' pleasure is framed on both sides by pain. At the moment of fulfillment Chaucer makes the contented reflection that joy is doubled coming on the heels of distress. The corresponding conclusion is not drawn a few hundred lines later when fortune turns against Troilus. Against Troilus, for the fates of the lovers are not symmetrical. He began as a lonely sufferer before she knew anything about his passion, and that is how he ends, for a long time unsure what has happened, and when finally informed by a gruesomely impersonal agency, unable to confront her.

Criseyde has found someone else, or fallen effortlessly into a substitute for the relation with Troilus, as Pandarus has been urging *him* to do. It isn't a grand passion; all the more disturbing that it effectively replaces him: Criseyde resolves not to hate Troilus and always to speak well of him. That is to say, the episode has left little trace and no regret.

Earlier, we had thought their love meant about the same to each of them. Separate after their night together, neither can sleep. Even then they exist and express themselves separately. Pandarus now for the first time finds her cross with what he's done, and, immediately after, hearing Troilus' love venting itself in rhapsodies, warns him against recklessness.

Then at once the boom falls: Criseyde is to be sent to the enemy camp in exchange for a valuable warrior (who later betrays Troy, as Chaucer points out). Her father the seer had gone over to the Greeks when he divined that they would win, and now he summons her. Being a woman, she can't effectively resist (and does she entirely want to?); Troilus can't publicly admit his love or argue against the exchange on humanitarian grounds.

Pandarus visits him in his darkened chamber, speechless with an unnamed mixture of emotions, then weeping as loudly as Troilus, but with different meaning. Soon he is saying find someone else, or steal Criseyde, or accept my whole family as fighters on your side. A combination of fears and scruples makes Troilus incapable of following any of the courses with practical chance of success.

The matching treatment of Criseyde's grief is one of the most satisfying parts of the poem. The rumour of her ransom is carried to her by Fame, a personage whose very existence in the story calls in question Chaucer's modernity. But really this device is only a vivid shorthand for saying that the fates of the two are very distinct. We get her response separate from Troilus', orchestrated by a crowd of women who visit her, to whom she must present a false front (as against his frank outpouring to a single intimate).

Now Troilus ties himself in knots over predestination and free will, which literal-minded critics have seen as the principal issue of the story. Chaucer finds an irony in such disputatious exit for intense pain, and makes Troilus dwell on the exemplum of a man *sitting*, – does he have to sit, etc.? – a telling instance for the man of action immobilized, among other things, by the great importance he assigns to the affair. If he weren't in awe of Criseyde, if it didn't matter so much, he would be able to act in order to keep her, perhaps.

Chaucer teases us with options which aren't going to be taken, saying if it weren't for ... then all would be otherwise – if Troilus weren't afraid of killing her in the mêlée, he would spirit her off as she rides out of Troy. Criseyde has argued that their plight isn't as bad as it seems – she will visit him, he will get news of her, and anyway rumours of peace suggest that soon the barriers between the camps will fall – which is what you would say sympathizing with a distress you didn't share. And her argument against running off together is the damage it will do to their reputations. Awkward circumstances have pointed up shades of difference in their commitment rather than burdened them with the insurmountable.

At first their paths appear to diverge only to stay the same. They both look longingly toward the opposite side which they can't actually see, and imagine receiving messages (odours, sounds) on the wind. But Criseyde's remembering is already a pale imitation of Troilus's – she wonders if he thinks of her, while he relives the whole experience. He has more memories and more chances of awakening them; the one left behind is always more likely to remain lodged in the past.

Chaucer relishes the irony that the usual social roles are reversed, and Troilus feminized by circumstance into the one who waits and guesses. The hero's speculations as he paces the walls, first imagining Criseyde's life, then expecting sight of her as she crosses the distance between the camps, are a painful depiction of wishful thinking under pressure, as Criseyde's predictions were of wishful thinking with little to lose.

At first he makes perceptual errors, thinking every moving object is Criseyde. Then he supposes she's been held up (by her father inviting her to dinner), or has thought of something which escaped him (travel at night is safer), and finally when the watchmen shut the gates Troilus wonders if he has miscounted the days. This history of his errors is one of the motives taken over from Boccaccio but deepened by being tied more closely to the rest of the drama. It is essential to Chaucer's story that much human certainty is imaginary without realizing it. In a way, wasted thoughts like these of Troilus' are more interesting than those borne out by reality, because they reveal more starkly the thinker's state.

Troilus on the walls wondering if his great love still exists is simply the forward edge, or the most grotesquely subliminal phase, of a drama which collapses like a paper model when one pushes too hard. Pandarus has led us here by deceptions which appear valueless once their moment of usefulness is past, whose success therefore depends on no one's looking back. The real proof that he is only contriving what Criseyde wants (or at least what she doesn't not want) is that his tricks never catch up with him.

They catch up with Troilus, who never objected to them either. At the end he is cast back into the plight of unsure beginning lover – will she come, reply, etc.? – waiting for hopeful signs however slight and pouncing on any which come to make them less neutral than they are. Like most in this spot, he feeds himself cues: he has terrible dreams which he takes not as reflections but predictions, refusing both Pandarus' optimistic and Cassandra's gloomy interpretations.

Chaucer's interest in dreams is a phase of the ironist's fascination with human error. In this case the riddle has a solution: Criseyde has crudely transferred her allegiance, as Troilus finally learns. Diomede's captured armour is paraded through Trojan streets and transmits an incidental message no one but Troilus can read. It still has pinned to it, like a barnacle which wasn't shaken off, the brooch which was Troilus' parting memento to Criseyde. So *that* is her long awaited re-entry to Troy, a surrogate of a surrogate, wordlessly and invulnerably signalling 'Now I belong to him.' The irony is deepened by Troilus' receiving the message, more sincere than her letters but not meant for his eyes, only because his vanquisher has been defeated. Diomede's misfortune in battle leaves his victory in love unchallenged.

Troilus is driven to absurd lengths by this bit of empty pageantry. He seeks death in battle or hopes to kill Diomede, the contrariness of these two results, both strongly desired, casting doubt on the whole structure of feeling. And he upbraids Criseyde – wasn't there any other brooch she could have given her new lover? – as if the added insult mattered, or is he wishing he had stayed ignorant, and had failed to recognize Diomede's badge as a gift from her?

Troilus and Diomede often meet and trade blows, but neither of them is allowed to kill the other. Troilus' wrath costs Greece dear we are told – but not *so* dear, for the Greeks win in the end. At last he dies in battle, and we have a final sight of him in the eighth sphere, from which human concerns appear ridiculous, both Troy's (and our) grief over him, and the lust he long lay subject to as well.

Chaucer intervenes here to cast aspersions on the paganness of his tale, and to offer Christ as a worthier love-object for the young, male and female alike. But he leaves a last doubt about how completely he has turned his back: the poem closes with a compliment to a special maid, the Mother of Christ, which is flavoured with ordinary human gallantry, the words of a man who doesn't forget he addresses a woman.

The astounding proportions of this poem, an immensely complicated bringing together, followed soon by an almost-as-complicated separation and betrayal, with none of the thing itself in the middle – long beginning, torturous end, no middle – this structure is a dramatic realization of the subjective view.

It is a world with little secure to hang onto, where one is always guessing, and where it makes sense that once out of Troilus' sight Criseyde should fall away, because what is real is so unsteady, liable to be overturned by a change of mood. It is a compelling vision, this feeling of flux at the heart of things, which follows from the lovers' acceptance of *feeling* as the controlling fact. The poem marks an important stage in the history of fiction and the concomitant emergence of subjectivity because Chaucer lacks the comprehensive view so remarkably present in Dante, where an achingly personal and egotistic response is somehow harmonized with a cosmic view, as if one could be under and out of a strong illusion of personality at the same time, to duplicate which in Chaucer one would have to combine the view of the epilogue to *Troilus* with that of the story. In some way nothing could be more intense than Dante's subjectivity, yet Chaucer in *Troilus* takes the personal view more seriously by seeing less often past it. Such an enveloping realization of what it feels like to be in certain plights requires the unlearning or forgetting of much old wisdom.

To our perception *Troilus* is in a class by itself and Chaucer's subsequent development a riddle and something of a letdown. If the poem meant to him what it does to us, could he have gone on from it to the *Canterbury Tales*, which whatever their virtues are less inward than *Troilus*, and give less startling views of what it's like to suffer individuality?

Perhaps the continuity is there after all, except that to our displeasure Chaucer follows the inquiry in a detached way, as if it were a philosophical problem rather than a compelling maelstrom. The famous story of the chickens and their dreams is about the absurdity of individuality and the pretence it inevitably requires; it makes the self's most precious concerns look silly.

But if individual tales are cooler, essentially comic even when gruesome, because of their subordination to the scheme – the frame which holds them has rightly attracted attention, and, seen next to comparable arrangements like Boccaccio's *Decameron*, enshrines a surprisingly Romantic view, gratifying to those of us who want Chaucer to carry them on past *Troilus*, further into subjectivity.

The *Decameron* takes place outside Florence while the plague rages in the city; a group of ten, forming five couples, have met in a privileged garden-like place to while away the time until it is safe to go back to Florence. This work is an unapologetic depiction of art as a delightful refuge: the tellers feel no obligation to pay for their leisure by dwelling on the less fortunate. Instead of guiltily remembering distresses outside the walls, this world concentrates on perfecting itself, civilization invented over again, as if after the Flood, without the familiar flaws.

Not that the tales aren't full of human venality, a little too full for most tastes, which is an ideal of a kind: people will always act brutally for their own advantage, Boccaccio's tales keep saying, though the behaviour of the tellers suggests this is a simplification in the interest of joke-like clarity of structure. Someone is usually outwitted, a clearer outcome than most of what happens in life. Many readers must have waited for these neat patterns to spill over from the stories into the lives of the tellers, but this never happens. There is reality, and there are stories.

Boccaccio's stories are something like a set of mathematical puzzles.

The numerical completeness of the set is very wonderful: when Chaucer came to duplicate this feat his endurance gave out for interesting reasons. Yet like Wren's City churches, Boccaccio's hundred stories must often have seemed too large a group, only superficially various at times, and built on an essentially prosaic idea of what a church or a story can be. Great compactness is one of the secrets of the successful completion of the huge project, and a refusal to be drawn into any single story very far.

Chaucer produces a fragment (but of what size!) or an armature because he loses his bearings by becoming absorbed in individual parts. And the frame, which one can see as introductory to the main body of the work, gets loaded with splendid complications which threaten the forward progress. From the beginning collection is a strongly centrifugal principle: instead of a homogenous group of nonentities, Chaucer imagines a group so diverse and incoherent, so rich in gratuitous peculiarity that biographies of his individuals have been written, histories of medieval occupations have started from his exempla, and most people's knowledge of life in the Middle Ages has taken much of its colour from these 850 lines of verse.

Like *Don Quixote* (the *Tale*-armature is proto-picaresque) the idea of this Prologue has transcended its exact location in time and language until it is bigger than any single literary object can actually be. Looking at the thing itself, less exciting than inhaling all which has come of it, one can still say that it is diametrically opposed to Boccaccio and other earlier examples of narrative made from telling stories.

Tales told on a journey rather than in a retreat, by characters strongly marked by trades and social roles, make a more unstable and fluid whole. The reader's sense of passage is accelerated or excited by the sensation that nothing holds still here. The tellers are in motion, one tale is underway, others are nearing the point of readiness, and every stage of the unfolding is conditioned by the jostling cloud of disparate splinters which travels along in its wake.

Of course in some degree Chaucer wasn't equal to his magnificent conception. To some extent there are the tellers and there are the tales, the tellers quarantined to little link passages and the tales sometimes heated-up leftovers Chaucer had done at an earlier time when he hadn't thought of anyone telling them or other tales nearby. So the tales are only intermittently under the influence of their teller and, otherwise, separate laws unto themselves.

There are thirty pilgrims in Chaucer's group and according to the plan announced, each will tell two tales going to Canterbury and two tales coming back, making 120 altogether. In fact what we have is twenty-four tales, some incomplete, only two of them by the same teller, so that seven travellers never tell a story at all. Could Chaucer really have thought he would complete the plan? How often did medieval pilgrims reach the place they set out for? Will all Chaucer's arrive at Canterbury? How can one imagine that their purposes will coincide long enough to bring them all back together along the same road? Previously we've caught sight of them at Southwark, near Rochester, and at Sittingbourne. In some sense then the pilgrimage ends, short of its goal, at Boughton under Blee.

It is one of Chaucer's more delicious jokes that so many unholy purposes should find shelter under the idea of spiritual quest. His motley group is not united by a shared aim except in the most trivial sense; one could more properly say that they represent a diverse if similar sounding set of lies, not that Chaucer is uniformly censorious about the impurity of his subjects. In part their nonconformity is a consoling emblem of the confusion of all human intention.

One finds similar dishevelment in the decoration of medieval cathedrals, like Chaucer's work in the impossible scale of their ambition and the waywardness of their working out. Things do not evolve or perfect themselves as planned, and a close inspection reveals many anomalies and deformities, many departures from and even denials of the single high aim which seemed originally to motivate the sculptural programme.

Probably one would find a kinship between the two different kinds of huge project (Chaucer's, the cathedral builders'), which flows paradoxically from a conviction of the smallness of human life, allowing a worker to embark confidently on enterprises without foreseeable ends. Other, quite different results can grow from the feeling that life on earth is a preface or forecourt, but we note in the Middle Ages a capacity for undertaking gargantuan tasks which express comprehensively the transitory quality of earthly life rather than a grand design of the Almighty. Dante's comedy combining the two therefore seems a more staggering and less modern work than Chaucer's ad hoc perambulation.

Dare we hazard that there were medieval builders with our appreciation of the unfinished gargantuan fragment, a piece of some barely imaginable monster-body like the chancel and transept at Beauvais, which stretches the mind more, grasping after the nave which isn't there, than any building which ever existed could? So we try to feel what the whole journey to Canterbury and back would be like, taking the vast existing fragment to be one-fifth of some unrealized whole. We cannot believe it is *always* accidental when books end over a void or break off before explaining themselves fully.

Appropriately Boccaccio's ten tellers perform their duties on each of ten days, and the symmetrical group of one hundred products of this industry holds still for analysis. Chaucer is a more slippery character, promising things he can't perform, intuiting worlds he won't survive to inhabit.

Boccaccio's tellers all agree. Their view of the world may subvert certain kinds of order, and even appear dangerous to some of the pious, but it is largely shared. Chaucer's parts do not seem revolutionary in themselves, but his way of combining them is. To put the Knight's tale with the Miller's is a more seriously undermining and relativist act than any narrator had thought of before. The idea of a single reliable basis is threatened by such diversity of view.

So it is not appropriate to consider particular Canterbury tales in isolation. 'The Knight's Tale' may have been written earlier and separately, but in its present location it is only one of the possible range of tales. We are meant to feel the story as a prim, archaic product with an outmoded charm peculiar to itself. No narrator before Chaucer places his narrations so carefully as characteristic human products, as themselves something like characters, with distinct, fallible personalities.

'The Knight's Tale' is coloured by its imagined teller's personality, and also by literary revivalism. An old-fashioned teller tells an old-fashioned tale. We underestimate the part conscious revivals play in the history of art. The further back we go the less well known or even recognizable such phases become. Nineteenth-century Gothic Revival is widely known, its eighteenth-century predecessor less familiar, and the Elizabethan Gothic revival hardly perceived at all by many observers. 'The Knight's Tale' is a milder case of course, the earliest Gothic revival, which is meant to seem slightly out of date and no more, perhaps a generation behind the times, not a strange messenger from a different mental world.

Perhaps this difference between archaism and revival is not so critical as we imagine, the essential innovation being to inhabit a medium which is not really one's own. 'The Knight's Tale' is a compelling example of its type, the courtly romance, courtly in an almost technical sense; it lacks the banter between men and women which the word calls up in the Renaissance – in fact it keeps men and women apart to an unusual degree. Chaucer's tale is courtly mainly in being presided over by a ruler who decides its outcome, and in the ritualized mode of its progress.

At the beginning persons and events are persistently paired. Two almost dead warriors are found on a scrap heap of bodies, revived, imprisoned (having been rescued by the enemy), and soon fall in love, one after the other, with a girl they see through the grating. This duplication is then undone for a while: one is released, and one left behind, and each envies the other – the one freed because he is banished from the city where she is, the one inside because prison bars still divide him from her.

The spacing of events is extremely elongated. After two years away, the escaper returns, spending three years outside the court, then two more as a server to Theseus, the city's ruler and the girl's stepfather. Such lengthening of our perspective, which seems a deliberate dissipation of narrative tension, is the key to the story, whose strands are now reunited and form again a non-individual bundle.

The remaining prisoner escapes into the same woods toward which the freed youth rides to celebrate a May morning. Events are doubling up in more senses than one. So that the hider will recognize him, the rider now recites his story from the start, which we are to believe works as a single sign or word, like his name.

The other springs out, and finding their *difference* – that they both want to fill the *same* space, as the unnamed girl's lover – can't be adjusted, they decide to fight, but as the escapee is unarmed, his ex-friend must bring him the gear which will make him formidable as an opponent. This dissociated motif could stand as an emblem of the entire story. Neither participant's thoughts are examined: the active one does not balk, the waiting one does not tremble, and when they come back together, each arms the other without a word. Civilized without civility, dependent without sympathy, they couldn't be less like the slaves of passion.

The course of the narrative is perverse to match. No sooner has the fight begun, than we switch to Theseus, who feels an urge to hunt, and accompanied by the woman in question, stumbles into the very clearing where the youths battle, parting them. One of them requests that they both be killed, and Theseus says yes, which would be extremely uneconomical (why all the jockeying if it leads to this?), though logical.

But it is a story desperately seeking to resolve itself, and Theseus is that antiquated figure, the actor with the power to end the story, who by this time in the history of narrative is felt as a throwback and a wish. In later tales the idea is occasionally resurrected in figures like Sherlock Holmes who solve reality as if it were a riddle someone has posed, and all except the young recognize such stories as a specialization of narrative, founded on an artificial premise. One would no sooner point to them as representations of how things are, than one would to crosswords as natural uses of language.

Theseus's decision is soon reversed, as if we are flipping through the range of possible results, his appearance having notified us at once that we are going to get a result somehow. Again the women persuade him to unbend, and his solution to the great traffic problem of the story – two applicants for one woman's hand – defies logical analysis.

Theseus acts as the bringer of peace by suggesting that more people take part in the battle. He imposes a delay of fifty weeks, during which time each contestant will collect one hundred helpers, and then a large tournament will be staged. He immediately sets about building a tournament ground worthy of this grandiose conception. It is a fortification of imperishable materials, *inside* which the fight will be held.

But the most surprising features, and the culmination of the story, are some beautiful chinks built into or grafted onto this new battle-armour, in the form of three oratories or temples let into the walls, each sacred to a particular god or goddess. Each exfoliates into shrine within shrine, crowded with art. There are rich materials, painted landscapes, famous personages, and a statue of the god at the centre: Venus half veiled by water rising perpetually from the sea, Mars accompanied by a wolf gnawing a human victim, Diana riding a hart.

True, it is essentially a pageant-like and inactive structure: like the threatening images painted on the wall in *Romance of the Rose*, a kind of depiction which can't come to you, which you approach in a chastened or awestruck mood. But the shrines are a more interesting compromise between animation and torpor than Guillaume's Vices, for they are enterable and inspectable, forging little imaginary 'spaces', as if while the oyster was making the pearl one could get inside it and follow its formation.

And these sacred nodes continue to interact with the story in unexpected ways. When the year is completed, the fighters arrive with a flourish. The night before the battle each of the principals (the two lovers and the lady) slips away from the feasting, to pay devotions to one of the enshrined gods, so at last we understand the confusing proliferation: two sides in the fight, but three foci in the boundary, like three impassable gates or lookouts.

Ambiguous omens are dispensed, and Chaucer revealed as a student of pagan rite. The next day Theseus's magnanimity causes him to substitute a capture-the-flag game for real battle. Many die anyway, but a decision is reached. As the victor (Mars' favourite) leaves the field, a Fury sent by Venus frightens his horse, who throws him. He lingers on between life and death, his medical problems carefully described. When he dies, Theseus has the ingenious idea of erecting his pyre in the old clearing in the woods, allowing the story to return to another one of its sacred spots. There is now a lovely description of all the kinds of wood the forest consists of, which we might have expected on our first visit, and which have regrettably been collected now only to be burnt up in the funeral.

A year passes; the remaining lovers hang back, two being a less satisfactory number than three in some unanticipated way. In the end Theseus pushes them into marriage, and at that point the story is done. But one senses that this tale has set in motion a problem which can't be satisfyingly resolved. In *The Parliament of Fowls* Chaucer feels free to leave the love-debate unsettled, because these are only birds. They have been boring each other all day with arguments for and against three applicants for one lady's hand, when Venus impatiently says 'Let her decide.' To which the lady's demure answer is that she would like a year to think about it. And at that, staying only for a brief song welcoming the summer, all the birds fly chattering off, eager for their various naps and dinners.

The moment of greatest fulfillment in such stories is when the forces are most evenly divided, among the three temples, surrogates for three candidates, each of whom (not just two of them) has his or her preferred outcome which can't really be assimilated to the others. Arcite wants Emily, Palamon wants Emily, Emily wants maidenhood – dynamic and quiescent desires don't match – but for the time being each is granted expression in the form of a small individual territory linked formally to the others.

This static arrangement is Chaucer's improvement of the allegorical preface to *Romance of the Rose*, the largely inert barrier to the Garden of Love, and more recondite his comment on the three-part structure of Dante's *Comedy*, where Forces are similarly divided (Mars=Hell, Venus =Heaven, Diana=Purgatory or waiting). Dante's is a pictured- and Chaucer's a mock-theology. In Chaucer the dominant role assigned to art functions as a deflating mechanism, as if Dante were to hobble us with the consciousness that the *Divine Comedy* is *his*, just another building.

However ritualized 'The Knight's Tale' seems, Dante's works are much more thoroughgoing in their faithfulness, more true *and* more artificial. *Romance of the Rose* begins with the most petrified state of the material and then has to back off from it, while Chaucer builds towards that phase. The *Divine Comedy* is told from inside the concentric shrine, as if Chaucer were to begin and end with the wall, telling the whole story as a circuit of it. Before readers got used to the conception, it must have seemed extremely bold of Dante to fashion an entire epic from a visit to the underworld, which had ordinarily been a tapestry-like interlude, more a kind of list than real drama. But then no poet before or since has possessed such capacity for invigorating static arrangements with momentary excitement and presenting eternity through one pair of eyes.

In the longest sustained narratives he wrote, *Troilus* and 'The Knight's Tale', Chaucer exemplified these two qualities as incompatible parts. Suspense in *Troilus* is matched by suspension in the 'The Knight's Tale', the poet in his modern and his archaic self. Though the first seems much more pregnant with future narrative possibility, the other strand is far from barren. Historical moments succeed this one in which the stylized delays of ritual incorporate the most pressing truths. Perpetually deferring crucial confrontations, circling the old shrines once more, that can also be a way of uncovering the strangest areas of the self. The courtier, of which Chaucer's knight is an unselfconscious type, embodies human possibilities which survive the disappearance of monarchs and awaken responsive chords in the age of Freud.

CHAPTER SEVEN

THE DEATH OF MAGIC: SIDNEY AND SPENSER

One could argue that narrative is something the Elizabethans weren't good at, and that therefore they might plausibly be left out of an account of it. They reach their greatest artistic heights in miniature forms, or in applying the techniques of the miniaturist unexpectedly to larger canvases. The archetypal Elizabethan artifacts – a Shakespeare sonnet, one of the queen's dresses, any of those architectural conceits built by noblemen here and there across England – are intricate, cold, and dazzling, aglitter with the unfriendly light of a jewel caught in tangled metal.

If one can leave aside most of Shakespeare's plays for the time being, which fight their way free of the straitjacket of Elizabethan artifice, though they are more outlandish than they are generally credited with being, one finds over and over a civilization theatrical but undramatic, defiantly secular (a great novelty) but hamstrung more effectively by superstitious ritual than the ones which preceded it. Such attitudes are the enemies of narrative, and the great Elizabethan prose fictions are quarrying grounds for anti-narrative impulses.

Not many readers of Sidney's *Arcadia* have realized that the intricacy and elaboration of the work were grafted onto it in a second stage of labour. The original version of the story, clearer and more straight-forward, remained unpublished until 1912. So it isn't part of the settled mythology of the work that Sidney himself needed to get the skeleton fixed in his mind before he could disguise it with the bewildering embroidery which is now the *Arcadia*.

The circumstances of its production are quasi-mythic: it is a noble-man's prank written deep in the country for the private amusement of his sister with whom he was staying, continued after his departure and dispatched quickly back to her. How satisfying to uncover such pastoral roots for a pastoral work and to feel it so nearly narcissistic and self-regardful.

For the book is one of the great demonstrations that extremes of artifice and subjectivity meet, that the most entirely externalized materials can, like the shell of a crab, be the self turned inside out, inner parts now surfaces. The *Arcadia* is an incestuous narrative in the sense that it is more self-referential than it appears, and constructs a closed circle of meanings in which many apparent-others turn out to be the self after all. Like the most elaborate Elizabethan clothes it departs from the body only to swing back to a closer mirroring of its form, flirting in between with farfetched analogues – jewels, metals, lacy filigrees – through which it aims to emblemize the person.

Depending on what level of magnitude one focuses on, the texture of a paragraph or the shape of whole episodes, there is either an astonishing amount of activity so the pages iridesce like a peacock's tail, or one undergoes constant back eddies and deflections, and makes no forward progress.

The later, expanded version begins with two shepherds who have small parts in the action which follows but are like carved figures on a doorframe or the allegorical border of a title page. They proclaim themselves rivals but speak identical sentiments. They have returned to the shore where they saw their disputed love embark, and they put their longing in the form of the speech Remembrance made to them in between the departure and now, a decorous way of saying they haven't forgotten. The ideal reader would never feel impatience, pleased for sentences to lengthen in front of him with no prospect of altering the mood into which they lull him. At any moment he is very far from an ending.

So he doesn't reach out for the events which occasionally float past, but registers them half-indifferently, 'Ah, there goes a lion, or a conflagration.' The shepherds' reverie-declamations break off when they notice an object on the waves – a coffer holding treasure? – no, it is a senseless man, like an object; naked, but his beauty is like clothing. He is carried shoreward and they attempt to animate him. When he comes round he lunges toward the sea again; they find a boat and take him to the burning hulk from which he came, fire in water. No sooner have they drawn level with the companion he wants to rescue, than the current, with a motion like Sidney's sentences, carries them out of reach. So from a distance they see the companion captured by pirates, who are in turn attacked, at which point the watchers' allegiance swings round like the wind to the opposite quarter. In the end the almost-drowned's friend disappears on the second alien boat and our party regains the shore.

They set off in a new direction, for the shepherds aren't natives here but promise hospitality in the adjoining country, Arcadia. So the noble youth has been doubly displaced, to a wilder stage outside a remote pastoral enclave.

This prelude at the edge of the sea has set the tone for a story in which human beings will be randomly wafted on an unstable surface, sometimes lurid but fundamentally soothing in its action, spawner of metamorphoses, suggesting a fluidity of human identity matching the sea's.

Musidorus and Pyrocles have decided to adopt false names when separated, which clears the way for confusions – how will they find each other, for a start? – geographical bearings lost, they set about obscuring others. One might think that a false identity was a rigid kind of fiction, but this turns out not to be the case. Not for very long will we have the disguise and the real self under it, for soon Musidorus, whom we are trying to call Palladius, leaves again to rescue his host's son imprisoned by the helots. His reading of historians suggests an ingenious ruse requiring another layer of disguise: some of his men will dress as ragged peasants and haul the others in carts wearing artificial chains, so that they look like Arcadian riffraff coming over to the helot side. This pageant works perfectly, and before the helots relize it, the masquers have overpowered them.

Now Musidorus/Palladius is in for a surprise. Instead of attacking, the helot leader kneels at his feet: have you forgotten Daiphantus (Pyrocles' pseudonym)? To understand this reversal, we have to unfurl and reposition the preceding episode. A residue of confusion remains, war is an unreal play, and a rhetorical figure – oxymoron (delightful terror, sweet enemy) – has grown into a dramatic incident.

This brings the story to one of its resting places (short lived): like meets like again, and several pairs are realigned before gathering strength for new separations. The rejoicing is barely finished when Musidorus notes that Pyrocles frequently drifts off by himself. He upbraids him, but is interrupted by an invitation to hunt, from which savage ceremony (lovers of oxymoron will love the hunt, full of gorgeous murders) Pyrocles slopes off, leaving a cryptic note, which propels Musidorus to assume a knightly disguise and set off in pursuit or symmetrical wandering.

At Kalander's house the host's own story hasn't been able to go forward because it keeps meeting other stories at every step, which start distinct but will become involved with each other. These stories are often sparked off by works of art; fiction reveals itself through further layers of fiction. At the heart of the host's garden is a house of pictures, and among many images of gods and goddesses is found one of a recognizable family.

That picture catches Musidorus, who questions its owner, who tells a long story about a king and two daughters. Although they are present in this bewitching image, no one can see them any longer because their father has spirited them away, hiding their virtues in two garden lodges he erects in the woods.

One has to come into a garden to scale pinnacles of art, and soon learns that this promise is held out only to be snatched away. Like Sidney's fiction the painting is a tease, offering us something which doesn't exist or isn't where it is supposed to be, so we must wait longer than we are initially led to hope.

The host regards the king's behaviour as a terrible theft. This selfish king has deprived the country of its ruler, youths of the most glorious dreams of marriage, and hence everyone of the future. Right in the midst of this relation someone comes up and whispers in the host's ear, at which he changes colour and disappears, like the king mysteriously absenting himself from society.

This provokes a story from a retainer about the son whom the host mourns, and the friend whom the son went to rescue. This friend loved a standoffish woman, disfigured by a disappointed rival who smeared poison on her face, transforming her from the most beautiful to the most hideous of beings. Because the son's friend, perceiving inward worthiness through obscuring mists, would not give her up, she took matters in her own hands and disappeared. He followed, and was soon clapped in prison by the rival, awaiting tortures too horrible to devise at once.

That anecdote intervened because the host's absence needed explaining, the story's cause forgotten and reclaimed only at its end. Sidney's work is composed of units like gigantic periodic sentences which keep us suspended for long intervals before leading suddenly back to the point of contact with the old thread which we are then re-encouraged to view as the primary tale. The friend's story can only take its proper seat when, at its close we are reminded why we had to be told it in the first place. We may feel that it is at that moment reduced to minute dimensions, as if we finally saw that a lustrous object which has filled our sight for ten minutes past is only a pearl in an Ethiop's ear, satisfyingly round, yet by no means as big as a world.

Most readers of *The Arcadia* must have grasped that art here consists of decoys and impediments. In later fictions it is common to pretend that the writer is as helpless as anyone before such convolutions in our passage to the story's end; in Sidney there is no such pretence. 'To make a long story short' would seem an impulse of inconceivable grossness here. Rather, to prevent meanings from declaring themselves, to keep other characters in the dark about the heroes' natures and intentions, or in the first place about their whereabouts, that is how a civilized story proceeds. The most beautiful tale would lose as many of its protagonists as possible and send them through the woods to bump into each other one at a time.

Here the resemblance to medieval romance is most marked, yet Sidney is defiantly less consequential: like pseudonyms, coats of armour are primarily costumes which wanderers don for short periods to take on brief chameleon identities. Musidorus finds empty armour scattered among the trees and decides to change it for his own. So clothed, he meets a troop in black and white who charge him without warning. After causing a few deaths he makes his way to the centre of the party, a lady in a coach so preoccupied with a painted portrait she hasn't heard the fighting, and only looks up when Musidorus' shadow falls across her picture. Oh unkind, she says, mistaking him for the owner of the armour and the subject of her reverie. Now her story, of which we have had fragments, is reassembled *in toto*.

The lady is whirled along in her carriage as later Musidorus will be spun by the king's ingenious revolving dinner table powered by a garden fountain, kept always the same distance from the loved object, though apparently in motion toward her and soon occupying the space in which she just now was.

That mechanical table is an epitome of the courtly view, decorous mockery of real motion or true activity, a kind of façadism, like armour conceived not as physical protection but flimsy covering or pseudonym, reaching its highest pitch of perfection in the mock armour which 'Zelmane' wears when Musidorus spies 'her' moving toward the secret arbour where she doffs her disguise in verse, and leaves him aghast to find it is Pyrocles turned into a woman by his passion for the king's daughter Pamela. Luckily for Musidorus – both of them having seen the same painting at different times and fallen in love with different parts of it.

Pyrocles' 'armour' is made of feathers, silk, and thin scales of gold, the nearest thing to an immaterial phantasm. Some will find it distressingly literal, like the table powered like a mill-wheel, an unworthy parody of Dante's concentric rotating spheres. Others will recognize the waning power of magical transformation on the point of waking up and finding its metamorphoses have lost their power to persuade. It is ritual in the last moments before a collapse of conviction, when it begins heeding the sceptical critic who says it is all an expensive and trivial waste. We can see what the illusion is made of: the fishes under the net on the horse's caparison are *sewn on* and their swimming is caused by the motion of the horse's knees. Perhaps that falsehood wouldn't be humiliating by itself, if it weren't also becoming clear that the idea of the tournament exists now only so that 'knights' can appear in 'armour' constructed of such illusions. Decoration ceases to be simple embellishment of a tool, becomes a compelling and overmastering spectacle in itself, a Protean *version of reality*. Until a sceptic points out that it is 'only a fiction', which was its strength and becomes its vulnerability. The same exposure suffered by knightly ceremony is finally undergone a generation later by Sidney's language, which from powerful magic tumbles down into hollow rhetoric.

The most interesting Puritan commentary on Sidney takes the form of a peregrinating romance more indebted to him and his aristocratic medieval models than it cares to admit. One can imagine Bunyan's stubborn reading of the *Arcadia*, his refusal to think of himself as a prince, his insistence on taking the pastoral literally and identifying with those excluded from the centres of the story, shepherds and fishermen, whom it is the king's aberration to put in charge of his daughters' education, with grotesquely comic results.

Someone, Bunyan or anyone else, hoping to free what is good in the *Arcadia* from the solipsistic aesthetic and social ideas would have a real job, because the two are seriously implicated in each other. All the narrative's most dazzling devices start off in a new direction only to circle back to the self after all. Statues and pictures, which cause such excitement, are other guises of art, which allow the prose to look at itself without seeming to, a Narcissus which doesn't recognize its own reflection. Sex changes and disguises, though in some way alienations of the most personal materials, like portrayals of people in tapestry, allow one to call something Other which is the self in new guises, prevented by unfamiliar stitches and patches of glitter from a clear idea what one is looking at.

This fusion of coldness and inwardness appears most plainly in the story's intimate ecstasies, like 'Zelmane' taking Philoclea's hand, a metaphysical symmetry pulsing on and one without prospect of end, which would be at home in Henry James. Or even better and stranger, because less resolved or definite still, their electrical rubbing as they sit side by side in the coach:

> Basilius and Gynecia, sitting in the one end, placed her at the other, with her left side to Philoclea. Zelmane was moved in her mind to have kissed their feet for the favour of so blessed a seat, for the narrowness of the coach made them join from the foot to the shoulders very close together; the truer touch whereof though it were barred by their envious apparel, yet as a perfect magnet though put in an ivory box will through the box send forth his embracing virtue to a

beloved needle, so this imparadised neighbourhood made Zelmane's soul cleave unto her both through the ivory case of her body and the apparel which did overcloud it: all the blood of Zelmane's body stirring in her, as wine will do when sugar is hastily put into it, seeking to suck the sweetness of the beloved guest; her heart like a lion new imprisoned, seeing him that restrains his liberty before the grate, not panting but striving violently (if it had been possible) to have leaped into the lap of Philoclea.

But Dametas, even then proceeding from being master of a cart to be doctor of a coach, not a little proud of himself that his whip at that time guided the rule of Arcadia, drave the coach, the cover whereof was made with such joints that as they might (to avoid the weather) pull it up close when they listed, so when they would they might put each end down and remain as discovered and open-sighted as on horseback: till upon the side of the forest they had both greyhounds, spaniels and hounds, whereof the first might seem the lords, the second the gentlemen, and the last the yeomen of dogs. A cast of merlins there was besides, which, flying of a gallant height over certain bushes, would beat the birds that rose down into the bushes, as falcons will do wild-fowl over a river.

This becomes ever more beautiful as it gets further from its goal, lodging itself in progressively remote surrogates. First the excitement is trans-ferred (as body heat, perhaps) to the construction of the carriage, and then to the birds flying along the river bank.

But as usual the effort to carry the story on by other, more indirect means, fizzles out. There is no way back from the flights of sympathetic imagination; continually needing other ways of saying it, like the evasions of Elizabethan clothes, leaves one outside the statement one wants to make in the end.

Sidney's fiction and many other Elizabethan works of art profess a fervent faith in *making* which extends even to machines, rarely seen before or since, which is really a faith in the transforming power of imagination. The strength of this is that it is viewed as a general human capacity and to that extent not an individual possession or personal accomplishment, a view unavailable to Nabokov, for instance. But this worship of art, or more properly of artifice, is without content to an unnerving degree.

In Elizabethan fiction it is a test of faith like reincarnation when a character who was gone appears again, or almost more mysteriously, when a *name* we have seen embodied in one way turns up more authentically borne. Pyrocles has masqueraded as Zelmane for ages when it is brought home to us that there is a real Zelmane: she appears disguised as a boy.

At times one thinks, yes, this is a truly modern supernaturalism, something akin to the movement of sap in trees, which has a chemical formula but not a specifiable meaning. Yet it is only half of a circle. Like William Morris in flight from Romantic ideas of personal originality losing himself in mindless pattern, the Elizabethan approach to character carries one giddily away from parochial dogmas to strand one far out on a limb, wondering if there is really no more than this – a graceful weaving of indistinguishable tendrils, of pairs splitting and recombining, impeded and temporarily out of sight, then reappearing and rushing on toward a destination which no one can be terribly concerned whether it reaches or not.

Their materials are not the same of course (Spenser's more consciously out of date, or timeless), but near enough so that comparison of these two constructors of endless fictions seems apt. Neither is a linear narrative, but we trust ourself in Spenser's hands, whereas – though we may enjoy the sensation – in Sidney's we are victimized or hoodwinked: often things get in such a tangle they need untelling rather than telling. Perhaps this is true in isolated patches of many stories, and then one has the agreeable sensation of needing to back up. Confusions in the *Arcadia*, though, take the form of 'who is who?'and in the *Faerie Queene* of 'who is this *really?*' So the deception isn't an entertaining flicker of the surface but a moral quandary which may deepen to a consuming gloom.

From the beginning Spenser lends sobriety and depth where we don't expect them. The dints in Redcrosse's armour, from fights before he wore it, are poignant signals of past stages in the narrative; we intercept two strange riders in their passage. And the bloody cross on his shield, emblem of his dying Lord, an astonishing deepening of the meaning of battle to a richer shade of red. Some will not like the feeling of responsibility in Spenser: nothing is neutral, even the landscape is loaded with moral significance which penetrates like the English climate rather than the preacher's voice, and is therefore less evadable.

Before we know what it means we notice how dark the darkness is in Spenser's woods, how believably things become hard to see. Redcrosse's armour gives off sufficient light to reveal Error stretched out in her cave, a beautiful but most melancholy vision. That is the real Spenser; he sinks naturally into these entranced or slightly torpid states, but when the tone lightens, we feel he is working at it, because he knows it would be healthier to move in such a direction.

Spenser's glooms contrast markedly with Sidney's decorative exuberance, which lends new and unexpected frivolity to the materials, new pagan insouciance. It therefore comes as a surprise that dogged, serious

Spenser is the one careful not to let debates obscure the story. When Una shouts advice to the entangled warrior, or they discuss what dangers might lie ahead, with overtones of the soul's welfare, it remains dramatic. Premonitions are semi-moralized and still pregnant with possibility. Premonitions, one of narrative's surest means of drawing us into its movement, carefully nurtured by Spenser, neglected by Sidney.

Sidney's courtiers engage in long debates which have forgotten their dramatic occasion. Spenser moves slowly but steadily on – how rare his unshakable devotion to the story is. Sidney pushes forward in bursts and then loses himself in tangles, which Spenser's characters would be penalized by the story for doing. It is obtuse of course to try to smooth out the inequalities in Sidney's telling: he is the irresponsible narrator par excellence. In the *Arcadia* morality is another part of the decorative effect: altruism part of the aristocrat's idea of himself, interesting for how it reflects or creates him, not as a social fact which it can't help being.

In Spenser the moral vision is so deeply infused he hardly needs to discuss it. The first enemy they meet is the female dragon Error, not a rubric one can imagine Sidney paying any heed to, whose whole conception of a story is the setting in motion of a thousand delightful errors. From the start *The Faerie Queene* undertakes the reader's moral education, cleansing his mind of various falsehoods. But Spenser's way of doing this is so discreet that before very long we begin to wonder what need he really has of old-fangled allegory, because he usually introduces a character or a place vividly before letting us hear its allegorical name. So to learn that the church robber is Kirkrapine, after his death and the good characters' departure, can be like the last piece of an almost complete puzzle slotting into place, or like checking one's already written out answers against the test key.

These questions of moral valency can be more a mystery needing solution at some times than others. Often the absent name is a neutral gap in our knowledge, infrequently – in the case of Arthur, for one – an active curiosity anxious to be set to rest – who can this intriguing champion be? The essential point for the history of allegory is that in Spenser the meanings aren't promulgated as dogma we must learn, memorize, or obey, but revealed at different speeds to different readers according to individual capacities for enlightenment.

An undeclared struggle courses underneath Spenser's fiction to which – and this almost saves him from bigotry – he rarely gives a name, the war between Catholic and Protestant conceptions of things. Archimago comes disguised as a priest muttering Latin prayers. Should we conclude, when this priest is revealed as a magician, that most or all priests are too? At the

House of Pryde the first rider among six vices who pull Pryde's car is Idleness, presented as a religious contemplative, with many sneers at inaction as a form of goodness. Before long we begin to recognize the sad and solitary wanderers with bowed heads as magicians in disguise. True goodness isn't so enervated and downcast. Yet here Spenser goes against his natural inclination: the life of a studious hermit is not intrinsically hideous to him. Like many English writers he finds that the battle with the Catholic residue in himself isn't so easy to win as he had hoped.

The immense divide between Spenser and Sidney consists, above all, of this: in *The Faerie Queene* it is taken for granted that one wars against one's natural inclinations, and the hero's most gruelling battle is fought with himself. Error is our principal enemy and our central dilemma. Archimago is dangerous most of all in making the good mistrust each other – not because he can corrupt them to evil acts, but because he makes them doubt the beauty of goodness. Thus he sends Redcrosse rushing from the castle thinking Una has forsaken him. The converse of this is that badness can impose itself as goodness on goodness, which is not resentful or suspicious enough to imagine such deceits.

However benighted by the ruses of malice good characters become, a reader never questions that under everything the truth waits to be found out. The distance separating this view from Sidney is unbridgeable. The idea that reality is a game, or that feigning is a good occupation for adults, so that we might enjoy, by dressing up, adding to the errors and illusions abroad in the world, how can anyone suggest this? When Spenser's good characters perplex us, there is a reason: Arthur can't tell his origins because he doesn't know them; the past remains a mystery to him too.

An impulse to see through disguises, not to let them be, and to explode ceremonies as hollow fictions, is an extremely dangerous scepticism to turn loose in stories, and Spenser's world survives intact because he seldom imagines he can draw the lines as sharply as that. Sometimes he seems dauntingly sure he knows what wickedness is, and many of the least convincing moments in *The Faerie Queene* are unmaskings of some lurid vice. In some hands destructive scepticism can be an energetic and almost a creative force. Fortunately Spenser does not trust himself to this. The poem is saved by his uncertainty he knows what goodness is, and his continual struggles to uncover or define it. It is a guiding principle of the *Faerie Queene* that goodness is active and can only be truly conceived as it engages with reality, must be seen in motion, undergoes continual change. Because he is a story-teller above all, Spenser's version of this, rather than a contribution to moral theory, is a new and unarchaic way of imagining a story, as something which happens in an individual.

And thus it is more fitting to see him as the ancestor of Bunyan and Richardson than as the feeble continuer of an exhausted romance tradition. Why Spenser the arch-anti-dogmatist should have borrowed so much inflexible paraphernalia from the likes of *Romance of the Rose* remains one of the most interesting literary questions.

In a letter dated January, 1589 (two years after Sidney's death), and addressed to Raleigh, Spenser provides rudiments of an explanation. If he were an historiographer (instead of a historical poet), he would begin his narrative with Book XII, that is at the end of the poem, and he now tells us what that book will contain: the Faerie Queene is holding court, and on each of the twelve days as the company meets, an adventure announces itself – a maiden, a palmer, or some other suppliant appears asking for help, and is put in the care of a particular knight. Each of these pairs will become a book of the poem, and by the time we meet them the suppliants no longer look prior, but *follow* the knights as their companions. Thus in twelve days the action of the poem is somehow contained, though it is hard to square this with the wide expanses and deep pools of time suggested in Book I.

From the examples he uses one gathers Spenser hasn't thought any further than Book III, or at least hasn't assigned the succeeding books to specific knights. Each book will be in the sphere of a particular quality, the twelve constituting a set of private virtues. If the work is well received, Spenser may continue it with treatments of political or social virtues in a further series of parts. In the end he finished about half the poem.

We have our misgivings about the orderly scheme, and find it hard to accept that the poem will end with the announcement or initiation of its constituent parts. Another unlikely ending is projected near the end of Book I: the poem will culminate in a great battle between the armies of the Faerie Queene and a Paynim host, easier to imagine in Faerie Lond than Palestine, a contest between England and Spain rather than an echo of the Crusades.

Spenser might project compendia of all the virtues and great final battles, but he is not a systematic or apocalyptic writer. His great themes are not noisy clashes but slow and imperceptible changes – like deterioration and recovery, which press wordlessly in on the observer: Redcrosse found deep in Orgoglio's dungeons with his flesh shrunken like a withered flower, companions waiting a few days after hard battle to *recure* (a favourite word) their strength with the help of physicians.

He calls the poem an allegory or darke conceit. One quarrels with the first, and accepts part of the second of these descriptions. Spenser isn't a naturally allegorical writer. The dullest parts of the poem are stretches like the House of Holinesse where insistent captions follow close on one another's heels and the verses are dutifully demonstrating the names.

But his mind is naturally obscure, winding or oblique in its progress, and allegory gives him a convenient excuse for why he might come at things in his peculiarly wandering way. Spenser's narratives don't begin or end, but link with something before and after. The returning hero meets one who is setting out, and our attention is divided comfortably between that which is ending and that which is just beginning to grow, as in a garden where among many plants no two are of the same age.

How does a writer make palatable a story which encapsulates this sense of un-finality, of slow growth and maturity in the presence of other lives growing at different stages and speeds? One way is by pretending that there is a single grand design which will become plain at a point rather far off in the future, so individual lives are not simply parallel instances of the same thing, roughly co-equal, but everything is orchestrated from a central node, a court in this case, and falls neatly into a compact series.

Except that every time Spenser mentions or presents a court it is a horrible place. The first court rouses him to the most comprehensive vision of doom he is capable of – Pryde's carriage sallies out to take the air, and the lines which describe the movement of the watching crowd and the descent of a mist on the land have a true flavour of Apocalypse. How could he have held up for all those years the vision of a court as his great goal? Doubtless he knew from early on that he had better not come too close to that fulfilment, that it was a beautiful prospect, like heaven, which couldn't be rendered with conviction.

One of the main strengths of his plan is how much distance he has managed to insert between himself and completion, how far he is from the story's final resting place. Even within a single book we see his preference for throwing forward the central business. Una's parents, the motivating cause of the first adventure, aren't more than casually mentioned until Canto XI. As we near the end of Book I perhaps it is time to apply ourselves at last to the problem which brought us into the field of battle in the first place.

It is true that once embarked on it, Spenser rises to a height in the ultimate battle of Book I. He may be at his best or most characteristic 'wandering in ways unknown', in the spaces *between* adventures, chartless, nameless lulls in which one senses man's lonely separation on the earth, and feels with excited horror that no one has been here before. But the fight with the last dragon is not a disappointment. Spenser achieves this by making the dragon a landscape, who casts a deep shadow as he flies, whose eyes are lamps *far within* making a horrid shade, whose cry sounds like a winter sea, and the spout of whose dark blood could turn a mill-wheel. So it is not a personal struggle but a contention with an adverse fate where the hero meets trial after trial, as if in disconnected episodes, on a series of days. The dragon comes apart into separate problems like a pervasive condition rather than a limited being.

As *The Faerie Queene* progresses it becomes more noticeably interwoven. In Book III many new intrigues are set going while very little is concluded. Only the peripheral story of Malbecco can be said to end (he loses his manhood and *becomes* Gelosy, an allegory). By this point in the story, concluding stanzas seem to exist to heighten the feeling of suspension. It is at those moments we realize how many things we await an outcome of. When Book III ends, Marinell is on the sea bottom having his wounds tended. Florimell who loves him is nearby, unbeknownst to both of them, in Proteus' sea-cave. Timias has undergone a similar tending and healing in Belphoebe's forest retreat, but the ache has only moved from his thigh to his heart. Most important, Britomart seeks the knight she saw in the mirror.

The entry of Belphoebe sets in motion one of Spenser's most voluptuous regressions, from her tending of the wounded squire, to the story of her birth: her mother slept naked in the woods, and the sun acted on her womb as it does on Nile mud, to implant two daughters, born without her knowledge in her sleep, taken by Venus and Diana to be raised as exemplars of lovable and chaste womanhood respectively.

This tale drives Spenser further back into myth, further from the story, to the Garden of Adonis, a perfected place where the rules of time (and of narratives) are suspended or collected: it is spring and harvest forever in the seminary of all things born to live and die. But this equilibrium crystallizes only a single aspect of Spenser's sense of passage.

For one of his greatest discoveries is the positive value of interruption, which naturally has no place in the Garden. We can tolerate Belphoebe's disappearance before we learn her name, or can accede to the replacement of a discourse on springs by a three-cornered fight because we *will* learn the missing details (or perhaps just others like them) in the fulness of time.

Book III begins with references which would come near the end of most books, to how *long* Redcrosse and Guyon have been travelling and how drawn out their journey has been. Spenser is remarkable for sounding tiredest, and nearest to giving up, at the beginning of the journey. It is the most revealing fact about his sense of time: that he feels most reluctance to move on as he sets off, and that he is just getting into stride and beginning an ascending curve as he approaches the close.

The reader comes to expect him to rise to certain subjects, often unpromising, like wounds and their tending, or imprisonment – immobilizing conditions which slow or halt time's unfolding, and convert ordinary existence into a muted version of the Garden of Adonis. But the essential thing about him as a poet, and the final importance of the knightly milieu to him, is his unpredictability, and the scope that the wide pastoral expanses of Faerie Lond give to it. The interest of the poem is diffused over a large number of sub-centres, the relations between which are essentially unbalanced.

One could devote oneself, not pointlessly, to showing Spenser's consistencies, how every emphasis within a book tends toward a general portrait of the ruling virtue and its antithesis. The voluptuous material of Book III (Chastity) is not paralleled elsewhere in the poem, because lasciviousness is à propos there, the contrary of Chastity, as religious hypocrisy is to Holiness (Book I). Even to go this far, though, shows one how tricky the idea of moral contraries is, for blasphemy and prudery would form equally plausible, but unseized, anti-types to these virtues. One *could* assemble the evidence of rational planning and argue that it ruled the poem, but this would be perverse. The discussion of chastity or holiness is left in a very dishevelled state, a numinous mist of half formed notions, not a hierarchical presentation at all.

Perhaps all large poetic achievements are syntheses of unmarriageable traditions. Milton has certainly looked that way to many observers. But the pagan and Christian enjoy an unheard- of cohabitation and mutual tolerance bread of unconsciousness in Spenser. The landscape is vast enough, the binding ligaments vague enough that confrontations are avoided.

The knight who bears Christ's insignia on his shield is driven into the woods of Error by a storm (the poem's first event) caused by Jove. Creatures of classical myth are equated with the members of aboriginal tribes. Most unresolved of all, is the problem of faeries or elves, a status both Recrosse and Arthur have thoughtlessly claimed, only to see it taken away by those who know their origins better. Even if its main inhabitants are not really faeries, the place remains Faerie Lond with its Faerie Queene, insensitively identified from time to time with our queen now. This does not mean that Faerie Lond is Britain however, for there is a Britain in the poem, from which some of the more reliable characters derive, but not a place one expects to spawn interesting stories. In spite of the tangle and the appearance of paths which may join up between the poem and life, it is another world, which when we near its border, will subtly repel our steps and send us off in another direction.

Before a reader has gone very far he has ingested one of the main rules of the place, that he cannot go straight to the real goals, that there is never an easy route and there may be none at all, but that his imagination can be sufficiently occupied with subsidiary objects at a great if unspecified distance from the Faerie Court, to which he has been promised admission in the end, a promise which cannot be kept because so many things must happen before that, that there isn't time for them.

Occasionally in Spenser the causes of events are placed after them in time. It is normal of course for causes to be told after consequences *in the story*: thus Book IV begins with an amusing account of the beginning of Amoret's far from amusing captivity, which we have just watched Britomart bring to an end in Book III. Busirane's mistreatment of her conceals an Aztec cruelty in pretty, theatrical ritual. When he first took her it was one of those jokes masque-goers are used to: she was picked out of the audience at her wedding celebration and made to join the players. Aftermath and origin, suffering and entertainment, are of such different tonalities it gives us serious pause, and we conclude that much of life is more momentous than the actors imagine at the time.

Sometimes distortions of sequence, where one event is cited to account for another which we know happened first, do not feel like the writer's meaningless oversights. We have watched Marinell carried lovingly off to the sea bottom after being bested by Britomart in a set-to on the beach. Following Britomart again, we meet an overheated dwarf, desperate to find Florimell, who fled the Faerie Court at the news of Marinell's defeat (Florimell has loved Marinell and been repulsed because of the prophecy that he would be a woman's victim, a curse Britomart has lifted by fulfilling, clearing the way for Florimell). Marinell's defeat is the freshest event in the story, too new to have caused others or even to be known to someone arriving here from elsewhere. Britomart after all is like a shock wave of that event travelling from its centre and bringing the first evidence of it to the places she reaches.

Something worse is wrong too. Britomart only ever met Marinell because she didn't go with the other knights who were chasing Florimell. That was a long time ago, the first event of the present sequence. Florimell appeared in full flight, and, without thinking, the men were off in pursuit, leaving Britomart behind alone, because she is less drawn to Florimell, as if it were always a mixture of altriusm and sexual arousal which prompted a knightly rescue.

So one could say that the flight of Florimell deflected Britomart toward the shore and Marinell, a route which is now understood to have led out from the other side too (from Marinell), to the flight of Florimell. Of course, nearness and farness in time *are* mysterious. One can be more intimate with a distant than a near occurrence, and feel a continuing kinship which keeps it present or active.

Part of the point here is that people and happenings are allied which we haven't yet thought of connecting, that there are simpler relations between parts than we first realize, which are like short cuts driven across expanses we thought no one could trespass on.

There are different perspectives on the same event, seen from Britomart, or from Florimell, and occasionally we feel the difference uncomfortably conflated, and grasp that time and space make an overlapping web full of knots like physical impossibilities, expressing the inadequacy of the individual focus.

To understand events is to unravel them and trace them to their sources. An intelligent or thinking story goes backward as much as it goes forward. That is Spenser's archaism in the deepest sense, a concern with the roots of action. But he begins from a number of points in the present, following them back, and finds that the results of the searches don't match. So he starts over with a different thread hoping that the contradiction he has exposed will subside like an old ache. From such sources comes our sense of Spenser as a man with his eye on something else, as if he always inspects what *is going to* happen for signs of what *has* happened, drawn in another direction from the one in which it's easiest to go, and into the murkiest, oldest reaches of it.

CHAPTER EIGHT

SHAKESPEARE'S ARCHAISM

Two groups of plays, from opposite ends of his career, mark Shakespeare's nearest approach to the romance tradition. One set, the four 'late' romances (or thee-and-a-half, since he didn't write all of *Pericles*), bear the most obvious relation to it. Still, they are an impenetrable mystery in various ways.

Even if *Antony and Cleopatra* is regarded as a dim foreboding of their spirit, the last plays body forth a radical shift of tone and scale into a relaxed and spacious world, which has been explained as the intrusion of court masque into drama (following a general fashion), or the transfigured reconciliation of the writer's soul to all life as he approaches death. But he had just passed forty when this phase began and was forty-five at the end of his stage career, which is not to discount the second of the two explanations, more profoundly true than the first.

So the naïve Spenserian phase Shakespeare came to at the end of his writing life, and not of his biological one, was 'late' in an ideal, almost metaphorical sense. He found his way to the earliest, most buried layer last, and *The Winter's Tale* takes much of its poignancy from our knowledge that this autumnal rebirth follows the winter of the tragedies. Now it is hard to imagine reading these plays, as Coleridge did, as inexperienced works, not difficult reapproximations of innocence, or authentic pastoral, but truly rude beginnings. Readers may sympathize though. For we would like to fill in Shakespeare's apprenticeship.

The other group, less evidently romance inspired, are strongly youthful, in excesses of ingenuity and skill above all, in overflows of wit and linguistic exuberance. These are the 'lyric' works of 1594-6 which include *Love's Labour's Lost*, *Romeo and Juliet* and *A Midsummer Night's Dream*, apparently written following Shakespeare's deflection from the theatre (an outbreak of plague closed them in 1593) during which he wrote *Venus and Adonis*, *Lucrece*, and many sonnets. Compared to contemporary works of other writers, even these extravagant, mannered narratives are clear-headed and strongly outlined. One has only to look at Marlowe's *Hero and Leander* to see how far Shakespeare at his most decorative is from losing sight of the wood in the trees.

One imagines him freed by this interlude to be more gratuitously gorgeous, lingering in the habit encouraged by the narratives in verse, of stopping to compose pictures or tableaux. The comedies of this period (which really deserve a more specialized name, taken perhaps from the realms of music or dance – minuet, rondo?) are among his most locally active works, his most static overall. *Love's Labour's Lost* begins in a complete dead end, except that something so tightly closed must explode: a king and three courtiers have decided to shut themselves away for three years to do nothing but study, eating plainly, sleeping little, and forswearing *entirely* (an unbalanced member of the series) the company of women. By a lazy oversight they have forgotten that the French king's daughter and her court, all female, are about to arrive to negotiate a disputed territory, which is the size of a royal dowry. In short they make their promises a few days earlier than they could begin to keep them.

The play opens with quasi-religious vows creating a secular monastery of intellect, immediately threatened by an enemy who barely need appear in order to win, for soon we see the defenders begging to have their surrender accepted. The central part of the play is a series of skirmishes in a tournament of wit, whose result is vows similar to the opening ones which the men proved unable to keep. If the king shuts himself in a hermitage for a year the princess will accept him at the end. If Armado, the over-refined courtier, follows the plough three years, the milkmaid will hear his suit. If the caustic wit Berowne closets himself with the sick and dying and makes them laugh, Rosalind will come round. In a way they are worse off: the penances and cures are more stringent than their original scheme, but the rewards are better, love at the end of it.

Still, this, play which gives one of the most sustained exhibitions of the darting fires of wit, ends by the waters of romance-bred melancholy. *A Midsummer Night's Dream* follows a similarly parenthetical pattern, but instead of two abstentions framing an outbreak of gaiety it is the announcement and the confirmation of union forming a circle around the painful conflict marriage arose to heal. *Love's Labour's Lost* is play and high spirits overlooked by misgivings and self denial, *Midsummer Night's Dream* bad dreams sheltering under an overarching concord, like Mozart in a major or a minor key, or Harlequin's clothes predominantly dark or light, but mottled in either case. *Love's Labour's Lost*, the more deliberately superficial of the two, is to our surprise the more troubled, whose wit conceals something nearer to unease.

Both are peculiar among Shakespeare's plays in being written for particular occasions in great houses, topical as most of his works are not. Read this way, their self-consciousness (verging on preciousness) has a richer, more human point. Like Sidney talking to his sister, Shakespeare is inhibited by particular watchers he knows will be there. *Someone*'s marriage is celebrated, *particular* prejudices are reinforced. The anti-marriage play (*Love's Labour's Lost*) will naturally have a less self-congratulatory sense of the present moment and the immediate future.

In that work, one feels a counterpoint between affairs on stage and goings-on in nearby rooms of this country house. Actors in such a situation can't help letting their eye fall occasionally on those in the house whose role most resembles theirs, or on those they fictionally love. *Love's Labour's Lost* bursts with complicated interlineation, a version of the winks and confirming glances which show that one's mind is in two places. Letters are read and commented on, sonnets are found and declaimed, or more often, impersonated by the writer, who isn't thinking them up at that moment, but gauging their effect on various hearers, intended, unwanted, or outside the dramatic situation altogether.

The play's most characteristic mode is a variety of interleaving, repartee formed of matching one-line assertions like shelling which leaves spectators wondering how long it can last it is so rapid, consumes such huge amounts of energy, and finds itself so often in awkward corners from which there is no exit except in paradox, leaving one alternately exhausted and elated at the sight of difficulty and its defeat.

If the play has long been underappreciated, that is probably because language is its hero to a degree rare even in Shakespeare. It contains almost no unaffected discourse, like an enormous bit of jewelwork which one may perceive as multiplied delight, but which is confined to a single tonality. Characters are chosen and introduced for aesthetic reasons, for their part in the pattern, like a certain colour of wool in a carpet. It has been thought an extremely early product, perhaps only because it is cold and so little personal, but like the Sonnets it seems dateless, a disguise which doesn't reveal the performer's age.

The presiding genius of *A Midsummer Night's Dream* is, most inappropriately for a marriage play, the cold and fruitless moon, gorgeously linked by Theseus with permanent maidenhood:

> Therefore, fair Hermia, question your desires,
> Know of your youth, examine well your blood,

> Whether, if you yield not to your father's choice,
> You can endure the livery of a nun,
> For aye to be in shady cloister mew'd,
> To live a barren sister all your life,
> Chanting faint hymns to the cold fruitless moon.
>
> (I, i, 67–73)

The moon is also the impediment whose cycle they must wait out before marrying, the force which rules the woods and drives the lovers mad for a spell, and the 'character' which causes the mechanics the worst headaches of staging.

If the moon is not the immediate cause of the troubles in the woods, it bathes all in a strange light by which they all look new. Sometimes the link is more circumstantial: the juice from an infected plant which makes lovers' eyes see unheard-of things is the product of desire crossed with moonlight. Cupid mistook his aim in that baleful glimmer and hit a flower instead of a nymph, making possible the transfer of the essence to later victims.

The play seems to differ with itself about whether the disturbances of vision associated with the fairies are fruitful or simply erroneous. At first painful impressions predominate. And then, on top of everything, the fairies are at war with each other, which one can take as signifying among other things that imagination is a chaotic power.

The first depiction of Titania shows her lulled by an assortment of flowers, as if so sunk in them she is almost changed into them, in a place where snakes throw off their enamelled skins, which thereupon become the clothes of fairies, the horrid quickly transmuted into the beautiful, as in Art Nouveau jewelry or small Mannerist bronzes. She tells her troops to war with bats for their wings which make sturdy coats, another diminution and civilizing of the ugly. A further, more upsetting stage in these alterations is *mistaking* the horrid for beautiful, which Oberon soon after forecasts for Titania. Snakes and flowers, music and poison, have been tumbled together harmlessly, phantasmagorically, but the next thing we know such aberrations of vision are experienced by the lovers as paranoid mistrust edging toward violence.

One would be hard pressed to say whether this is a believing or sceptical treatment of imagination. The subject often rouses Shakespeare to wonderful flights (about creatures in clouds and the kinship of lunatics, lovers and poets), but the enthusiasm often turns back on itself.

The power of art has never been more beautifully mocked than it is in Bottom's play, one of those miniature versions of what the writer himself is presently doing which he includes even in sublime works like *Hamlet*. As the fairies provide a reduced, exquisite commentary on certain human preoccupations, the artless mechanics are allowed by their literal-mindedness to concentrate certain puzzles of artistic illusion to a gem-like hardness.

It is a moment of transcendent generosity when, the weddings themselves skipped over and the rustics convinced they have missed their chance, Shakespeare catches them up and propels them to the centre of the stage, where they are entrusted with the task of sanctifying by their innocent music ('like a child on a recorder') the turmoil which has gone before.

Rapture is something one will wake from, imagination is a cold and treacherous power, the best plays are only shadows, we have been told, yet the end of *Midsummer Night's Dream* gives the lie to these surrenders and disclaimers. The greatest divisions of intellect and taste have been bridged by an eye for similarities in disparate expressions, which recognizes in Bottom's wish to *show* moonshine, not to frighten ladies, but to take more parts than his share, some of what is best in ourselves.

The end of the play, when the 'tedious brief' tragedy, a little obverse of the larger comedy, has faded, is turned over to the fairies who troop through the house after we have gone to bed, showing us both the world outside, and our own hearth without us. It is one of those moments when Shakespeare is able to look on the whole experience of being human as if it were something outside us. We are told or at least allowed to hold that the play is a dream, 'You have been asleep, now go home to bed,' but at this moment we experience an illusion which is just the reverse of this: through art, all life has become a figment one can disengage from momentarily.

At this point in his career tragedy remains a conceit and death a tantalizing idea, like a black costume. The extravagances of *Romeo and Juliet* seem so far removed from comedy because the play *says* they are. Romantic tragedy is a consciously contradictory artefact, whose building block is the oxymoron (Romeo's first utterance a flood of them:

> O brawling love, o loving hate,
> O heavy lightness, serious vanity ...
> Feather of lead, bright smoke, cold fire, sick health ...

some of which describe the play) and whose overall shape resembles that figure of speech, a perfection of structure as in a universe where the largest objects repeat the smallest, solar systems and atoms. Very perfect but self-regarding in a way *Midsummer Night's Dream*, which refers more openly to itself, escapes being.

In the right hands unresolvable contradiction as the basis of the most impinging experience has been a profound if still Romantic and paradoxical idea. But in *Romeo and Juliet* Shakespeare reminds us only superficially of Wagner or Freud. Although oxymoronic structure penetrates the drama through and through, he does not want to take it seriously but to display it as a bewitching pattern.

We cannot know it at the time, but Romeo is introduced immured in a love he will momentarily discard, to plunge further in than ever. Those around him will continue to talk of the old love as if its power lasted. The most intense experiences come and go like lightning, and only those further from the centre give them the permanence of everyday reality. Not that the first love is false or immature, the second real, for it is in the nature of such obsessions to replace one another. They consume their practitioners for the time being, thus all the lovers' talk about *names*, signs of the separate identities lost in this experience.

Romeo is first seen making a night for himself in the daytime, shut in his chamber, obliterating and obliterated by love. He meets Juliet at night in the presence of torches, rich foods, crowds – ensigns of life and vitality which after their first eruption in consciousness look primarily perishable.

They meet in preposterous figures drawn from religious observance and pilgrimage, dividing a sonnet between them. Timid, abstemious, devout is just what Romeo isn't intending to be, and the sonnet glues them in a profane union and shows the piety to be a game. Earlier, Romeo's sincerity had taken the form of suggesting his tears be burnt as heretics if he forsakes Rosaline. We are so dazzled by the idea of tears individually burnt, colourless but containing the whole genetic code of the love so each is a perfect miniature lover, that we will never try to collect on the promise of which they are the astonishing vehicle.

Both lovers only find out afterwards that they've fallen in love with the enemy, a contrivance Shakespeare took from his source but improved on. This story gives a painful or a ridiculous twist to the old habit of regarding the beloved as a 'fair foe'. Here they are technically at war, as members of opposing factions, which makes official the opposition between disparate, competing egos always suppressed in love. As was his wont at this stage, Shakespeare improves on an artifice by making it more artifical, making an airy nothing literal.

Lovers meet by night, for though it is a prompting of life, not of death or sleep, that is the easiest time to find the privacy, even secrecy, which the exclusiveness of the passion needs. Romeo and Juliet thus have an extra reason for obeying the common rule. Risk is always part of abandoned love, for such open admission of desire invites various rebuffs: here the lover will be killed if he is discovered. So they enjoy their sunrise at midnight and undergo ecstasies of contradiction, saying goodbye thirty times, appearing and disappearing until the prosaic observer may well wonder whether the occasion is mainly notional after all, a meeting about the idea of meeting.

Founded on impossibility, the union becomes still more impossible. The answer to the replacement of Romeo with an unwanted suitor is for Juliet to appear to die, with the assistance of a priest-magician, after which she will be resurrected to join Romeo in another town. This imaginary death is conflated with the second of two festive gatherings which frame this play like the vows in *Love's Labour's Lost* or the marriages in *Midsummer Night's Dream*. In delicious terror Juliet foresees herself among the mummies of her ancestors, and is set against the spices, dried fruits, and consuming logs of the feast, preserved in a way none of them realize.

Next she is in the tomb, a womb, a maw (Juliet a delicious morsel), or rather a lantern or banqueting pavilion not a grave. This last is an idea supplied by Romeo, the second preying presence who arrives at the tomb, descends to the bed of death, and decides never to get up again.

Of course it isn't either-or, grave or feast, extinction or consummation. The one is the other, or is fulfilled in the other, and each is richer in the mixture than either is alone. The difficulty with *Romeo and Juliet* is that though the play's language finds ecstatic fulfilment in a love-grave or death-feast, the poet hasn't lost his grip on reality so thoroughly as to leave it at that, and follows the consummation, a lovers' union seasoned with corpses round the central orifice, with a feeble retraction showing the Veronese reharmonized, as if all contradiction had died with the young couple.

If *Romeo and Juliet* is too tidy to be a tragedy, *Hamlet* is in some deep way so untidy there must be an explanation, except that the untidiness is so fruitful, so artistically productive, that it seems an awful failing of criticism to view it as Shakespeare's inadvertence, a helpless sign of his involvement in the play. For this is the usual explanation of what makes *Hamlet* different, that there is more, perhaps too much, of Shakespeare in it.

This feels true, if hard to prove. Whatever drove him to it, he discovered in this play a new conception of character. Hamlet is a descendant of Chaucer's Troilus, and having seen him, we can say that, yes, drama is a natural place for such fluid renderings of individual identity. Nowhere else, though, does Shakespeare present anyone in such discontinuous flashes, to make us feel we cannot fully know him, and that although we understand a great deal there is much out of view. Repeatedly it's that we know too much, or have too many reasons for certain acts or failures to act, and don't know how to weight them, or to decide which are the really controlling ones. At the same time there are other undiscussible motives which may matter more than the ones receiving attention.

In spite of the view of Coleridge and many other critics, *Hamlet* is not a very explicitly philosophical work. If it is about the difficulty of knowing and, last and most impenetrable of all, of knowing oneself, it doesn't obtrusively say so. It is true, nonetheless, that the atmospheric opening generalizes a problem like Hamlet's to a metaphysical issue strongly present to simple as well as complicated minds: are there ghosts, and what are they there for? How big an attack on our peace do they make?

The ghost has something to do with Hamlet before they meet, but it is extremely important that Hamlet didn't invent him, although we might have expected him to. Hamlet has been haunted already, more than sufficiently haunted, without the ghost. He inhabits a private reality consuming and alienating like madness, which causes him to mistake or improve on people's words or stand silent much of the time, like an emissary of the night which the ghost comes out of, his black mourning only a disguise for a more pervasive condition.

The ghost's revelations are shocking (Hamlet's father murdered) but only improvements (or worsenings) in the same vein Hamlet was already tracing. And his first 'mad' replies are semi-involuntary answers to words of the ghost which no one else hears. Once he has made contact with Hamlet, the ghost ceases to be evident to anyone else, or is it that, external confirmations now removed, Hamlet is from then on hallucinating? He has cause, having heard terrible things, and being intensely moved, so the response though aberrant is not disproportionate.

Like other questions in this play it is more tangled than that, insolubly but not futilely tangled. Hamlet quickly decides to use the appearance of madness to throw his newly confirmed enemies off the scent. The first employment of this disguise is reported by Ophelia. Hamlet has appeared *like a ghost* from hell and entirely convinced her he is out of his senses. Why Ophelia? Because most vulnerable to attack, and most vulnerable to *his* attack? As part of a ruse it is extremely hard to fathom: the principal effect of Hamlet's 'madness' will be to drive Ophelia mad.

If it were pure ruse, Hamlet's behaviour would be cruel in the extreme. But when we see them together, what we have suspected is confirmed. After this we have no doubt that the ruse is a disguise for true distraction, that the feigned madness hides or speaks for powerful torments. His ferocity is all the more convincing because obviously displaced – Ophelia has not offended him, another woman has. His mother is never mentioned here, though constantly referred to. Incestuous passion is the most obscure and crucial motive of the play, which sullies all his efforts to straighten out his motives and responsibility. Even Shakespeare finds it undiscussible. It would be easier if Hamlet could admit that he was *jealous* of Claudius, but if that were done his relation to his father would come under suspicion. In some sense the essential and immovable fact about the play is that it can't even occur to Hamlet that his motives for hating Claudius are suspect, or at least mixed, and that this defect in his hatred without his knowing it undermines him.

The mousetrap play is another example of displacement which becomes more mysterious the more one thinks about it. Ostensibly it is a way of checking the ghost's story in a publicly evident manner, like a trial. Claudius will reveal himself before everyone, which will be extremely satisfying even though most of them won't be able to interpret it. But Hamlet also lets Horatio into the plot. He now feels the need of intelligent company in his agony of conscience.

It is exceedingly appropriate he should lay a trap of words and art, this brooder drawn to the players' profession by obscure promptings, not only because presently engaged in a prolonged and strainful feigning but because his feelings have always sought release at points distant from their sources. We have no trouble believing that it is more satisfying to stab Claudius with suggestion from afar while dallying in Ophelia's lap, than to make an immediate end of him. In between the first encounter with the players and the public performance, interrupted like the ghost's appearance by its own too-great success, Hamlet has a chance to kill the king but isn't satisfied with the setting. Not just a death but the right death is required, a fastidiousness like the artist's, which enters inappropriately to halt the action.

It takes an intricate mind to find in the players an intensification of, not a distraction from, the main business, but this is how it seems to Hamlet and is meant to seem to us. Hamlet is the histrionic man par excellence, not the intellectualizer (Coleridge's view) so much as the representer. The episode of Priam and Hecuba is the quintessence of this instinct in Hamlet and his author, and so readers like Dryden, who supposed Shakespeare didn't write these overpoweringly rich speeches, or like Pope, who thought they were meant to seem ridiculous, have fallen out of sympathy with the imagination at work in the play.

'The rugged Pyrrhus, he whose sable arms,
Black as his purpose, did the night resemble
When he lay couched in the ominous horse,
Hath now this dread and black complexion smear'd
With heraldry more dismal; head to foot
Now is he total gules, horridly trick'd
With blood of fathers, mothers, daughters, sons,
Bak'd and impasted with the parching streets,
That lend a tyrannous and damned light
To their lord's murder. Roasted in wrath and fire,
And thus o'er-sized with coagulate gore,
With eyes like carbuncles, the hellish Pyrrhus
Old grandsire Priam seeks.'

(II, ii, 448–60)

Lines which Hamlet quotes from memory, *becoming* one of the players, an actor imitating actors dressed as actors, embodying briefly the purest conception of language as constituting a world, standing up of its own accord like an armour made of nothing but baked blood.

It is the most serious confirmation of this drama as occurring not in the world of action, nor in the realm of ideas, but in a place – a stage or an imagined stage – where both acts and ideas are converted into words which are a displaced echo of the events recalled.

Hamlet is frustrating at some level as a narrative, appearing to be the story of how something could not be brought to pass, because it has put a person who finds satisfaction in contriving representations in the place of an *actor*, as if one were to make a playwright the hero of a play. Hamlet considers and discards, or leaves as suspended possibility, numerous courses of action. He draws from everything he sees surprising instructions tending to action: the players' tears awake in him a self destructive bombast as he compares his withdrawal unfavourably with their excitement. Fortinbras' futile war in Poland gives him ideas of other people's energy which he admires all the more because of its uselessness. He is a marvellous reflector who focuses any number of things for a moment but loses the previous resolution in the next one.

The mysteriousness arising from this inconsistency, the excitement of something which remains, after the most extended exemplification in any of Shakespeare's works, much more potential than actual, helps explain the enormous mountain of commentary the play has disappeared under. Like Hamlet offering any number of reasons for acting, and not doing so because absorbed in this unravelling, we are reduced to saying that so many solutions have been offered because the riddle of this character is finally insoluble.

Hamlet's most effective act is inadvertent: killing someone whose identity is concealed by a shrouding curtain. But the serendipitous aftermath makes one wonder if this accident isn't a way of broaching the crime which can't be named after all. For now Hamlet has killed a father as well as lost one, landing Laertes in a plight like his own and provoking a grotesque inversion of the play's subject: he becomes the *object* of a revenge plot.

Laertes holds Hamlet responsible for Ophelia's death too, on the theory adopted by the other onlookers that the corpses who surface in her mad raving are her way of grieving for her murdered father. Madness in Shakespeare is often accompanied by such choral interpretation, alerting one in a general way, 'How pregnant his replies are', or suggesting specific under-meanings which might not otherwise occur to us.

His interest in madness is one of the most novel and profound reaches of his meeting with the world. He begins, in *Romeo* for example, with the Gothic or picturesque view of the subject common in his age and for several centuries after. Like ghosts, madness is one of those terrors of the night like dark shadows at the edges, which remains a fringe never entered or experienced except as an alien intruder on one's daytime consciousness.

Shakespeare is the first writer to make us feel he is not just dabbling in madness, but uncovering in it the most serious and widening truths about the mind and reality. Superficially it is a linguistic disturbance, in which surprising subjects are juxtaposed, animals and men, lewdness and grace, gaiety and despair. Not that the experience madness brings is simply dichotomous, a way of proving that opposites meet – but that there are all sorts of kinships and affiliations, which only disturbed states can perceive or face, having less to lose from the ending of illusion, or because their defences have been utterly shattered. In *Hamlet* madness is the destination to which the widened inquiry into personality, that results in the character of Hamlet, seems to be leading. At times the richest psychic existences look (from afar) or feel (from inside) like madness. Then, in spite of ourselves we begin to take raving more momentously than normal speech.

Everything stops when the madman appears, we become all ears, attend a taxing school. It is the bizarrest form of a truth which spills over into other parts of the play. Welcoming madmen and women into the most solemn category of drama, and admitting laughter at funerals, these are allied acts. The grave-diggers are the first of a series of disruptive presences in Shakespearean tragedy which ruin the high consistency of tone in the interest of a previously unimaginable inclusiveness. Death does not become trivial because it is joked about, but more intensely present, as in Grünewald's paintings. Instead of cultivating the seclusion of the study for his reflections on death, Shakespeare consults humble practitioners who have had to find defences against it most people don't need. Their irreverent songs are thus new evidence of its power, which show that one can sing and eat and get tired in its presence, for seen close-to, it is not a pageant.

Yorick is rightly remembered: though only a skull he is one of the quintessential expressions of his author, and brings to a focus these contradictions: jokers die, nonchalance and fun grant no protective exemption, all will turn to dust. Such generalizations are already a long way from the pangs the scene induces; even Hamlet is old enough to harbour a few such amputations, and now tramples one who used to carry him.

However gross, low, and vivid, the gravediggers' talk is still exemplary, but in what follows other illusions are dragged lower into the dirt. To Hamlet the grave is still a grave in general, he doesn't know whose it is, doesn't know its occupant is someone he will mourn, and thus for all his melancholy, he will seem to have played the trifler.

Laertes, whom Hamlet doesn't expect to find in Denmark, jumps into the grave, followed by Hamlet whom no one else expects there either. The unwitting treader round the effects of his own actions – for he killed Ophelia in a different way from that the others suppose – has now fallen in. But here both Laertes and Hamlet seem untrue to their grief and better selves. Hamlet's love of the girl, which we have seen to be in its odd way real, now vaunts itself in competition with the brother. They are diverted toward their own rivalry and vent their reverence for Ophelia in a disgusting brawl.

A spectator can only gasp at the sublime incongruence of it, watching people quite beside themselves, like primitive howls from distant centuries. *Hamlet*, which initiates the cycle of tragedies, is perhaps the first of his plays in which one feels that opening oneself unreservedly to the language is at certain moments like demonic possession. Hamlet's vituperative attacks on his mother, for instance, must have seemed at the time about as far as one could go in turning loose the forces of language, inviting the enemy into the hallowed space of art. Before long of course Shakespeare was to go further still.

Such distances cannot be precisely measured, but it seems roughly fair to say that *King Lear* is as far beyond *Hamlet* as *Hamlet* is beyond *Romeo and Juliet*, along the line of loosening boundaries, widening field, diffusing focus and increasing metaphysical uncertainty. *Romeo* is a beautiful embroidery, *Hamlet* a tortured diary, and *Lear* a symphony in which the instruments sound inhuman, and not like voices at all.

These unearthly effects are produced with means we have already seen Shakespeare using, albeit pushed further and including, in a form more emblematic than literal, an astonishing forecast of Wagner's drowning of the voice – the storm which bellows like the ghost's warnings, in unwelcome echo to Lear's cries, a reinforcement so powerful it obliterates the spark which set it off.

From almost the beginning the scale of this drama is cosmic, and man, who is still the measure and apparently the subject, is in danger of being lost or swept up. It begins with an inversion of its main theme, it shows two fathers mistreating their children, and in a way which will become familiar it makes two cases feel not just a pair but sufficient evidence of a pervasive discord. How can this be? How can we take Gloucester's slanders of Edmund and Lear's abuse of Cordelia as a universal cataclysm in the moral world? Because each is so stark and uncaused, because Lear goes on from there to sweep more away as well, stripping Cordelia of her suitors and himself of his most faithful retainer. It is the first instance, but there will be others, of laying bare, tearing off clothes, getting at the truth in semi-involuntary frenzy as a wounded man worries a wound.

Lear's error is obvious to everyone including its beneficiaries. Goneril and Regan's unaffectionate analysis of his faults following his gift to them is a chilling caution against taking the rational approach ourselves. Lear causes shudders, but initially we share Gloucester's mistake. We too find a resemblance between Edmund and Cordelia the abused children, pitched against siblings who take advantage of them. Admittedly we are allowed to wake sooner than Gloucester does: his eyes freshly put out, he thinks of turning for help to Edmund and is at last brutally disabused. Lear continues almost to the end thinking of Edmund as a dutiful son and envies Gloucester that good fortune. The blindness of goodness, and its continual misapprehension of badness, is one of the most humiliating motifs of the play.

There is a half-obliterated, even desecrated, structure of religious ideas in *Lear* into which this fits. Very few traces remain of the sacramental relinquishment which explains Lear's odd act at the start ('Unburthen'd crawl toward death'). Certainly such an abdication is not psychologically credible in this particular king. Yet if no willing hermit, he has set in motion a sequence which will drive him into the wilderness. It is as if a malicious impresario had got hold of the idea of *As You Like It* or some such pastoral idyll and decided to make it as embarrassing as possible, 'See, this is what it is like to live outdoors, when you have no choice.'

Lear is a sacrament of purification in the same cruel way it is a pastoral escape: the many references to the gods (pagan, for safety, to avoid imputations of blasphemy) are taunts: though characters can't get the idea out of their heads, they are clearly talking about something which isn't there. The only notions of justice which tally with what happens are disgusting:

> The dark and vicious place where he thee got
> Cost him his eyes

says Edgar to Edmund concerning their father, Gloucester. Yet the play gives this some credence. Lear's powerful diatribe against copulation is called forth by the sight of ruined Gloucester stumbling about near Dover, 'Blind Cupid' as the other old man names him to express Gloucester's absurd involvement in the toils of generation. He continues in spite of everything to represent adultery.

It is a possible though fearsomely harsh view of twentieth-century extermination camps that they were a refiner's fire incinerating human motive and pretence in search of a tiny beatified remnant or core, not that anyone ever imagined the camps' organizers meant such a thing: if this is a possible view of these ordeals, it was God's work carried out by the devil. This is the insuperable task of *Lear*, to imagine the most senseless suffering and see if it is in any way redeemed.

But in looking for hopeful signs here, one is picking among the ashes, seeking mementoes when one should heap them on one's head. Lear's purification is to be driven through demented rages to confusions between himself, the weather and everything he sees, pausing for a moment on the brink to identify himself percipiently with all human suffering, then to to enter an elemental stage, 'mad as the sea' and crowned with noxious weeds, running wildly across the land formerly 'his'. This is followed by a peaceful childhood, very beautiful in its way, which he imagines as endless games and pantomimes with his daughter, who is in fact too old for these amusements. Such an aftermath is not permitted: she is killed by someone anxious to prevent peace or happiness, and Lear must absorb her death before being allowed his own.

The play's comment on this is 'we that are young shall never see so much nor live so long', showing that Lear's case is much more consoling seen from outside than inside. Edgar's words are spoken with a mixture of envy and relief. Whatever happens there are some things we will be saved from, which makes us less.

The trouble with such schematic summaries of the play's course is that they omit its essential core, an initiation into a maelstrom nearer to the true heart of reality than we have come before. It is an experience presided over by the unlikely figure of the Fool.

Lear first thinks of his fool when the trouble with Goneril worsens. He calls for Goneril, who won't see him, so like a child diverted with a toy instead of his mother, Lear now summons the Fool. The court fool is an institution we know mainly from Shakespeare, which enshrines the human tendency to lump all forms of mental disturbance or abnormality together, and then to see them as a spectacle. It is exceedingly strange to us that someone should sit down and devise a costume to represent madness: particoloured for the jerks of illogic, eruptions of suspicion, splinterings of thought, dangling tassels of incomplete feelings and ideas. Like other deeply brutal institutions though, the office of fool left room for feelings of kinship for which we have no happy expression, having (mercifully) lost the confident knowledge of what idiots mean or how they fit into the economy of the world.

One of Shakespeare's most radical inversions of common wisdom (how erroneous the idea he only formulates what everyone is already thinking) is, like Freud interrogating dreams, to sift the dregs of the court for the most profound insights, and to make from this figure of absurd fun an oracular voice. In talking about the Fool, modern readers always sentimentalize him, a failing his creator avoids by preserving a high quotient of irrelevance in the Fool's words. They are mainly cockeyed, and only secondarily probing. Every one of his lurches into speech is shocking, travelling on from the last in an unforeseeable way, as in a game where the lights are periodically switched off, so even when his message is prudential (as in the first scene: hang onto what you've got, don't upset the status quo) his ways of conveying it are alarming.

Already before venturing onto the heath, we have been schooled in the mental-abyss style of thought, which by showing powerful figures of speech shorn of the route toward them, mines reality with dangerous voids. Perceptions come like hammer blows, e.g. 'when thou madest thy daughters thy mothers', always suggesting all is over, never imagining a way out, only inert, horrified contemplation.

The Fool is like a poet in vigorously seizing the aspect of things, while remaining passive before what he sees. Thus he has a far from tranquillizing effect on Lear, making enormities more enormous and more insoluble than ever, starker and utterly disconnected.

Although the Fool drives Lear further into alienation, we have no misgivings about his motives. He is a convincingly motiveless character.

But there is a mock-fool who seems more problematic. After Kent has been shut in the stocks like a tethered beast, Edgar appears and announces a programme to assume the basest shape, to become a mad beggar roaming without a home. It is one of those accident-seeming convergences in which the play is rich; the audience reads separate fates progressively, finding a logic in disaster no character can see.

Later, when Lear's hardships have made him for the first time solicitous and brotherly toward the Fool, and prompted a sublime slackening on this side of uncontrolled collapse:

> Poor naked wretches, wheresoe'er you are,
> That bide the pelting of this pitiless storm ...

all the more moving for the unexpressed 'just like me', which inspires and infuses it, weakness calling to weakness, he turns from this still-Olympian view of wretchedness (for it is *all* wretchedness seen surveyor-like) to enter the hut and encounter Poor Tom-Edgar among the straw, an exact answer to his speech, full of spleen, paranoid fears, and self disgust.

It is a too-perfect echo and precipitates the king's collapse, making the Fool's bitterness look harmless. For Edgar's ravings have a tendency – that human nature is bestial and human motives corrupt. In spite of Lear's attempts to interpret Edgar as himself (it must be Edgar's daughters who have brought the beggar to this pass) enough is coming through to cause an overload. Edgar's case is one injustice too many, and it ends with the three of them gibbering in their different ways.

Except that by now the Fool has been silenced. The others have outdone him, passed beyond him. His sort of craziness, sufficiently awful at first, now seems mild, reliable. It is a chastening progress: the unstrung approach which the Fool announced has assumed such proportions in instances which continue to accumulate that he appears only its harbinger and feeble annunciator. At the close his fate is unmentioned except for one strange splutter. Just as Lear realizes Cordelia's death he calls her his fool, and one has a déjà vu that, yes, there was a person named Fool who meant something once, long ago.

In its twenty-three years Shakespeare's career encompasses that sensation of constant fruitful change and of successively transcended stages we find in very few, in Titian and Rembrandt say, both of whom stretched the development over a much longer span. To be able to step back and see the career as a single work, all thirty plays making a rounded narrative, is one of the great heights in anyone's imaginative life.

A frequent miracle in careers like his is that a satisfying close is followed by yet another last soaring flight. *Antony and Cleopatra* is an extended valediction, like an imagination dispersing itself or undergoing gaseous expansion which leaves it nowhere and everywhere. But as we know, this vision of an Oriental fecundity bursting gently like a noiseless firework into non-existence is only a pause on the way to an even gentler close, an even more reconciled statement of the blurring of individuality.

As in the late works of Titian or Rembrandt, one traces the relinquishments and relaxations of age in a loosened brushstroke, or, in Shakespeare's case, in a grammar one must call impressionistic, absolutely unclogged, taking astonishing freedoms which pass without a hitch, small ellipses or extra particles which work equally in the service of a wave-like motion mildly hypnotic or analgesic, never casting so deep a spell that one loses track, never creating such difficulty one pauses or even slows down.

In spite of a sprinkling of geographical references and the oft-remarked volatility of scene, *Antony and Cleopatra* suggests huge spaces mainly by what happens to the poetic line, which runs off the edge or levitates as it approaches points where one expects endings, like a glider caught on a new draught.

It is an ungrateful task to translate such impressions to metrical analyses, or to explain, brushstroke by brushstroke, how intelligible images are formed of units which seem to lack sense themselves. One example must serve for the shorthand of the play:

> And the ebb'd man, ne'er lov'd till ne'er worth love,
> Comes dear'd by being lack'd. This common body,
> Like to a vagabond flag upon the stream,
> Goes to, and back, lackeying the varying tide,
> To rot itself with motion.
>
> (I, iv, 43–7)

Perhaps more is needed to convey the sublime effortlessness of this writing properly. But these lines are a special tour de force, because it is Caesar speaking, about a lazy motion and nonchalant style he hates, forced by the verse to execute the blurring together of the hero and the crowd.

The play is a mild allegory of imagination bested by reason or calculation, or of imagination floating free, bodiless, while the earthbound power stays behind to anatomize its undignified victory. Both the negative and positive renditions of the hero's end carry much the same grandeur, Cleopatra's vision of Antony striding the world larger than the weather after his death, and his own troubled view of his dissolution in the wide Egyptian skies:

Ant.	Eros, thou yet behold'st me?
Eros.	Ay, noble lord.
Ant.	Sometime we see a cloud that's dragonish;
	A vapour sometime like a bear, or lion,
	A tower'd citadel, a pendent rock,
	A forked mountain, or blue promontory
	With trees upon't that nod unto the world
	And mock our eyes with air. Thou hast seen these signs;
	They are black vesper's pageants.
Eros.	Ay, my lord.
Ant.	That which is now a horse, even with a thought
	The rack dislimns, and makes it indistinct
	As water is in water.
Eros.	It does, my lord.
Ant.	My good knave Eros, now thy captain is
	Even such a body.Here I am Antony;
	Yet cannot hold this visible shape, my knave.
	I made these wars for Egypt; and the Queen—
	Whose heart I thought I had, for she had mine;
	Which, whilst it was mine, had annex'd unto't
	A million moe, now lost—she, Eros, has
	Pack'd cards with Caesar, and false-play'd my glory
	Unto an enemy's triumph.

(IV, xiv, 1–20)

Casting back to the clouds in *Midsummer Night's Dream* and *Hamlet*, which this improves on, one is staggered by the triumphal seamlessness here, which sails on as if over the heads of the voices, unslowed by the change of speakers, which converts grandiose self-reference into unselfish description, or has arrived at such flexibility of exchange between the thinker and the thought-about that neither is tainted by personality, neither insisting on primacy, so that the order ends by being insidious and surprising, but right.

For all its magnificence there is something low-key about *Antony and Cleopatra*, because some of its most powerful meanings are practically unstated. Like late Rembrandt taking leave of paint, Shakespeare is here taking leave of writing. Antony is not just a single character dissolving, but his creator's appetite for drama gratified and on the point of extinction. For those who have followed the whole career this meaning dwarfs the larger than human personages: Shakespeare is expressing the half-regretful fulness of someone nearing the end of an enterprise bigger than any of its episodes. He approaches the limit of his imagination, and there is a not entirely foreseen, but finite amount left to say.

Those viewers are right who feel there is something unreal about Shakespeare's last plays, and the most antique, the most stiff with gold or silver thread is *The Winter's Tale*. Here he returns to archaic tale-structures, full of odd hiatuses, sudden eruptions, unplausible reversals.

Mamillius the pure boy infant is just beginning to entertain the women of Hermione's court with a sad tale for winter when Leontes bursts in, halts the tale after one enticing line ('There was a man lived by a churchyard'), takes the boy from his mother and packs her off to prison, initiating a winter which lasts sixteen years.

Though not an empty pageant, this is abstract or at least abstracted like a pageant, as if the actors withheld themselves a little, moving in a trance with one eye on heaven. Thus Leontes' suddenness doesn't remind us more than faintly of Lear's. The disasters which follow from it possess from the beginning a strange gaiety. Perdita, as she will be called (named by her mother appearing in a dream to Perdita's soon-to-be-devoured carrier), because long lost though finally found, is dropped on the seashore as a storm begins, and her protector is chased off by a bear who tears him limb from limb. Compound of innocence and violence, the new and the old, seeds and death, it is a spectacle which inspires one with half-formed notions, less impinging than the storm in *Lear*, like its filtered echo.

Next comes an unconcealed gap in the action which has seemed supremely awkward to many viewers, but in the flatness lies a weird power. It is a hiatus like winter, when no one knows what is happening under the soil. When the characters re-emerge above the surface they are as if reborn, having passed to the next stage of growth.

In the seasonal masque at which we first see her as a sentient being (only a germ before, a premature birth) Perdita is playing a figure from myth, Flora, and presiding over the alignment of the human with the vegetable world. She gives all the participants flowers appropriate to their ages, or imagines doing this, because although all seasons are co-present in the world of man, the most crucial flowers are lacking: it is late summer so the young, whom spring would suit, can only be matched in grandiloquent verses, for she has come before (after?) her time, out of phase. A hypothetical marriage is initiated, but blasted, as by an unseasonable shower, when her lover's father, the king, strips off a pastoral disguise and shows himself Leontes' equal in arbitrariness at the other end of the play.

Another flight is precipitated, and the action flows back to Leontes' court, where the winter's tale begun by the lost child is concluded, at Paulina's remote house or chapel, the play's equivalent of a churchyard. The reunited families have gone to worship at the shrine of their most important missing member, Hermione the generatrix. Through the long dearth Paulina has preserved the principle of life secretly and now savours her wizard-role to the full. She presents Hermione in the form of a work of art, a clever painted statue of the same age she would be now had she lived.

It is a bit of childish playacting which keeps the separated couple apart a few minutes longer and ritualizes or makes deliberately awkward their coming together. For Hermione must step down from her pedestal with all eyes upon her, and these first movements will seem unpractised, falling short of the grace we can imagine, however unembarrassed they are.

But the audience is fooled by the pantomime too. Which is really stranger, life or art? To see a statue come alive, or a person turn into an idea – we are bewildered between these and feel them both intensely. The playwright has brought onto the stage in a painfully slowed form the moment when the first tip of growth appears above the soil, or when the embryonic leaf unfolds revealing its familiar shape for the first time. Parents are folded back into children, or spring forth from them as if reborn. The highest reach of art is to make the beginning and the end of the longest human span essentially indistinguishable, in a last reunion like their setting out.

CHAPTER NINE

PURITAN CONSCIENCE IN BUNYAN, MARIVAUX, AND RICHARDSON

Pilgrim's Progress is the first Dutch still life in English literature, which takes the humblest reality and lends it spiritual dignity. Bunyan's book is father of a whole class of fiction, a new Evangelical strain which regards art as an instrument of correction, a warning, or a pattern for home embroidery. His book, unlike most of its descendants, resembles Dutch painting in its emptiness or depopulation, in spite of Hills of Difficulty, Valleys of Humiliation, and traps or snares which pop up on demand like a series of momentous carnival rides.

Bunyan's seems an unnaturally cleared space because it cuts the protagonist off from his old life at the start, not in order to replace it with another, but with impermanent adventures like painted phantoms. Don Quixote has Sancho Panza; for half of his progress Christian has his book, or his parchment roll with its alarming message, 'Fly from the wrath to come.' The streak of madness in Bunyan's sobriety must be one of his strongest attractions for many readers: sometimes not far from Kafka, obeying obscure but overpowering urges. One moves forward because followed by a fear like a large shapeless presence.

Like Kafka's heroes, Christian has false friends who travel beside him briefly but underminingly, and he meets people going the other way who try to convince him this is a one-way street. Then, fairly late in the story, he comes upon Faithful, who set out after him, claims to have travelled more slowly, and has ended up in front. For Christian, listening to Faithful is not unlike reading in his book. The way Faithful tells it, the road is quite different from how Christian found it, as if he had selected different amusements or been selected by them. And the moral of that is, that we can't copy the set of instructions Christian has been giving us out into our own lives as neatly as we thought.

Another whole journey like Christian's is telescoped into the first line of *Pilgrim's Progress*: it is the narrator's own. Only from the marginal note do we guess what suppressed intensity this sentence conceals: the note identifies the 'den', where the narrator lies down and dreams the *Progress*, with the jail in which Bunyan was shut for preaching the sort of thing the book contains. The minutely reported trial in Vanity Fair must be thick with details of official procedures which the author had endured before landing in the place where he could write the book.

Like Malory's, this work is a dream of excursion imagined in forced immobility. But it is also evidence of a struggle in the author's mind between doctrinal insistence and the requirements of the story. For narrative appears in some essential way a false vehicle for eternal truth. In the light of eternity, *Pilgrim's Progress* is simply a record of mistakes made on the path to a long-foreseen goal: the story is a necessary or unfortunate evil stemming from the weaknesses of human protagonists.

Often Bunyan sounds superior to his story. Its reader is a child, who needs to have the truth broken artificially into instalments, 'And what happened then?' or 'What did he say next?' Enemies are invented, loaded with error, and then refuted point by point by Hopeful and Christian in turn, like the famous interrogation system called the escalator. They never tire of being right, or at least never admit it to the misguided. But their 'Let him go, it's no use talking, he *will* be damned' is perhaps a form of disgusted surfeit with having too much of the truth on their side.

Though it is the only admitted conflict in the book, the contest between right and wrong is not a real one, in part because wrong keeps changing its face and right continues the same. The idea of the journey requires that each opponent should soon be left behind, after which there is no danger of meeting him again, for he belongs to that stage of life and that only, and collapses like a defeated argument.

The real contest in Bunyan's book is between different modes, between prophecy and daily life, between story and instruction. It is this war in Bunyan's mind – for it is much more that than a dispute between his temperament and the task he has set himself – which makes the great interest of *Pilgrim's Progress*. It would be a perverse reader who wished for perfection either of story or argument in place of the speckled object we have. The book compels us to think, not that Bunyan should never have told a story, but that he was violently torn between the attractions of drama with its uncertainties, sinuosities and surprises, and the unswerving assurances of sectarian belief. Perhaps we relish the duplicity of a story pretending to be something else, so that the snugnesses and intimacies of narrative – characters chattering on in a relaxed and unstrenuous way as they walk, or waking in a large chamber facing east – feel like illicit pleasures stolen from under the nose of a watchful guard.

Though we prefer the vivid, humble Bunyan who points his Christian toward a Little Wicket Gate as toward the most sonorously unattainable goal, or has the burden of sin dropping from Pilgrim's back and tumbling like a parcel or dislodged pebble until it finds the mouth of a sepulchre and falls in – though we prefer this Bunyan, we couldn't safely excise the smug or the harsh Bunyan. Especially not the harsh one, because that hateful energy is the negative side of his sturdiness.

Even the heavenly crew are sometimes a little rough with their protégés: Christian finds himself given a sharp tug just as he is passing the wicket gate. 'Why did you do that?' he asks. Here the explanation (to protect him from arrows fired from a nearby castle at those nearing redemption) is almost superfluous. Relations between God and the sinner have some Hebraic ruggedness about them. Later a man appears unexpectedly from behind and knocks Faithful down; he turns out to be Moses, and shows how man will fare judged simply by the Law. Doctrinal schemes aside, the bluff suddenness, even violence, of these events carries a conviction and contains a truth of a different order from all the controversial discourse.

Not that the controversial discourse in *Pilgrim's Progress* is all the same kind. Least dramatic are the conversations between Christian and Hopeful, like the long investigation of Hopeful's spiritual history carried out to help them keep awake as they cross the Enchanted Ground, and probably the sleepiest part of the book.

Then there are a few examples of what wickedness talks about when it is off by itself, like the discussion among By-ends and his friends, which shows sermon technique turned backwards, all the paraphernalia of Scriptural citation and exempla brought out in the service of selfish lack of stringency. Bunyan doesn't trust himself to show bad characters from the inside very often. The only other instances are the conversations at night in bed together between Giant Despair and his wife Diffidence (an inexplicable name: she is more inventive than Despair and eggs him on).

After settling all the matters of dispute among themselves, By-ends and his people catch up with Christian and put the questions they've just answered, to him. His response is vitriolic, as if pent up, as if he's been waiting through their misguided discourse (which he didn't hear) to have his say. He calls them heathens and witches (albeit in involuted form). They don't answer back; Christian's opponents seldom do. They go off shaking their heads, or drop back and let Christian and Hopeful travel on alone. It feels like an authentic glimpse of the effect Bunyan must sometimes have produced on the world around him, a condescending tolerance which maddened him to further insults.

It may not be very edifying, but it's one of the liveliest sorts of encounter in the book. Without noticing, Bunyan turns one of the worst tools of the oppressor onto his imaginary opponents: he becomes an inquisitor and harrows the bad characters through a series of questions to which he knows they cannot give the right answers.

Like all such interrogations this resembles at times the inner dialogue with one's own guilt. Perhaps the pain of self-accusation whips Bunyan on to be the harsh judge of others. Or perhaps, a more fruitful speculation for the history of narrative, these arid debates full of bad feeling are the forebears of the agonies of (Protestant) conscience prominent in a large class of subsequent fiction.

In Bunyan there is a strong, anti-dramatic drive to reduce the results of such debate to system: the three infallible signs of true fear of the Lord, the nine stages in the cooling of the Towardly Professor.

Among the strangest instances of this urge to turn spiritual complexities into diagrams are the frequent lists of bad people's names, of which the most outspoken is the catalogue of jurors in Vanity Fair:

Then went the jury out, whose names were Mr Blind-man,
Mr No-good, Mr Malice, Mr Love-lust, Mr Live-loose,
Mr Heady, Mr High-mind, Mr Enmity, Mr Liar, Mr Cruelty,
Mr Hate-light, and Mr Implacable

Bunyan is often praised for his fertility in coming up with these lists; some might find it an alarming exuberance. The flood feels hasty and unreflective, like a series of explosions. Perhaps it is a capsule version of the arrangement of the whole work: schematic, yet without a convincing sense of overall plan.

There are some entertaining nineteenth-century maps of *Pilgrim's Progress* which show all the incidents in order, laid out along a path which has, for convenience, been curled up on itself like a seashell's whorl, but they only make plainer how many anomalies the plan contains. There is no careful grading like Dante's of those you meet along the path of your spiritual progress. Atheist, for example, is one of the last, who casts doubt on the very existence of the Celestial City when virtually in sight of its walls. As a subjective event this is potent just where it is, but if it's as hard to reach this spot as we've seen it is, how did Atheist do it?

This is one of the persistent problems of the story. Many of its personages create serious discontinuities in the narrative, beginning with

Evangelist, who arrives out of nowhere and accosts Christian in the field. Never afterwards is he given any circumstantial link with affairs in Christian's town. He isn't a neighbour, or a stranger from a nearby place. He issues from another sphere. One can say that he is the spirit of Christian's reading, and that a thread of Otherness runs through the whole narrative, which is the alien perspective introduced into provincial English life by the strange body of ideas which constitute Scripture as Bunyan and those like him conceive it.

It makes a stronger story that Bunyan should present this discord without quite grasping it himself. How fully does he perceive the starkness of his initial vision? Christian alone in a field reading and beating his breast: it is a sort of nowhere, not *in* the village, but in an indefinable proximity to it, for one doesn't just walk out past the town-end a certain number of paces to come where Christian is.

Like this one, all the most arresting moments in the story are partly inexplicable and left unexplained. When Christian leaves his home, he goes running with his fingers in his ears, uttering cries in an unknown language. Where did he learn them? In the same place he found out about the Hill Lucre, which he recognizes and can explain though he has never been there. And in the same place where he was prepared for such sequences as writing his name in the book outside the castle and then rushing violently through its gate, or where Faithful was told about people with writing on their foreheads, whom he encounters without batting an eye. All this lore was learned in a secret place to which only members of Bunyan's sect are admitted, the closed room of the knowledge which one is smuggest about.

One of the oddest features of Christian's departure from his home in the City of Destruction (a name pinned on it retrospectively, discordant with the place we saw) – putting his fingers in his ears – is perhaps illuminated long after, when he tells the ladies in the castle that he fled a horrible noise which only he could hear. This is the first we have heard of it: other, less concrete reasons for leaving have been alleged before and have seemed sufficient. And though having that explanation didn't dissolve the gesture's strangeness, we assumed the fingers in his ears were there to keep Christian from hearing his family's pleas that he stay behind.

Bunyan's readiness to reinterpret or amplify earlier versions of an experience this way sits oddly with doctrinal rigidity. More often than not it is a further delving which brings to light new aspects of a started topic, rather than a perspectivism like we find in Spenser which undoes our prior understanding. The strangest instance is the dreamer coming one or two steps behind the pilgrim and interrogating the story (asking questions of the helper called Help) more persistently than Christian about the history of the Slough of Despond. Readers will naturally want to know more than characters need to, seems to be the idea. For the reader the character's past is not really past: we go on inspecting it and elaborating its meanings (the steps up out of the Slough as promises, but promises of what?). The headings which pepper the margin are often a sign of this process of rumination (as well as helping a reader looking back over the text trying to locate a favourite spot). They crystallize points half buried in the story, and form a series of markers, which are also just words, like the warning pillar which Christian and Hopeful erect at the edge of Giant Despair's territory once they are out of it. Future pilgrimages will take a different route. So the headings represent the journey, one can almost say, pictorially, but this is only another evidence; like the formulaic titles for places and events, of how verbal Bunyan's universe is.

When Christian notices that he has dropped his roll (containing a short message long ago memorized) while lolling in the arbour, he returns to collect it and berates himself for covering the same ground three times. Yet there has rarely been a story which held up to itself more constantly the ideal of covering the same ground over again, fixing by recapitulation everything which has already happened.

Christian goes back to collect his text, as we are sent back to re-examine old events in pretty nearly the old locutions. It has been noticed often enough, that this exegetical assault on experience is a sort of structuralism *avant la lettre*. The text-hungry will here be fed: even monsters like Apollyon argue things out, and one defeats them by the Sayings one remembers appositely to hurl.

The approach has its legalist side. Admission to heaven is by certificate. The bureaucracy responds affably to those who carry the right papers. Poor Ignorance, who has an easy time with the river Christian finds hard, is absolutely stymied by the paperwork, receives a typical official brush-off, and is bundled off to hell, providing a curious coda to the tedious gloating over harps, crowns, gold robes and streets.

If the weaknesses of the vision are verbal (or perhaps *literalist*), so are the strengths. Christian reiterates with ox-like tenacity that Talkative chews the cud (a point in his favour) but does not divide the hoof (a damning omission). One may find it an illiterate (there is a fascinating glimpse of the difficulties involved in reading script as opposed to print when the pilgrims meet the inscribed monument made from Lot's wife) twisting of Biblical dietary prescriptions, but one must admit the doggedness produces impressive results. Translated, it means Talkative seeks knowledge, but fails to separate himself strictly enough from the way of sinners. Once Christian has enshrined this thought in the intractable, derived form, he will not budge, having withdrawn into a verbal fortress.

Even moments which appear graphic or spatial often confess to verbal inspiration, like a sight Christian sees from one of the Delectable Mountains, men walking among tombs a great distance off. It turns out that this powerful spatial sensation is an attempt to illustrate a single cryptic verse of Scripture, and thus to supply a sense for familiar words.

One of the most crucial aspects of *Pilgrim's Progress* as a barometer of cultural history is the powerful sense of visual self-denial it exudes, of an imagination almost entirely non-pictorial. When images occur they are usually flat and unadorned, like the door in the hill, representing the mouth of Hell. Compare that with representations of the idea in early Netherlandish painting, for example. We end up loving the bleak prose of the image, like a cuisine based entirely on potatoes, but we are still starved in our sturdiness.

One of the most impressive figures in the book, the river as an emblem of death, is more spatial than visual, and these two crazy pilgrims are still shouting tags to each other as they struggle across it. Even at its best moments, *Pilgrim's Progress* is like a story told by a blindfolded man in a strange room, a powerful but deprived sensation. Bunyan is certainly a man of the Book. It would be fascinating to know how much he saw of and what he made of the emblem books of his century, which even at their most exuberant seem, like him, anti-iconographic in some way, putting images under the supervision of words, confining them to small pages, to be pored over like texts and fulfiled in inspiring further words.

Bunyan was on the winning side. His strengths and his weaknesses now seem prophetic. English visual culture has laboured ever since under the curse of blindness his century pronounced so vigorously. It is tempting to see an omen in the convergence of the ascendance of Protestantism, the birth of the novel, and the end of the last strongly visual moment in English culture, the Elizabethan, before an eclipse lasting almost a century and a half. One follows the change in architecture, the theatre (from Shakespeare to closure), and perhaps vividest of all, in decoration of the person (seen in costumes in painted portraits). The eventual revival of a powerful visual art came most unexpectedly at the furthest remove from the person, in a cult of landscape and artful approximations of it in the contradictorily named landscape-garden, a form which apparently bore little relation to the Catholic iconography of the past.

It no longer sounds strange to us that Pilgrim's most famous and numerous descendants were women. Various causes coincide, and before long we find it taken for granted that novels are written for, by (though this less often), and about women. *For* them, because they admit more openly to an appetite for imaginary lives and feelings. *By* them, because women (sometimes anonymously or under male pseudonyms) are better at imagining the sorts of things novels come to embody. And *about* them, because their situation in Western society has been more problematic and hence more interesting for three hundred years.

One conceives life as a pilgrimage or journey, a discovery of the meaning of the self in action as it encounters new situations, and then one looks round and sees that half the human race is more or less held prisoner, if not by the other, by a large social construction in which the other cooperates.

Eighteenth-century women can't have adventures because they can't travel alone, can't strike off on their own, unless like Defoe's disreputable heroines they leave decent society behind and become outlaws – whores, thieves, businesswomen. We may take the view that all interesting fiction concerns outlaws of one sort or another, not often, except in the Newgate novel and police thrillers, those who deserve hanging, but more subversive resistors, like Pilgrim, who run foul of the law because they are right and it is wrong. The subtlest form of outlawry, which we find in Marivaux or Jane Austen, is a silent disruption of the rules about marriage and hence of the present constitution of society, which is confused and opponents throw off the track by professions of self-abnegation and grisly spectacles of heroines excoriating and attempting to murder their own egos.

The protagonist of Marivaux's *La Vie de Marianne* is one of the most insinuating cases of self-realization in the history of fiction. She is discovered, the only remaining life, as an infant of two or thereabouts (her finders can only guess), in a carriage attacked by thieves, who have killed all the adult travellers. Marianne is wedged in the doorway of the half-empty conveyance, crushed under the dead body of a young woman travelling under a false name. This may have been her mother, as the male incognito may have been her father. These seem people of gentle birth; on the other hand there is a chambermaid close by, also a candidate for the role of Marianne's mother.

The accident has frozen this journey, of which no one can recover the purpose, in the middle of nowhere, but near a village, to which Marianne is now transported and handed over to the curé, also a refugee, also more refined than one would expect in such a place.

Protagonists in stories are frequently 'discovered', as if emerging helpless into our view from an egg or hollow womb dropped on our doorstep. The existential loneliness of Marivaux's little pilgrim keeps receiving reinforcement: the manuscript itself is said to be a kind of orphan; it was found in a womb-like cupboard in a house deep in the country just purchased by someone from outside, who felt a pang of sympathy for the unknown writer whose name (Marianne) means nothing to him.

This femine presence, who speaks with unexplained confidence now, is under constant threat in the past where we meet her. Even the protection offered by the kind curé and his sister is a spawner of delayed insecurity; they are old, will soon die, and then what will happen? Like the carriage stuck in the mud at the centre of another Marivaux story, Marianne is both trapped and exposed, a prisoner and an adventurer. If motion had been maintained her situation would have improved, but having come to rest where she has, she is neither here nor there, and lacks acceptable ways forward or back.

The curé's good sister takes Marianne to Paris against her better judgment to tend a dying relative. The experienced reader will already be apprehensive (apprehensiveness the human faculty which Marivaux exercises most) for the prospect is baited with money, the promise of the sick man's fortune. Superficially the city carries extremely different meanings from those it bears in Bunyan. Her first ride through Parisian streets is Marianne's awakening. Yet its multitude of excitements is a population of snares.

The aged relative has been dead twenty-four hours when they arrive, but it takes them three months to establish that there is no longer any fortune here. The unfamiliar complexities of urban finance do not work to the advantage of people like them. This disappointment sends the 'aunt' into a decline, news of which reaching her brother finishes him, and the shock waves from his collapse into senility make the aunt's illness mortal.

Marianne is boxed in on both sides, like someone trapped indefinitely in what was meant as a temporary conveyance. Staying on at the inn consumes her small capital at an alarming rate. Sympathetic 'friends' strip the old woman of clothes, jewels, and trinkets, while Marianne watches in horror or lapses into semi-conscious grief. But the kind old lady has made a sort of inept provision for the girl, turning over a slim remnant of cash (too dangerous to leave it in the hands of a virgin) to a priest. Marianne's anxiety, a constant mild tumescence, now erupts in fears of abduction, and she begs the priest to remove her from the inn at once.

From the frying pan into the fire, or from an exposed position near the highway to a true home in a more hidden corner of Paris? The priest takes her to see a pious philanthropist, more capable than he of securing her future. It is the first in a series of traps or locks made more unpickable because she is shut in by religion.

After an interview Marianne finds herself alone in a carriage with this charitable gentleman, who is taking her to the shop where he has found a place for her, a shop dealing in intimate items of clothing. Bumping along in the carriage, he takes her hand and notices she has no gloves: he will buy her some. Three hours after dropping her, he is back visiting Marianne in the bedroom she shares with a vulgar shopgirl (who leaves when he comes in, and not from delicacy), stroking her hand again and proposing that he buy her a dress. Without suspecting his motives, Marianne feels intense shame at these proposals, and thinks initially that she must refuse them. Shame is implicating even when absurd. In the end she decides to accept, an act tinged with surrender.

The reader may feel, rather callously, that Marivaux's purpose is to make *all* acts compromising: even keeping quiet can seem guilty acquiescence in whatever passes before one. To see things through the eyes of an observer as innocent as Marianne has the unforeseen effect of overstimulating our suspiciousness. She is slow to get the point of men's designs, which makes us quicker to imagine meanings which may or may not be there, readier to turn the bluff shopmistress with whom she is lodged into a procuress, and to posit conspiracies against her virtue.

Even his menacing way of discussing chastity encourages prurience. The good old lady says 'virtue' but means only sexual abstinence. Marivaux has stumbled on a secret Bunyan couldn't imagine. Once the idea of violation is set going, nothing easier than to make readers dwell on something you've sworn never to mention, which you would die before devoting an explicit sentence to. One sees only the pure surface, and may have imagined the riot of suggestion which seemed to follow in its train.

Marivaux finds intense dramatic possibility in passivity and weakness. Marianne continually flirts with the idea of throwing everything up and becoming entirely defenceless again: to avoid the slightly coarse imputations of the shopwoman, she will leave this haven (after one night) and cast herself adrift in the streets, a proposal aborted by the two of them collapsing together in tears when she voices it. The only decisive steps open to her would in fact be surrenders or abstentions, however vigorously executed.

Marianne soon finds herself the object of all male eyes (or all visible male eyes), an experience most concentrated in church. One day when she has singled out one of these starers as specially interesting she leaves the church, as always avoiding meetings or verbal exchanges with her admirers and, wrapped in a dream of this man, fails to hear a carriage behind her until almost too late. The driver shouts, she flees and escapes, but in doing so falls and hurts her foot.

Imagine her shock and pleasure to find that the offending carriage belongs to the interesting man, who makes up for this attack from behind by having the powerless Marianne carried to his house nearby, where she is put to bed and waited on by a doctor who, like the priest lubricating the old lecher's approach to the maiden, makes it feasible for Valville (the young man's name) to admire the prettiest injured foot in the world.

We pay for pleasure with peripheral pain, if we can even separate them any more, they are so mixed together. How miraculous to progress, through the agency of the carriage, from passing in a public place to practically inhabiting a bed together. Of course this dream of powerless bliss is too good to be true, and Marianne feels she must wake herself, so she asks for another carriage to be sent to end her pleasure.

Now come some of the sinuous twists Marivaux must have been famous for. Valville presses her to stay, which thrills her, but she must notify the woman she lodges with, and the idea of the shopsign hanging outside her house stops Marianne dead. Valville (a rich aristocrat) mustn't know she is virtually a shopgirl, so she will leave at once to prevent his finding out. Will she succeed at self-sabotage, caught between her two imperatives? Marianne's precipitance, ready to choke off the infant passion, works: it throws Valville into fervent declaration: he can't let her go off into the unknown, he loves her. Though truly speechless, Marianne is also cagey. Asked point blank if she cares for him, she gives no reply. What excitement Marivaux extracts from her paralysis.

Getting home becomes hugely complicated. Valville will send his own carriage, or will accompany her, alluring options she cannot allow. The name of the shop slips out, and all is ruined, but Valville doesn't understand, supposing that Marianne is hiding her true address and using the tradeswoman as a screen. Marianne tearfully sets him straight, and is about to tell her whole tale when the door opens with a loud noise to admit ... her old lecher-patron, who is Valville's uncle, and very embarrassed at the sight of Marianne.

Hardly has she enjoyed his discomfiture when she realizes that she has given herself away again. What will the nephew think seeing that she and his reprobate-uncle recognize each other? It is the old story, to be pulled first one way, then the other, to be vindicated and then have doubts about whether one really looks as pure as one should.

The rhapsody at Valville's has gone sour by the end, and Marianne returns 'home' to a wrangle between her landlady and the cab driver over the fare, in which the romantic fumes of the lovers' meeting are dispersed.

Then, in the nearest thing to quick succession this story can muster, the tables are turned: the old lecher visits Marianne when the others are out, warning her against his dissolute nephew, who appears unexpectedly, draws the wrong conclusion, and turns on his heel without waiting for explanations. The uncle reveals he will no longer pay for Marianne unless she moves to a more secret hideout whose address the nephew won't know. Rejecting this, Marianne cuts off her retreat still further by refusing to sell the older man's gifts to her landlady to pay the rent – she will return them to him.

Now she feels a longing to see her priest-protector, and finds him closeted with the lecher, who leaves having misrepresented her, so that now the priest upbraids her for her slanders of the good old man. Every avenue blocked, Marianne is on her way home when she falls into a new alignment of her affairs.

An obstruction in the street ahead halts her progress, and Marianne finds she is standing opposite the open door of a convent church. From a mixture of motives she decides to go in. Besides true religious feeling, embarrassment propels her into this gloom. She has been crying and consequently attracting stares, which she doesn't like. Part of the explanation, we suspect, is that Marianne's sexual power is suddenly too much for her: sometimes it isn't exciting, but simply tiring, to feel that you awaken interest in strangers.

Like Valville's, the convent presents both a temptation and a threat, though of contrary type to the man's den. Subjection to a man and immurement in the safe feminine world of a religious order are the extreme poles of experience in this story, and it is surprising that their physical forms share so many qualities.

In both convent and nobleman's bed, Marianne is an interloper – thrusting her way into an unguarded opening in the first, lured into a space which isn't hers and may be a trap in the second. Though both escapes occur in broad daylight on city streets, they are not unlike being captured by bandits. The church is a deserted place where you lose yourself as in a forest, an escape from entanglements, as Valville's is a focusing of one's bonds down into a single intense one. Though it is less easy to identify, the convent too embodies a threatening impingement on the person. Marianne is more unguarded, but feels safer, and thus to our eyes runs greater risk of being drawn in unawares. The idea of the convent as a possible solution to Marianne's problems has already been intimated by the priest. Taking religious vows is alarming because like loss of virginity (the ultimate threat at Valville's), it is irrevocable. Opting for permanent maidenhood is like sealing up the body; male ingress is no longer possible.

Marivaux feels these contrasting dangers so powerfully that both settings look like prisons or even torture chambers. The church is a theatre of grief where mournful murmurs and suppressed sobs are the only sounds in the semi-darkness. Marianne, prostrated by practical difficulties, here seems sunk in devotional passion. Because she is well dressed (having worn the lecher's gifts in order to convince the priest of her accusations) and carries herself well, she attracts the interest of a lady who has just arrived from the country – is somewhat displaced, that is, but clearly a person of consequence. Given the rules of the book and the setting, this almost-meeting does not occur now, though it will later.

Marianne's visit to the church, which began in a casual way, deepens into a stable grief, and she is still there when they want to close. She has really nowhere to go, as she has somehow avoided facing. Shown into the abbess's presence, she finds the sympathetic lady from the country again (a missed chance retrieved, which may yet slip away). Now Marianne tells her story once more (we cannot hear it too often, it being one of the functions of the whole narrative to impress this primal pattern on us again and again in hopes of getting a clear and permanent print). Like other religious in the book, the prioress draws back when she finds Marianne needs something, disclaiming any power to act. Her anonymous interlocutor on the other hand quickly offers to pay Marianne's keep at the convent.

So it is arranged. She is safely extricated from the old lecher's clutches, not without swinging too far in the other direction. We didn't want to see her as fully protected from sexual danger as that. And somehow the prioress has given one the idea of a *negative* sexual threat.

Marianne's obligation to her benefactress will come, in time, to seem a straitjacket, albeit of a different kind, like that to her first patron. But for the time being all goes well, and Marianne is encouraged to call her new friend *mother*, and thus to fill one of the greatest voids in her life. That this completion might ever come into conflict with her passion for Valville is as yet only a suspicion on the horizon. Drowning people don't have time for inquiries about their rescuers, but some readers will remember that Valville's mother was expected from the country. The more she becomes the daughter of her new protector, the greater impropriety Marianne is storing up in her love.

This situation is turning into one of those double binds Marivaux specializes in. Marianne insinuates herself with the mother who hasn't yet realized the threat to her son. She ends a fervent admirer of the girl, yet her sense of propriety continues to say that, however marvellous, this marriage must not take place. Marianne's gratitude is so overmastering she rushes to acquiesce in this, self-division and inhibition pushed toward an excruciating limit.

After twists too numerous to recount, however, this resistance is broken down, and she is scheduled to marry Valville, when one evening she receives a mysterious visitor. The next morning a coach appears, purporting to be from Valville's mother. Though she recognizes neither the equipage nor the servants, Marianne docilely gets in, to be whisked over an unfamiliar route and find *another* convent door closing behind her.

Now a sweet abbess delivers an ultimatum. Either Marianne will marry someone they have selected, or become a nun. She is taken to visit this prospective oaf somewhere in a garden, an experience verging nearer to rape itself, though no violence is actually offered by these people, who do exactly as they please with her. Who are they? Other members of Valville's family? Someone connected with rivals for his hand? His mother's minions in disguise? Or allies of someone who knows Marianne's true past and wants to nail her (a valuable property?) down?

All one can say is that in her peculiar way she continues to rise in the social scale, because her oppressors are increasingly important people as time goes on. She is granted an interview with a wise old minister who is behind the current plot. Does it make everything better or worse that those giving her such trouble should be so civilized? At least it makes us feel she might seriously consider submitting.

Eventually, however, the choice seems to be made for her. Valville has fallen in love with someone else. Now the idea which has been mooted so long finally looks attractive: Marianne decides to enter a convent. At the very door she is met by an unhappy young nun who warns her off, telling of how the nuns seduced *her*. This girl harks back to her own arrival at the convent, where she was met by an unhappy sister who handed her an unopened letter from a corrupt lover, a young abbé she herself had met in society. She describes how this glimpse of corruption killed her vocation, and she returned to the world.

After this she relates a series of vicissitudes not unlike Marianne's own history, though a lurid, Gothic version of it. The nameless girl is in fact more like a back-up set of batteries than a true, contrasting double plot: parentless, imprisoned, threatened with unwanted marriages. The interpolation grows to such considerable size that we forget from time to time it is not Marianne we are reading about. When we leave her the prospective nun is heading toward marriage. A stranger has entered the coach, who is found during a stop at an inn to be her lost mother. At this point the nun is called away to devotions, and Marianne must wait until tomorrow to hear the end of her story.

We will never hear the rest, though, because Marivaux, who lived another twenty years after reaching this point, never carried *La Vie de Marianne* any further. It is a classic instance of breaking off, permitting himself to be interrupted in a parenthesis. So successful has he been at diverting the main flow that he has stranded us forever in a back eddy. How did the girl become a nun after all? And, the parallel question in Marianne's case, how did she become the countess she tells us at the beginning she now speaks as? There is a kind of perfection in the impasse: the girl who ends as a nun is shown heading toward marriage, Marianne, who ends as a countess, is left about to become a nun.

More important, a question from further back, but looming larger for us – who were Marianne's parents? The greatest mystery remains to be solved. And yet, the story 'ends' with someone finding a parent. That is the motion which will complete the cycle, and it occurs. Events began with Marianne's emerging from the carriage: they end with the nun's mother getting back in, at a stop somewhere in the country which means nothing to those passing through.

It is the occurrence one has waited one's whole remembered life for, and it comes gratuitously, casually. The journey is completed at a point somewhere in its middle, not by our all arriving or getting out, but by the inconsequential act of accepting one more passenger. The fact that this moment in a journey brought him to a standstill, accidental though it seems, is the strongest confirmation of the overpowering significance for Marivaux of the idea of transit and especially transit by carriage. A carriage is a snugger, more intimate dwelling than more stable homes, and it is a nameless, placeless experience of constant change. A story about a coach is evidently doing what stories exist above all to do, it is moving forward. But at some point it must come to a halt, or at least hint at a destination, and at that moment all the fun goes out of the idea of conveyance.

The first part of *Marianne* appeared in 1731, the eleventh ten years later. Samuel Richardson's *Pamela* came out in 1740 and soon took Europe by storm. It is the story of another helpless girl, a lady's maid in a great house who after her mistress' death is placed under siege by that lady's son. Almost at once the idea is broached of whether Pamela should return to her parents' home to escape these assaults, which quickly take overtly physical forms – he kisses her, pinches her finger, grabs her arm so tightly it comes out black and blue, or detaches a piece of her skirt before she disappears behind a door and locks it, falling down in a fit which her master observes through the keyhole. Richardson is more direct and graphic than Marivaux, and early critics, though perhaps also influenced by the aggressive class-message of *Pamela*, were right to complain that it is a coarse product. Those mixed emotions of trouble, pleasure, and fear which are the wellspring of such fiction, are more delicately rendered by Marivaux, and the entrapments in which Marianne is placed are more subtly concocted of her own scruples as well as the demands of others.

The core of the two books is the same, and Marivaux is more ingenious, far more tasteful, a more persuasive moralist, and yet ... however much one despises him, one must admit that Richardson has done more for the novel. One cannot even say that the book's overarching hypocrisy was not tremendously fertile in other hands. But Richardson's greatest discovery was a certain intimacy with time. Incredible as it seems, he wandered into his great technical innovation, epistolary form as a way of telling a story.

It is far from obvious that such a method might work, letters being highly ritualized and formal as a mode of transmission, though often studiously informal in style. For one thing, no matter how assiduous the correspondents, they are perpetually out of synch. By the time the answerer hears of a happening it has been overtaken at the other end by something else. Part of Richardson's shrewdness is to dispense with the other half of the correspondence for the most part, and even better to exploit the inefficiencies and failures of letters as communication. It is a frequent potent irony that Pamela has been outrun by events which go too fast for her reflective capacities to keep up.

The letters began as a Practical Instructor in letter writing, and much that is irritating in the book as we have it is residue of this didactic origin. It is no longer epistolary style, but propriety of sentiment and behaviour in which we are instructed: Pamela is an example to be studied, a kind of modern saint. This feeling that there is something rather pressing to learn from it distinguishes this story from Marivaux. *Marianne* is a reverie, *Pamela* a tract, not a demanding or gruelling one, but pleasurable and pleased with itself.

Its sense of rectitude and its sense of passage are closely linked; to us the second feels much less tainted. We have a story about someone who writes it down as it happens, under conditions in which the manuscript's fate forms part of the story. It has virtually to be smuggled out, and the adversary may at any time (has once already) get his hands on one of the instalments.

Richardson isn't even afraid of showing Pamela consuming a whole day writing what we are now reading. Such is the continual tension under which she matter of factly lives that she can be *surprised* writing – she hears a noise and, frightened that it may be Mr B, puts what we are reading quickly down the throat of her dress. In a moment, after this intimacy which we can dwell on if we want, an intimacy which is like a blanking out of consciousness in intense pleasure or fear, the flow is resumed. It wasn't Mr B (a threat) but Mrs J (a comfort), but it is too late to tell us this. We have had it both ways, and trembled for a second while Pamela suspended her pen, and we (the letter) slipped down her dress.

Richardson writes almost continually under this delightful pressure, overlaying the rhythm of leaving off and beginning again on the events which the prose chases after, catches up, briefly outdistances. In this book time wells up, paradoxically more palpable because nothing is happening. A large part is consumed with the question of how soon and, finally, of whether, Pamela will go home, thereby discharging the tension and ending the tale.

The question is first broached in fantasies of escape and second thoughts of what might go wrong and how her act may be misinterpreted. After that, Mr B unexpectedly proposes Pamela's departure (imagining it a sort of rebuke or punishment) in the interview like a court trial which follows his first real assault. From then on the book is a cat and mouse game with the idea of leaving. Pamela's mind rushes ahead to how her parents will meet her, how she will travel, how alter her plans in bad weather; then she is pulled back by the need to finish a sewing job, a waistcoat she is embroidering for the predator. In fact a series of trivial (and finally less trivial) accidents intervene to separate the seamstress from her stultifying goal.

There is a very simple question which seems to demolish *Pamela* like a house of cards: if the girl wanted to escape, why didn't she? Gothic novels are more lurid, but if we can accept that the woman has been captured, more plausible. The Gothic heroine is actually locked up in a terrifying building in the middle of an unfamiliar landscape. What stops Pamela from leaving Mr B's? Not the few details which must be tied up (sorting out her clothes, waiting for Mrs Jervis to join her), and are the only excuses offered. For they are entirely different in scale from the magnitude of the threat. The clue must be sought in odd signs like Pamela's falling immediately to her knees when given the chance to return home, and bathing her master's hand in tears; or in her asking solicitous upper-servants not to think ill of Mr B (though he has been tormenting her).

The success of the book and its continuing hold on us, though it consists of one long impasse, lies in the confusion which these anomalies give sign of: *Pamela* is built on a set of unresolvable ambivalences, which manifest themselves in the ego's feelings about itself, in ideas about the class structure, and in sexual passion, its suppression or disguise.

Richardson is so powerful an upturner of established habits of narrative because all these things come together in him – class resentments, thwarted ego, and greedy instinct. He makes one aware for the first time that the quintessential protagonist of the new kind of fiction will be a lower-class woman just finding her way past the inhibiting pressures of religious ideas on behaviour. She is in several registers hampered or disadvantaged, and the unconfessed goal of the book is to achieve untrammelled expression for these thwarted strivings of the personality.

Her goal is to make herself known and admired, famous for her virtues, not obscure; to rise in the social scale while pretending a superstitious awe of the distance between masters and servants; and least discussible of all, to achieve legitimacy for strong sensual urges. Of course this programme is not presented as a programme, but pushed forward hesitantly with many stiflings and claims to want the opposite of the goals finally achieved.

But it must at any stage have been a rather innocent reader who was not thinking *Shamela* while reading *Pamela*. That is to say, this heroine never completely fooled people. Though she isn't allowed to think it, we are: it will be good when satisfactions no longer have to be deferred, and one can admit (as the heroine does in Fielding's parody) that the bedroom is exactly where one wants the man; looking nervously under the bed is a way of putting him there.

Except of course that Richardson's hypocrisy is deeply true, and Fielding's good sense is rather superficial. Pamela and her inventor scorn the noble ladies (both she and he a little unclear exactly what the ladies' rank is), blurting out roughly, 'I'm just as good as you,' mixed with 'I'm not up to this exalted company.' Pamela expresses a creditable nostalgia for the humble cot, 'Oh if only I'd never left my little bed in the parental attic,' but she knows her story is only worth hearing because she has put the attic behind forever. Every Christian soul is as good as another, but for safety's sake why not climb to the top of the heap? One doesn't really want to be kept down by one's illusions, but one isn't prepared to give them up either.

As Fielding pretended not to see, hypocrisy can be a way of expressing complexity, and so it is in Richardson. Hypocrisy is the strain caused by feeling in oneself two incompatible views of a situation, even two different natures. Pamela is not angel or whore, or even sometimes angel and sometimes whore, but both simultaneously. Like Marianne she is strongly drawn to fine clothes as an extension of the personality. But she is also suspicious of this leaning, or has been taught to be, and so feels the need to disown finery as she accepts it, mixing together class consciousness and Puritan conscience: her new clothes are good for her. Then when she begins planning her return home she realizes that she will stand out from those surroundings by her unwonted fineness. So very laboriously, she confects a suitable wardrobe of plain stuffs in modest style.

This nunnish garb spawns some odd rites. She has produced it secretly in the old room where she no longer sleeps since moving in with Mrs Jervis to escape her master's attentions. Now she goes there to enjoy trying it on. Pleased with the effect, she wants Mrs Jervis to see it, and this leads to further complication – Mr B bursts in, doesn't recognize her, asks to see the new girl, and then takes new liberties by pretending she is Pamela's sister. So in the end she reaps every possible advantage from the furtive project.

She has mortified herself and won acclaim for the sacrifice when found out. She has even created an alluring new style, being one of those who look good in anything. From the beginning Pamela has retold the compliments others pay her, disowning them the while. 'I hope it does not make me proud to hear this, heaven knows I can take no credit for it.'

Of course the way to take no notice of compliments is to ignore them, not to give them further circulation. But the novel isn't a spiritual medium where social definitions of the person have no place. Clothes are one of the purest cases of self-definition through others, as too are physical charms, which only come back to the possessor secondhand as it were, reflected in the stir they cause around her.

The bind Richardson finds himself in arises from the contradiction in the idea of a Puritan first-person narrative, impelled to call many things vanities which it realizes at the same time are what the story is about. The most interesting of these contradictions are those which occur in Pamela's feeling about Mr B. Marivaux forged an occult connection between the oppressor and the beloved: they were kin (uncle and nephew), which is to say older and younger versions of the same thing, so it qualified our feelings about both; there was seepage from one to the other.

Richardson's innovation is to combine the two meanings in the same person: Mr B is overbearing, uncomfortably powerful, teeters on the edge of violence – how can one stand up to him? Yet Pamela knows in spite of these appearances that she is in control, so that she can repulse him as strongly as she wants and he will come back for more.

The great demonstrations are his three forays into the bedroom, hiding in closets the first two times, waiting for the women to undress and get sleepy, then creeping out and approaching the bed. The third time he dresses as a maid known for drunkenness, and pretends to be so soundly asleep in a chair he can't be dislodged. Though he comes toward the bed full size, he is trembling like an aspen, emasculated by his fervour. This doesn't stop Pamela from going into hysterical shock, screaming, fainting, sweating. The onlookers fear she has died. Maybe they've never seen anyone have an orgasm before, Fielding might pipe up. Pamela's ability to faint at these moments, like the catatonia of prey-animals, is a great preserver of purity. Outrages offered to unconscious victims, like trees falling in unvisited forests, don't count.

The more one details exactly what has happened, the more one feels that the book's picture of Mr B as a devil is the wishful dream of a melodramatist. He is persistent, but his worst crimes take place in the mind of Pamela: he rouses some dreadful apprehensions. This gives us an answer to Dr Johnson's observation that anyone who read Richardson for the plot would hang himself. Plot in a dramatist's sense of the word has virtually disappeared, only to be internalized. The outer parameters of action remain strangely locked in place, which throws the feverish racing of the feminine mind into higher relief. In some sense Richardson is the true fruition of Protestant conscience as the mainspring of narrative. The buffetings of faith have become enticing proposals offered by men with obscure intentions, and the Purgatorial journey has become an open-ended flirtation with reality.

Some of the most radical treatments of feminine rebellion have been produced by men. Jane Austen's place in the history of this subject is extremely puzzling: is she the most dutiful of daughters, accepting with a good grace the prison of the little world of Highbury, or does her dismissive wit utterly shatter the pretensions of the constricted place in which she finds herself? Is it natural when reading her to wish she had a wider range in which to test her powers? There is plenty of evidence that she considered and rejected the idea of writing about a wider world.

The Prince Regent's librarian asked her to try a novel about a clergyman, which she professed herself too ignorant to attempt. But at that or some other time she sketched out a sentimental treatment of the subject which gives a ludicrous synopsis of everything missing from her own books. The clergyman and his daughter, who share an ambiguous, passionate attachment, are chased across Europe by a relentless suitor for her hand, putting down roots in a new country every fortnight and forced to sever them by the lover's threats. They are supported by her devoted labours, though she is continually cheated by depraved employers. They end in primitive conditions in Kamchatka where the father, finally worn out by trouble, lies on the ground lecturing and advising her for five hours before finally expiring. She then begins crawling back to Europe, passing through twenty narrow escapes and as she turns a corner, meeting a long lost lover who is just setting out in search of her, having overcome powerful if absurd scruples.

In exercises like this Jane Austen has turned herself into an enemy of stories, letting a Protestant asperity and mistrust of imagination get the upper hand. In her best books there is only a distanced residue of feminine subjectivity. Sensibility, the secret of these novels' power, is a bad word, and imagination a treacherous faculty. Both Emma Woodhouse and Elizabeth Bennett (in *Emma* and *Pride and Prejudice*) fail to grasp that they are the objects of others' desires, and put an irresponsible fancy to work imagining romance for a protégée or sister. That is like an inversion of the standard romantic plot in which the heroine hallucinates various passional connections with the world for herself.

Seeing her wage such vigorous war against imagination we are tempted to suppose that this writer felt threatened by it. She might have given in, and we would have novels with great heights and depths, betrayals and corruptions, sublimities of landscape and sentiment. But instead of such a Hawthorne-like figure, we have one of the most powerful renunciations in literature; she sees very exactly the spiritual nullity and emotional smallness of her world, and she accepts her place in it without a fight, as if to say that only men could be silly enough in society as we find it to indulge in rhapsodies of the untrammelled Feminine.

CHAPTER TEN

GOTHIC TERROR IN WALPOLE, KLEIST, HAWTHORNE, AND KAFKA

Resisting the idea of a novel about a clergyman, Jane Austen was digging in her heels against a whole class of fiction full of priests and abbeys and pine trees. Beginning with Horace Walpole's *Castle of Otranto* of 1765, Gothic had been a notable vogue in English fiction for the last decades of the century. To Jane Austen, as to many people nowadays, it was the bogusness of these tales which mainly stood out: their interest in the Middle Ages, Italy, and religion only a superficial pretence, which created vague exotic flavours bearing no great resemblance to specific cultural realities. Like the supposed history in English landscape gardens, the foreignness in Gothic novels was just scenic or picturesque.

Though there were enthusiasts who become Catholics on no firmer basis than the ideas contained in pre-Romantic literature, and though travellers actually existed who looked in Italy for the landscape of castles, caves, hermitages and forests, it is true that the best Gothic novels were written by Protestants who had never been to Italy, or by witty critics like Walpole who suspended their habitual scepticism to enter unwonted trances.

But it isn't true that the pretences of these books were hollow, or that just because Catholicism isn't its historical self in them, it lacks another kind of profundity. Gothic novels *were* prescient, Romantic literature before its time, uncovering new layers in the psyche and new possibilities in narrative by returning to archaic forms to which these writers had only dubious right, strictly speaking.

'History' in *The Castle of Otranto* takes nightmarishly physical form. The past haunts the present in buried secrets which the story will exhume: if one is to have peace one must disinter the dead. The ideal of the Gothic novel is to numinize as much of the landscape as possible and hold off the moment when one learns that the graves contain ... skeletons. At first it is ghosts not corpses which we keep stumbling upon, a spiritualization of terror.

The heroine finds herself alone in an obscure part of the castle, and a thousand thoughts crowd in on her like ghosts. These frights are the featureless epiphanies of a religion without a god. Every building becomes a church of this creed, infested with spirits, a mouth from which dark powers issue. Instead of refuges or sanctuaries human constructions seem more dangerous than the surrounding woods.

In *Castle of Otranto* Manfred's castle is connected by underground tunnels to the church of St Nicholas, to which are attached two religious houses, not expressions of piety but muffled ventriloquisms of guilt. The secret passages are child's play and enshrine a key Romantic principle at the same time, short cuts between opposites.

Pursued by Manfred's quasi-incestuous desires, Isabella's defence is to hide in the convent. But church and convent are *his*, staffed by his appointees, another kind of prison. The commerce between castle and convent is that one of the tombs is sending emissaries to the castle. Pieces of armour from a former ruler's monument keep turning up there, magnified to many times lifesize. In spite of numerous pious protestations by its narrator, religion is subverted in the book to a demonic affair – something seeks revenge for crimes unknown, and we are caught in the middle, non-believers in the idea of vengeance after a long lapse.

Isabella leaves by the underground route and immediately a gust blows out her lamp. She hears retreating steps in front, and meets their owner who offers help. Now voices threaten from behind, and they must locate a hidden entrance, from which dark stairs descend. Before long the two are on different sides of the locked trap door, at opposite ends of an obscure corridor guarded by a demon whose power for some reason is waning.

Gothic novels work by keeping readers outside the centres of the story, like the ignorant believer to whom the faith is a mystery. Manfred's motives are a closed book, making his sudden movements seem unnatural. Explanations are invariably less involving than the uncertainties they dispel in these books. In *Castle of Otranto* the main form of fearful suspense consists of searching through empty rooms for one knows not what, the cause of a noise one has heard, the wind, a groan, or a voice in rooms where no one should be. Caves and inaccessible chambers are metaphors for secret parts of the self, 'inmost recesses' of the soul, of which there are many, containing things one is reluctant to know. Finally Gothic novels baffle us in ways that aren't fruitful, as well as in ones that are, and remain cultural documents rather than works of art, follies rather than temples.

Even so their significance is extreme. They seem parodies rather than true observances because they are the reconstructive efforts of non-believers. Here the miracles of myth are given great swathings of sentiment, and rituals are seen from outside by Protestants who have lost touch with them. But it is a bold intellectual enterprise, and in the next generation more probing and successful efforts will be made at recovering these huge lost territories.

The flaw in the Gothic novel is perhaps only that it doesn't take its terrifying suggestions seriously enough. These central intuitions would include the presence in every psyche of promptings toward incest and violence, unseemly closeness and horrible remoteness. And the swallowing up of the individual and the carefully hoarded significance of separate identity: in *Castle of Otranto* generations are mistaken for each other and the two maidens twice exchange identites, the second time permanently, so it ends like 'The Knight's Tale' or the chaotic centre of *Midsummer Night's Dream*.

What seemed passing madness in earlier literature has become for us the central truth about personality. It is not consoling to note that many of the mysteries Freud uncovers in the mind are the motifs of the Gothic novel. This is the modern supernaturalism, to subjectivize the dark forces which had been ranged round about man in earlier myth. When he ceases to believe that the world outside is really inhabited, it isn't long before he has to find new homes for the demons within himself. So these frivolous Gothic fictions have a special poignancy as early inklings of terrible new intellectual burdens.

The eight stories which Heinrich von Kleist wrote between 1805 and his suicide in 1811 are among the most striking products of spiritual crisis in existence. Kleist's materials are even more archaic than those of Gothic novels, but like them he subjectivizes the old motifs, and lends them new psychological depth. And like Gothic novels his little narratives exhibit an intense attraction-repulsion to religion.

The proportions here, of that which is idiosyncratic, and that characteristic of the historical moment, are hard to determine, which only heightens the interest of the ecstatic convergence of personal peculiarities with the strains of that moment in history. Kleist came from a Prussian military family, studied music and mathematics, and entered the world at a moment when rational certainties and stable political orders were receiving a perilous shake.

Stendhal's response to Napoleon is well known; Kleist's of a contrary sort (he became rabidly anti-French) carried such primitive force that it appears the deepest levels of his nature were engaged. Likewise a reading of Kant produced effects on him which not every reader suffered. Far from comforted, he felt threatened by the philosopher's effort to protect moral absolutes by internalizing them. The picture Kant gives of knowing, an event less securely tied to external measurement than heretofore, was like a mathematical proof of what Kleist's sensibility was already telling him.

These 'scientific' stories seem to make contraries inescapably clear: that life is intolerably painful, that perceiving this evil consistency produces euphoria, a parody of rapturous union with God. The second of the feelings, though more novel, has a shorter life and fewer possibilities of development: it is a godlike calm unstable like a radioactive isotope.

The stories begin with matter of fact statements of impossibility: at the moment when the great earthquake struck Santiago in Chile, a young man in prison was about to hang himself. He paused, and when he looked again there was no longer any place to attach the rope. So he fled through the chaotic city, down streets where earlier his beloved had been drawn toward a public execution, which may have been disrupted as his suicide was. Their passion had been forbidden by her father, who stuck her in a convent, in the garden of which the love was consummated. Later the girl feels the pangs of childbirth on the cathedral steps in the midst of a solemn religious procesion.

Kleist's Chile, like Kafka's China, is a place we're ignorant of. Ignorant and also suspicious, for unlike China, the seat of a venerable and exhausted civilization, Chile shows us fervent Catholic morality sitting right on top of a savage past. Although the events of the story are highly questionable, they are presented as facts already achieved, not the subject of debate or searches of conscience. Both passion and the vindictiveness it calls forth are forces of nature inexorable like an earthquake.

We are rushed along through enormity after enormity. Jeronimo (the would-be suicide) gets free of the town, climbs a hill and feels oceanic bliss as a breeze hits him. Refugees nearby, heaving their saved possessions, deflate him with eye-witness reports of his beloved Josefa's death. But in a secluded valley he finds her, and the earthquake seems their salvation. Now they plan a retreat to a nearby coastal town, 'Concepcion', and flight to Spain. At this moment an acquaintance approaches who wants Josefa to nurse his baby, and the couple change their minds, reconciled to the world again by catastrophe. But already we feel warning tremors as the party sets off for a thanksgiving Mass.

In the crowded church a priest is painting artistic pictures of doom, holding up the couple as an example of what God uses earthquakes to condemn. Now they are accused by worshippers who confuse the borrowed child with Josefa's and its father with Jeronimo. The viciousness unleashed is lurid beyond belief, until someone asserts there's been a mistake of identity, and begins leading them to safety, when a man claiming to to be Jeronimo's father attacks him, Josefa throws herself into the crowd, and the convulsion is stilled by smashing one of the babies (the wrong one) against a pillar of the nave. So the bastard survives, strangely valued by its adopted parents.

After the earthquake is over, its cruelties and random destructions are duplicated *in church* by human malice calling itself by the most sacred names. Opposites spring from each other: lulled by incense we are hit on the head with clubs. Events are unreal or incalculable in proportion to their momentousness: when Josefa goes back to the nunnery to rescue her baby, the abbess and most of the nuns are killed by a falling gable just as she is about to embrace them.

There is a subtext which is only allowed to peep out, but looks like a truer set of meanings: the young parents' purity of feeling and the miraculous birth on the church steps remind one of Christ the infant-God. In another Kleist story, the Marquise of O has become mysteriously pregnant. She gives birth like the Virgin without knowing sin or the father, and though outcast by her family regards the unheralded child as divine.

As in certain Baroque poems, the paradoxes of religious imagery are heightened or exaggerated, until there are two incompatible realms: muddy earthly understanding which regards the innocent bearer of new life as a criminal, and a more precarious intuition which sees in earthly life glints of a harmonious order beyond our grasp.

We feel so excluded in these narratives because the writer gives powerful flashes of what we are excluded from, in little oases like the perfumed night the young family spends outside the city, and in the embracing divine patterns which the world insists on inverting.

'The Marquise of O' is the only Kleist story set in contemporary Europe. Exoticism of place or period is ordinarily an important part of his effect, estranging the happenings from us and, most of all, helping us accept the part that superstition plays in the way things unfold. Superstition, that is to say beliefs tenaciously held which we see to be without foundation, a human manifestation Kleist ranks among the most compelling. But if we compiled a dictionary of man's illusions from his stories we would not need to leave out 'The Marquise of O'. This story turns on the idea of dishonour, and is pervaded by an even more drastic sense of shame than *Pamela*. Can a woman bring opprobrium on herself by something done to her without her knowledge while she suffers a fainting fit? Yes, is the unyielding answer. Or rather, that certain occurrences cannot be unwilled.

'The Marquise of O' has restored the primitive state of mind in which the link between intercourse and conception is only half believed. One needs to prove that that is how it happened. Except, of course, that securing a man's agreement is a dissociated victory, like finding a Joseph to endorse one's pregnancy. The husband, like the baby, is in his way a miraculous birth. He appeared out of nowhere during upheaval, disappeared, died on the field of battle, and re-emerged in the family drawing room around the time morning sickness began.

The woman wants to disown him, but he is so honourable he is hard to shake off. She retires to a self-constituted nunnery of one, whose defences he breaches, to be repulsed again. He finally succeeds in making contact through the newspaper, but when the truth of her pregnancy is out she rejects it hysterically, and he takes a house in town in which to bide his time after their wedding, before approaching her again and winning relatively unfeigned acceptance.

Looking at its outline, we can see the plot is an alienated depiction of courtship. Sexual intimacy with another person is so profoundly wanted *and* unwanted that for a long time it seems there is no way to achieve it. It is the story of *Pamela* all over again, with the ideas of angel and demon naturalized because the dreaded consummation *preceded* everything else and must be reapproached from ordinary life, yet the distance continues to seem unbridgeable. The luridness of the sexual encounter informs everything else, but is more credibly off the page's edge than lewdness is in *Pamela*. Such inversions, to have the wish fulfilled before there's been time for the desire to enter your mind, to be married before you've met, are not unknown in fairy tales. Kleist by an uncanny, and how witting? knack, found narrative situations which reverse the normal sequences, giving the result and then the cause, the catastrophe and then the steps leading up to it. Some of the same resulting hopelessness attaches to events in fairy tales. Much magic power is about, but it is a matter of luck whether it works on your behalf. Watching the unearned successes of fairy tale princes does not make us more optimistic about the outcome of our own plots. If anything it encourages the feeling that it isn't what one does that counts, and that outcomes are unpredictable.

Kleist's morals or conclusions are more concentrated than that. We find ourselves perpetually disagreeing with the common sense of mankind, a dispute fairy tales couldn't tolerate. One of Kleist's characteristic motions is to bring us to the verge of success or release and then to call us back to prison again. Hopes are repeatedly raised to be carefully dashed. His most extended narrative 'Michael Kohlhaas' is an elaborate reiteration of this rhythm as the motive principle of a story.

What keeps us going through its unbearably prolonged series of humiliatiohs and miscarriages? and why does it continue to feel magical? Because the deviousness of the forces we negotiate with are endlessly interesting, a slipperiness like Protean transformations. In this illogical and hence unalterable shifting of the whole ground of debate just as the story nears a gain in the old terms, Kleist's work comes nearest to Kafka's *Castle*, though Kleist is more conclusive, and depicts a real if tortured progress, the mirror image of fairy tale triumphs: an exhilarating because unearned series of failures.

The most treacherous and Gothic of Kleist's tales is called 'St Cecilia, or the Power of Music', which the reader suspects is about a more sinister power than music. Like 'Michael Kohlhaas' it is set in sixteenth-century Germany and uses religious controversy as its central conflict. A group of Protestant iconoclasts have decided to disrupt the patronal festival at a convent, smashing images and storied windows. The nuns rely on the music for which they are famous to soothe their opponents. On the day before the celebration their organist falls ill with brain fever. So the sisters are surprised to see her walk in at the last minute with the old Italian setting of the Mass tucked under her arm. Their singing and playing is inspired and holds the congregation as speechless as the dead.

Six years later the mother of the four young iconoclasts arrives seeking her sons, who have vanished without trace. Four youths of unknown origin were admitted six years ago to the local lunatic asylum suffering from melancholic religious mania, but this does not sound like her boisterous sons. Seeing them in their long robes seated around a table adoring a crucifix all day long, mute except for one howling rendition of the Gloria every midnight (and an hour's sleep soon after), she is horrified to recognize the boys. We infer that they do not know her and can give no account of themselves, for she travels to another city to hear a report of how they fell under this spell on the fateful day.

In the end she returns to the cathedral where the metamorphosis took place, and sees the mild abbess, in whose room the score of the Mass lies open, like a textbook of magic, at the fatal page. A letter from the Pope has just confirmed that St Cecilia intervened six years before to direct the nuns' choir, the sister she personated continuing delirious, attended by another nun. A year later the mother is received back into the Catholic church. Her sons die happily after a few thousand more Glorias.

Of all Kleist's stories it is most betrayed by summary, which reveals the tale's manipulative designs on the reader. It begins by telling events from the iconoclasts' point of view, but at the service it blanks out on them as if in a sort of amnesia. Later we learn that their former consciousness ended there, and they lost their old selves, so that in subjective truth there were no longer any such characters to follow the further history of, a cessation represented in the story by a bland sketch of the convent's vicissitudes until its dissolution a century later, followed by the mother's arrival after an interval.

The iconoclasts' later behaviour is more seemly and civilized than that which they were thwarted in, has not been imposed by physical force, but by sweet feminine agency, and is still, as the mother feels, terrible, because utterly unchanging, and unresponsive to its surroundings. It is worship as a form of death.

Our response is more divided than the facts seem to warrant. The mother's conversion is a way of acknowledging the hypnotic pull which this vision of the death of the self exerts. Though a religious phenomenon of some sort, the youths' conversion cannot be accommodated by the church, is not recognized or sponsored by it, which gives their piety a purer psychological status. The fact that it has a clinical name distances the new identity or non-identity from either demonic possession or true if obsessive belief.

If the story is showing us that spirits control the world, they are malevolent, but it seems nearer to the style of its crooked and deceitful unfolding to conclude that the mind contains fatal weaknesses within itself, and has a significant potential for bringing about its own demise. Religion, in this view, is simply the human construct by which we are most likely to be defeated, because it is our way of discussing our vulnerability.

At Hawthorne's moment, if not permanently, American literature appears to be out of synch with European, in relation to which the romancer of Salem occurs almost a generation late. In some ways he fits most naturally with the creators of philosophical fictions who include Wordsworth, Blake, and Kleist. But if like them he is an anthropologist of, more than a participant in, the antique superstitions he catalogues, unlike them he seems at the deepest level hardly to have moved on from Spenser and Bunyan. Most of his stories are tinged by an overpowering nostalgia, not for childhood, but for old age now lost, as if the usual progress of life was to grow up into the insecurities of youth.

Although they are in many ways antithetical types as artists and as men, Kleist and Hawthorne are alike in this: that they feel impelled to disown much of what attracts them, and that their most fervent moral assertions violate their instincts and temperaments, so that they give inverted representations of their true selves. Hawthorne expresses a terrible fear of being separated from the group. The devil's cleverest way of damning a soul (in 'Young Goodman Brown') is to make a young man think he's spied on respected elders worshipping evil, so that when he returns to civilization after this Walpurgis night in the woods he is alienated by the belief that he sees through people's goodness. The separate individual is Hawthorne's archetypal protagonist, separate as if diseased, carrying some secret he cannot share, or draped in an obscuring veil which frightens children and makes sensitive ladies leave the room. Such alienation is presented as the most awful curse, usually self-inflicted. The silliest case is Wakefield, the unimaginative Londoner, who tells his wife he'll be away three days, and then moves into a house in the next street. For twenty years he watches her from a short but uncrossable distance as she grieves, recovers, and stays relatively young as he grows old.

Hawthorne *says* that Wakefield is a fool, who loses life and warmth for a senseless prank, but most readers will feel that Wakefield is substantially Hawthorne, his strength and weakness as an artist being that he is cut off from life and returns to survey it from nearby like a ghostly visitor.

This may sound like a circumstantial description of the artist's position in any provincial society, but Hawthorne isn't much like Jane Austen. Outside the town boundaries in Massachusetts one found, instead of a progression of similarly enclosed worlds and eventually London, a vastness with its incidental delights and central terrors, savage Nature and savage man. Which goes some way to explain why the attraction-repulsion to Puritan society is more aggravated in Hawthorne than in any other writer of comparable mildness. He is allied on the one hand with writers in acute spiritual crisis like Kleist, and on the other with visions of the world exfoliating comfortably from stable poles of allegory like Spenser's.

The resting places or Houses which *The Faerie Queene* recurs to have their parallel in a kind of Hawthorne story which is essentially an elaborated image, a maypole, mantle, birthmark, or enclosed garden, around which the characters are symmetrically arranged. There are other stories without such powerful pictorial focus, which tend even more to static pattern – the four old people in 'Dr Heidegger's Experiment' are shown seated round the table which holds the crystal goblet from which they will drink the rejuvenating fluid. In that type of tale there is a tendency for the organizing image to disappear or to turn into a notion, as if Hawthorne were happiest when he can get the bodies to vanish.

Likewise, he is most moved by pieties detached from creeds and by guilt which stems from misunderstanding of a blameless or neutral act, so that you have the penalties of crime without needing to commit one.

One can fairly say that imagination and the senses which nourish it are the enemies in Hawthorne, where evil is presented as physically more vivid than its rival. 'The May-pole of Merry Mount' is the most frontal statement of this impossibility, impossible for how it deprives the artist of joy in the seasons and colours of the world.

A bizarre remnant of pagan England has found refuge in the woods, where escapees from Salem re-enact the vanished rural festivals, dressing in finery, disguising themselves with masks, playing, and dancing. In other words allowing transmuting powers of fiction to have their way. Hawthorne cannot indulge in this riot deep in a Spenserian Wood of Error without feeling it monstrous. In the story pleasure is killed by a group of grey Puritans who have stolen up on the hideout and pop out of the bushes just as the young Lord and Lady of May are about to be married. They tear down the maypole and disperse the revellers. There is no room on the new continent for alternative communities; Hawthorne's imagination is not really dialectical, but reductive, and strives for a triumph of one of the warring forces over the other.

His melancholy is perhaps not something of which we should expect easy explanation, yet at moments like this we feel it might spring from such suppressions, as if we have watched him kill pleasure in himself by this figure of exterminating it in the wilderness. Elsewhere we find a recurring effort to identify beauty and disease, as if by turning things into their opposites to convince oneself of the correctness of one's perverse beliefs. This inversion produces two of his most powerful stories, 'Lady Eleanore's Mantle' and 'Rappaccini's Daughter', both of which leave more room for the exotic than he ordinarily does. They are both more full-blooded, *and* more artificial or Gothic, than the bulk of his works, as if in this writer vividness and falsity went hand in hand, and rhetoric always cast a blight on richness.

Hawthorne is the sort of storyteller who likes to give his products Romantic pedigrees, in order we might suppose to put them beyond the reach of criticism, or, if we did not know he was a Puritan, in a typical gesture of the relic-monger. 'Lady Eleanore's Mantle' is the story of a profane relic, the magical garment contrived by a dying witch to make a young woman fatally attractive. Except that the special piece of cloth can no longer be worshipped or stared at in horror, because, we learn at the end, it was consumed by fire. To bring us to that conclusion is to snatch palpable satisfactions abruptly from our grasp, a purpose achieved more gently by the receding pair of tellers, like a voice growing fainter. Plying him with old wine, the group meeting in an old inn cajole from an old inhabitant this fragment of local history.

Lady Eleanor is an arrogant cousin of the colonial governor, who arrives like a cargo of foreign, almost Babylonian, luxury, and makes an uncanny impression at a ball by flaring hot and cold, seeming to give and withhold herself. Having fascinated and repelled the province, she is found to be the carrier of plague in the form of smallpox, which embroiders the face obscenely as the witch did the garment from which the infection stems. The wilful rhythms of Eleanore's behaviour match the incipient stages of fever. Illness looks like heightened life in its early phases, and draws adherents in its wake.

Hawthorne's nearest approaches to religious intuitions unveil anti-cults, in paranoid discoveries of a web of evil threaded through a society, an individual's body, or his motives. This writer found himself powerfully hypnotized by what he identified as evil. To him it felt like being drawn to worship the devil.

On the other hand the failing he most often castigates is cold egotism, with such insistence that we recognize the writer himself in these depictions of narcissists wrapped up in themselves. Thus in a story called 'Egotism, or The Bosom-Serpent' he broaches the surprising theory that everyone chronically ill is an egotist.

The curse of such a temperament is the inability to worship *anything*, or to look up from the self long enough to let external reality make itself warmly felt. Perhaps the idea of worship and the sense of evil are so strangely linked in Hawthorne because worship threatens to carry one out of oneself, breaking the charmed circle of self-absorption.

Unlike Kleist, Hawthorne repeatedly writes about the artist, in the unexpected figure of the scientist, who to many might appear his antithesis. In his stories the figure of an abstracted experimenter, frequently old, recurs, probing spiritual and physical process without regard for the human beings who form his material.

Dr Heidegger doesn't attract much censure because he only brings out the evil dormant in his old victims. The experimenter in 'The Birthmark' ruins his own universe by his insistence on removing the blemish from his beloved. The most interesting of all is Rappaccini, a lapsed physician, drawn into the study of poisons, who ends by setting his precious daughter off from the rest of mankind.

'Rappaccini's Daughter' depicts an Eden or anti-Eden (but the original Eden too is an anti-Eden, a treacherously beautiful place in which things go wrong) set like a trap for innocence to wander into. A student from another part of Italy takes a room overlooking a walled garden inhabited by an old man and young girl. In some uncanny way the girl *is* the garden; and the wizard her father is tampering with her. The most beautiful and alarming plant, placed at the centre, whose colouring resembles hers (rich, blood-derived purpled), is her special care. In fact it is a hybrid devised by her father, which appeared the day she was born and is linked to her survival: if it is pulled up, she will die and vice versa. Like her it is extremely poisonous, and kills the insects lured by its perfume.

But this story's mystifications, not its certainties, make it involving: can the plants really be poisonous? Does the maiden cause natural flowers, from outside this protected realm, to wither, or have we imagined it? At first the garden looks impregnable, but the hero forces his way in, believing he eludes the yellowed old father. Soon he discovers his visits are an experiment overseen by the wizard. What is their object? To swallow him up, his death contributing to the nurture of the plants?

The garden isn't as honestly malign as that, a fact which allows for the subtlest cancelling in the working out. The daughter has remained innocent of soul while the father fills her body with poison, so she wishes the youth well, and truly loves instead of luring him. As a result he is slowly acclimated to the poisoned air and becomes almost as lethal as she to life outside. A good doctor at war with the bad one gives the youth an antidote to rescue the girl from the garden, not realizing that by this time the youth is poisonous too, and apparently not foreseeing that just as poisons are benign to her, cures will be malign. The antidote kills her, and leaves the hero alone in the empty garden.

It is untypical among Hawthorne's stories for its foreign setting and utter absence of consoling moral. It makes one wonder if the true Hawthorne is more irresponsibly manipulative than readily appears, enjoying inversions for their own sake, and engineering alchemical transfers of strength from persons to things, so that characters are swallowed up in vaguer auras, like the girl dispersed into the garden, a permanence only achieved at the expense of life.

This notion of art as a method of preserving its subjects by killing them is the Romantic extension of a fairy tale motif to encompass the production of the tale as well as its constituents. Hawthorne's power and his modernity lie in a superstitious mistrust of his own function, so that the circumlocutory style, by which one will never be ruffled, the home-returning rootedness of his subjects, and the un-Kleistian slowness, are undone by misgivings about the fictionist's trade, which surface also in his ambivalence toward his main themes. Hawthorne's credulity and indecisiveness are his greatest strengths as a storyteller. The allegorist finding rigid systems in the world outside is finally a man unsure of his own mind.

For private reasons which are well known, Franz Kafka was able to give even more extreme form to this dilemma, which resembles that of the Gothic heroine, in which one has become a timid victim and finds all power lodged in an enemy to whom one is at the same time intensely attracted.

Kafka is torn between a very inward sense of the individual's plight and an effort to objectify his view of this apparent suffering, which leads him to such strong self-repudiations that few readers have had the stomach to follow him, so that these parts of his stories remain forbidden territories of feeling.

His stories are like machines running down, which put up a brave front, pretend not to recognize how serious the threat to their bare continuance, and hatch unworkable plans for how the future will be better than the past, except that from time to time the hero lets something slip which shows he has already made every capitulation internally.

Their poignancy often derives from complicated backsliding along the downward course. Although these protagonists are very weak, they do not give up easily. There are many stages between finding that one is a large beetle and agreeing that it will be best if one quietly removes oneself. We cannot even say that *Metamorphosis* describes Gregor's acceptance of the fact that for all his humane urges he is repulsive, for he has always felt it. From the beginning he contained within himself two opposed perceptions: that he had tender feelings and good instincts, that inseparable from his self were horrible sticky secretions, uncontrollable leglets, and senseless cravings to roam the walls and ceiling.

By certain unlucky accidents also physical (the twittering which drowns his words) the good in him is hidden from everyone else, and gradually those outside cease to connect his lost goodness with his present unredeemed self, and after tolerating him a while, openly wish for his extinction. At almost any moment the critic can reduce this drama to sordid proportions: the fate of one mediocre family (whose leader acquires importance by becoming a bank messenger) can look very tiny indeed. And yet the fate of a soul is the most momentous of questions.

The old melodramatic struggle has been internalized, though imperfectly. One is now the monster oneself, safely locked in the castle, but still, somehow, able to terrorize the inhabitants. One is also the forlorn and unfriended prisoner, to whom the whole world has become alien, like a race of unfeeling giants. Except that one's tormentors are not unfamiliar

Italians, but one's nearest and dearest, the oldest inhabitants of consciousness, too much part of oneself to be expelled.

The need to externalize born of these enmeshed dependencies
produces strange diagrams in place of feelings and the family. Apparently
there are three doors to Gregor's room, one for each of the other
members, like the three bears' bowls. At one point his father barks from
behind the one on the left, while his sister sobs behind the one on the right,
as if each has one of his ears, a negative image of Gregor's divided self.

Similarly, in 'The Judgment' the father hits on a powerful vision of
Georg's distant friend, who is seen holding the father's letters up to the
light with his right hand, while crumpling Georg's unread with his left. It
is an absolute distinction, like a legal judgment, which is at the same time
linked to the body and therefore natural. That is why in spite of its parodic
exaggeration, more like something on the Yiddish stage Kafka liked than
ordinary behaviour, it feels irrefutable.

There is a strong urge in Kafka toward such intellectual tidiness, which
is always liable to grow into something more, to attract belief, like the
surviving fragment of a vanished creed, or the seminal one of a creed yet
to emerge. The two aren't so far apart: embryonic intimations of
something which is almost certain to abort, or the tail end of a complete
system which now lacks believers, these are the two forms in which
Kafka's metaphysical orders occur, and both only whet without satisfying
one's appetite, inconclusive and nostalgic like de Chirico's paintings.

Kafka's great charm comes from his knack for normalizing metaphysics, making us feel that producing fine distinctions is like keeping up
appearances – Gregor falls with a *thud*, which could not be called a *crash*
– an expenditure of thought which is likely to be swept away the next
minute by some crudeness in the world's response, but gives one an
intense comfort while it lasts. The solidest-looking mental structures will
collapse, including those no one else could have an envious stake in and
therefore wish to threaten.

At the beginning of 'The Judgment', for example, Georg has just
finished a letter to his friend in Russia, but as he sits dreaming he unthinks
first the letter and then the friend, until nothing is more unlikely than that
he could write a letter or maintain a friendship. As so often in Kafka the
disappearance of the familiar markers of everyday reality – removed by a
dry, close-packed process of reasoning, any step of which is hard to take
exception to – produces a strangely magical feeling. To bring unheard of
things to pass, to cause oft-heard facts to disappear, these are unexpectedly similar in how they leave us feeling. We are drastically set free by our

ability to de-imagine so much of reality, even if it is a freedom we feel we didn't invite, don't like, and are frightened by.

At the beginning of *The Metamorphosis* there are interludes of normality in which Gregor turns from thinking about how to manage his chaotic legs, his lack of arms, his inflexible shell, and plans how he will get to the office, placate the chief, recover the ground he's lost. Because these boring scenarios depend on impossible assumptions – that he can dress, catch a train, speak to the chief – they are more farfetched than the oddities he leaves them for, which are by ordinary standards far stranger. Through a peculiar inversion of vision Kafka has convinced us that everyday facts are in some way more unthinkable than the wildest flights of imagination, which are after all an internal matter, giving laws to something which can't choose but obey. While we are under his spell, Kafka makes us believe that, unlike most tellers of tales, he is locked in serious battle with the recalcitrant forces which rule the world.

Sometimes, not often, we wonder if, instead of the most terrible infliction we have ever undergone in art, the metaphysical terror in Kafka's stories is a kind of hoax. The answer is yes (or both, a hoax *and* an infliction). The literary form of the terror is inevitably that of a joke or parody, which is to say that the stories do not present themselves as sacred texts pure and simple, but confess their origin in a single mind, while imitating the form of more generalized emanations. If one could imagine a marriage of Swift and Blake one might come as near as English literature allows to the spirit of Kafka, a profoundly undermining and sceptical intelligence, addicted to parables which make science into magic, allied to metaphysical passion (nearer to Dante than Blake), which is never allowed to enjoy its products properly because some other part of its creator's mind is already busy thinking up a numerous family of opposing cases.

His greatest ingenuities are the destructions of his main dramatic ideas, destructions which he appends to the original notions. Texts so brimful of contradiction can certainly be profound, but they cannot be solemn. The executioner in Kafka is too ready to change places with the victim for that, a metamorphism such as we find in myth, but exaggerated in Kafka as if for an observer who finds even the wildest myths too gradual or static, less mercurial than his unreliable psyche.

Kafka's joking use of scientific style and format is in fact defensive. He takes refuge in patient explanation of how something works to avoid direct confrontation with feeling. Being a bug becomes a series of specific technical problems – how do jaws without teeth work? How does one move this unwieldy object from a higher to a lower plane without damage? Feeling is only apparently missing of course: everywhere denied, it is perpetually on the point of breaking loose.

The most extreme case of this diversionary approach to telling a story is *In the Penal Colony*, which has a central mechanism like one of Hawthorne's. A lecture-demonstration of a beautiful conception has to be given using a malfunctioning remnant. Every crudity or grotesque absurdity in the present state of affairs is somehow an inverse intimation of the old purity, present clutter a sign of former concision.

The absurdity of physical suffering as the doorway to spiritual truth is here doubled. Christ's nailwounds become infinitely multiplied pinpricks which are at the same time the scratchings of a writer's pen. For the punishment ordained in this colony is that the sentence, in the form of a gnomic saying, should be very slowly inscribed on the prisoner, not by a human hand, but by a tracing machine working from drawings inserted in its superstructure. It is a parody of the transmission of culture through written documents handed down from one generation to the next, deified artifice like one of the table fountains or triumphal cars the Elizabethans delighted to eulogize, and also a devilish engine, which makes human cruelty untouchably secure because it has been delegated to a functionary incapable of taking any responsibility itself.

The words occupy only a narrow belt or girdle around the victim's waist but the rest of the body is entirely covered by tattooed embellishment, flourishes which lead away from and return back to the focal band of meaning – 'Honour thy superiors' (for humble guards), 'Be Just' (for judges who've come to doubt themselves). Like all thoroughgoing punishment, this is, in some practical sense, absurd: low prisoners aren't told the sentence, they learn it during the twelve-hour period of its execution, and when they have completely absorbed it, they are dead and are cast into the pit, into which they fall (in the words of a prejudiced onlooker) 'with an incomprehensibly gentle wafting motion'. Judges are inscribed with something terser, though it takes just as long to set down, which they learned by heart long ago. The more intelligent surface needs a different kind of scribbling on, we might have thought. But no, the story says, the same will do for all; though to be embarrassed this way by language suits intellectual types best of all. The story has the air of a revenge taken by Kafka on his own complexity: much refinement is marshalled to exit in bestial cruelty.

Certain stories (*Judgment*, *Metamorphosis*) will always have a special place for Kafka's readers because they give the most nearly autobiographical form of his central myth. But all his fragments are versions of the same story and could be replaced by a single whole. *In the*

Penal Colony contains no father and no son, but is another lament for the disappearance of the father, who was objectively a curse, but also the organizing and dignifying principle of the lives subjected to its crushing influence.

Only through the father does a son get his intimation of a transcendent order. So each story is part of the hollow depression left by a vanished fulness, an empty tomb or perhaps one stone of a sepulchre whose interred subject eludes us. We gain an inverse impression of size from the distance between Kafka's flat prose and what it aims at, one knows the heroic nature of narrative through the meagreness of these slivers.

In the penal colony all the functions have moved down a rung – the commandant himself used to strap down the prisoner as the officer does today, the judge used to act as guard, a post now filled by the uncouth soldier. The only hierarchies we find beautiful are disrupted or decayed ones. The idea of a centre, the Emperor sending out messages to far distant parts of the Empire, the Law sitting deep within its concentric doors and barriers, such cosmic order only succeeds in touching us because, far from having us under its thumb, it has retreated completely beyond our reach. Kafka has come full circle from narrative's rude beginnings: his gift is to feel with a superstitious intensity the disappearance of myth.

CHAPTER ELEVEN

THE PERILS OF IRONY: STENDHAL, ALAS, MACHADO DE ASSIS, HENRY JAMES

Some of the most interesting nineteenth-century writers occupied themselves with importing back into realistic narrative the abruptness, unaccountability, and magical transformations of myth. The old elements slip by in more or less cunning disguises, and one sometimes finds that scathing and dismissive writers like Stendhal are at the same time the most fantastic and wish-gratifying. Such paradoxical descriptions are deceptive, for paradox is a central technique in the resurrection. Rhetoric can salvage what metaphysics has lost, and we aren't inclined to rigorous questioning of these positive and negative extravagances (myth-making and demolition) if they are witty; they follow on each other's heels with no breathing space between.

A name for Stendhal like Romantic ironist would encapsulate how things are stood on their head and right side up again until one no longer knows which of the conflicting points of view is more extreme. Perhaps the most sophisticated observer comes back to taking the simplest view. But only for a moment, Stendhal's aim being to keep one's standpoint in flux. If (as is the case with the older characters in *Chartreuse de Parme*) one's feelings stay the same, what one proposes to do about them, or their relation to the world, undergoes continual change.

Stendhal mounts insincere defences against imaginary accusations of immorality. The truth is that morality in the conventional sense has been willingly sacrificed in the interest of narrative exuberance. The cover or passport for this relinquishment is the Italian setting, or more literally (but not confessed in his pages), the sixteenth-century chronicles on which he draws. No sixteenth-century original has made anything so positive and hence perverse of such characters' wilful gratifications, like a counter-morality with which to berate the nineteenth century.

Only naïve readers, however, will suppose that Stendhal's anti-morality is a morality after all, which would survive exportation outside the charmed world of the story. Our lives are neither as consistently game-like (no one will play with the required stamina), nor as profoundly successful as his heroes'. *Chartreuse de Parme* attempts to conceal how many things are going right for these characters by how much it causes to go wrong.

Pinning down this work is like wrestling with mercury or a firework: it resembles an old chronicle in its inconsequence – Fabrizio's rash excursion to the battlefield of Waterloo is a shapeless forecourt to the exquisite tangle of ministerial life in Parma, and more or less thrown away, though it is the excuse for intricate plots which follow (the Ultras apparently believing the rumours that this brainless teenager is an important French agent). The heroic escapee is a very Stendhalian idea, like prison as the scene for discovery of one's strongest desires, but neither of these antithetical notions could blossom as fully without the archaic stimulus. This writer psychologizes the sixteenth-century motifs so the rapist becomes a soulful rapist, the bandit becomes a poet of woodlands, but he also preserves the brilliant succession of murders, banishments, and false treaties which he finds in Renaissance sources, and which represents, such is his contrariness, an unrealizably ideal politics.

It sounds a facile primitivism, that poor bureaucratic us would be healthier if we could poison our enemies with more relish. But in Stendhal this is not superficial pretence or affectation. Goaded by who knows what boredom or by the suffocation of ambitions he mistook for political, he retreated into a bristly and sharp-edged dream.

Irony is always a disguise for frustration, like the controlled restlessness of a horse which is basically tamed. Of all writers Stendhal is the one who comes nearest to erecting irony into a philosophical system, or even acknowledging it as a god. Which means that like a horse who thinks he's being given his head, only to be reminded of the bit by occasional sharp tugs, Stendhal appears both the most untrammelled and the most arrested intelligence. Which of two people is he? The Duchess, a victim of passion and loss of self, or Fabrizio the cool ego, representatives of the sixteenth and the nineteenth centuries respectively? – except that in other relations each of them also embodies the contrary. Both of them are drawn toward one love-object and pursued by a different one, so that they appear hot and cold, ruled by heart or head. The Duchess pursues her obsession with Fabrizio through the most rational ingenuity, like a head of state following the nation's interest.

Such confusion between large and small aims (in the world's terms), between diplomats organizing governments and mature women promoting the careers of their boy-lovers, make Stendhal so stimulating as a political novelist. For public and private realms trade places like mirages. This is the greatest beauty of the old chronicles, speaking from a time when the lives of princes *were* the histories of their domains. So the fact that the new prince is shy or squeamish makes itself capriciously felt in how prisoners are guarded and rebels are hung. The administration of justice is rash like human impulse, not predictable like the rotation of a flywheel.

Most of all, the chronicles give Stendhal leave to imagine a world infused throughout by the wilful inconsistency, boundless generosity, and ferocious anger which constitute for him the most precious displays of individuality. A few nineteenth-century imports are allowed into the enclosed realm, unexpected ones like the propensity of newspapers to get things wrong and report that Count Mosca the Prime Minister has been made Archbishop (instead of Fabrizio), substituting one of the main characters for another, and one generation for another, a senseless error unthinkable to anyone on the spot, *and* a magical multiplying of what is possible.

Like the story's most antique and knotted intrigues these absurdities further the author's project of arriving at his own truth by mishandling our sense of fact. The more often and variously it can be violated the more surely we will see what he means, that there is nothing sacred about the nineteenth-century version of reality. So the most sobering experiences will produce a powerful impression of unreality.

Stendhal brings forward archaic social categories: *Chartreuse de Parme* is a story about the high aristocracy, and only allows a distant rumour of the bourgeoisie. But as it was written in a bourgeois century, this is achieved by setting it mainly in a small outdated autocracy. He relishes the arbitrariness of one-man rule (as he does many other arbitrarinesses), which is given a modern shade of meaning – it is another realization of ego. Likewise, 'aristocracy' is an idiosyncratic notion; it is simply the most complete imaginable freedom for the self. So we see, instead of hidebound aristocrats caught in the set of regulations from which they benefit but to which they must pay their allegiance as well, entirely unconventional people who use their position at the top to flaunt society. It is a fanciful, outsider's version of the truth, for no social class would long survive if composed of those determined to violate the pieties on which it rests.

One of the surprising pleasures of the *Chartreuse* is that we *half* believe it, and no more. Just as there is little of such pure and contented selfishness in our world as Stendhal's heroes embody, there is less than little of the ecstatic abjection of his lesser characters, who love being lorded over, insulted, even kicked. A grandiose fantasy of power lies concealed in the contrasts between the highminded, confident, innocent protagonists and their envious, conniving, mercenary opponents. Beneath the sophisticated surface is an infantile model of human behaviour. Because of the social position from which they start, and the strength of their emotions, the main characters are able to proceed without making the slightest concession to the world outside themselves, in spite of living in a despotism which leaves little room for individual expression.

Fabrizio is the younger son of a stuffy old nobleman who plots against Napoleon in blind adherence to his ancient privileges. The boy is an uncontaminated natural aristocrat, who believes in nothing but his own superiority and the supremacy of personal happiness, his own, not that of low rivals he kills without compunction, or of women he has pursued, and then become bored with. This character, whose distinction it is to lack a single grain of respectability, piety, or deference to anything except his own desire, whose course is repeatedly smoothed by women he chances to meet, who are instantly enamoured of him, becomes toward the end of the story Archbishop of Parma, an elevation hastily announced but long forecast.

Perhaps that is Stendhal's boldest joke against authority; nonetheless it is proof of a fascination with rulers. Likewise the Duchess of Sanseverina (as she becomes after a series of promotions matching Fabrizio's capricious rise through the hierarchy), despiser of society, hater of small talk, is the hostess to whose house everyone flocks, whose 'Thursdays' are so important to the welfare of the body politic that the ruler changes ministers and policies to keep her from moving to another city.

Love or amorous attachments govern the characters' political careers. The Duchess is brought to Parma and made a duchess by Conte Mosca, the Prime Minister (who rises from Minister of Police, not the only instance of Stendhal's intellectualizing of secret, cruel power), who falls head over heels for her at fifty in a theatre box. Mosca comes loaded with titles and renown – which he brushes aside to chatter unaffectedly with this amusing lady. He is bored by success, the Court, and Parma, all of which he pursued only to outwit the insolence of the powerful and eliminate the rungs above him. He finds fulfilment in evenings far from home, at La Scala with the Duchess (then still a countess) where he can forget or ridicule his life at court.

Duchesses are the first to admit that the idea of being a duchess is absurd. Yet Stendhal goes on calling his main characters by their titles not their names, a holdover from the most ancient and superstitious kind of story. No amount of ironic disavowal can overturn that simple fact: by continual reiteration it is impressed on us that we are reading about high personages, not ordinary mortals, however often they may attempt to simulate the latter by incongruously low behaviour.

Stendhal finds a number of further devices for having it both ways at once: it is an ordinary story, an extraordinary one. Fabrizio is disguised as a peasant, but is a prince underneath, and those around him make an error which tells a good deal about Stendhal's technique: the rumour gets around that the actress' incognito lover is actually the crown prince. An archaic story which has gone underground can get away with more encompassing delusions of grandeur than one which forgoes such camouflage. This novel by virtue of its nineteenth-century disguises is more unaccountably strange than the sixteenth-century chronicles themselves.

Some of the consequences of Stendhal's duplicity are so bizarre one wonders if he foresaw them or fell into them by lucky accident. When Fabrizio comes back from theological studies in Naples he has an interview with the Prince in which he is tested for the correctness of his opinions. He acquits himself well, expressing absurdly conservative views. After enjoying these extravagances, the reader is told Fabrizio *believed everything he said*, which is impossible. For he was advised setting off not to contest the opinions he would be taught, but to view theology as a meaningless and inflexible system like the rules of whist.

Stendhal wants to include the most complete cynicism and the most unspoiled simplicity in the same character, or bolder still, in the same act. So in one of his escapes Fabrizio's first relaxation is to enter a church as he would a café, and after rejoicing in the quiet, to catch himself in irreligious feeling, then to fall prostrate in an ecstasy of humble devotion, praying, weeping, and lighting seventy or eighty candles to make up for a long period of negligence. The wary reader will observe that this incident is unique in the book, that nowhere else does the future bishop experience a religious impulse. He is occasionally *credited* with one – tired of parties because he's given up hope of Clelia, he's supposed devout. And when he begins preaching as a desperately indirect way of wooing her, he gains a reputation for sanctity which only increases when he loses his voice because she joins the congregation. What delicious jokes against religion, the reader hastens to think, but this would denude the story of some of its complexity.

For the charm of it lies in incongruous mixtures. We may be privy, as his hearers aren't, to secret under-meanings in Fabrizio's sermons, but the love affair acquires its special quality from these elaborate sublimations. Fabrizio spies on Clelia from a dark cell, meets her briefly in a prison chapel, and lures her with sobbing proclamations meant for her alone but delivered for months to large groups of which she is not yet a part.

Fabrizio's preaching is an allegory of the relation between a writer's subject matter and what he really wants to say. All statements are inevitably generalized from their local cause in the speaker's own experience, and to learn the peculiar little causes doesn't simply invalidate the wider meanings, though it casts them in an ironic light. So, in the end, we are given an enthusiastic version and an ironic rebuke which appears to cancel or qualify it, the two phases sometimes presented in reverse order. The effect is more like foil and counterfoil than cancellation: we only learn how eager we are to retain the romantic illusion when corrosive acids of irony threaten to attack it: such threats make whimsies more precious.

In this book religion imparts a magical feeling to sexuality, and superstitious practices give structure to the Romantic ego's black apprehensions about its own continuance. Fabrizio is instructed in the science of omens by the old village priest, by whom astrology is confusingly viewed as a pagan and scientific pursuit. As found in Fabrizio, susceptibility to this kind of thinking is original and unorthodox. The intuitions always take the same form, however: he foresees himself imprisoned. In spite of all signs to the contrary that is his ultimate destiny: he is too good for the world and will be expelled from or raised above it.

The most beautiful expression of this premonition is his surprise visit to childhood haunts and his adoptive father the priest, after a long absence and much success at court. This is a forecast of prison in more ways than one: he finds the priest high above the town in his belfry, where he goes not for prayer but star-study. Like the boy's veneration and tending of a special tree by the lake, which he planted years ago and sees as a kind of alter-ego, this encounter is a heavily disguised negative – far from court, and above human life, which appears ant-size at that elevation; inhuman in its sweeping grasp or lack of personal affect, it is really a way of saying 'I don't need you.'

Such epiphanies are convincing because rare and brief. No one could want Fabrizio to retire to the country for good. When he does, it is a signal that the book will end. And yet the title of the whole novel is taken from the place to which he withdraws three sentences from the close, showing that Stendhal wants to give this idea of retreat from the world more in credence than it can ever have in fictional space. It is used up as soon as uttered. Fabrizio survives his religious seclusion just one year, and the Duchess in turn outlives him very briefly.

The boy's visit to the priest is a foretaste of his incarceration in the famous Farnese tower, as the result of an atrociously complicated intrigue, in which the Prince (his only herioc action) betrays Mosca and the Duchess. It is the central paradox of the book that Fabrizio finds fulfilment in this lonely tower, finally able to forget the Duchess and the court entirely when forced to live apart from them. He can see the Alps from his window and this helps him neglect to be angry or sad and feel a secret contentment.

Then he gets a glimpse of Clelia, whom he met long before, when her father – now the prison governor – for whom Fabrizio had just been mistaken, was arrested. The shoe is on the other foot and pinches delightfully: Fabrizio is kept busy cutting holes in heavy shutters so he can maintain these distant, infrequent glimpses of his shy beloved.

Eventually the Duchess sends signals (lantern flashes) from a corresponding tower, long and tedious letters of instructions, and various ropes and passports, so that Fabrizio ends up fleeing from the sublime happiness he has discovered in prison, only because he will be poisoned if he stays. As he foresaw, as soon as he is out he wants to go back, and spends his days sketching the horrid masonry in which he was shut, so downcast he can't even make conversation with his saviour.

This supersession is the kind of perverse fulfillment Stendhal's imagination seeks: the penalty which so much energy was spent to avoid is now fervently desired by the one from whom it has been taken away. We can predict with absolute safety that goals to which the way is cleared will lose their charm.

No sympathy to speak of is wasted on the older woman who devotes herself to a youth who can finally fool himself no longer about his feeling for her. But Fabrizio's coolness cannot stop the somewhat automated execution of an awful plan. As soon as he was free the Duchess authorized two outpourings of joy: lavish wine rations at her country place, the uncorking of a reservoir at the palazzo in town, flooding the streets of Parma. The second of those was a sign to a patriotic poet hopelessly in love with her to find a way of killing the Prince whose revenge on Fabrizio had now been thwarted.

Thus another catastrophic success occurs, grotesquely misplaced in time. This in turn will breed its own unforeseen effects. Mosca will fall, the Duchess succeed too well at seducing the new Prince, precipitating her departure from the city and absentation from the story. Perhaps one's own wishes are the most dangerous enemies of all, at least if one is able to empower them.

This novel has an insatiable appetite for the unforeseen, and a wonderful fertility in uncovering unexpected purports in the actions it presents. The Duchess comes back from seeing the Prince out the front door, and all the guests imagine her glow is the smugness of great success. Actually, the reader is told, it is the consciousness of danger and risk: she has just played with throwing away everything by pretending she is leaving Parma at the very moment when she has lured royalty to her parties. There is the low, and the mystical or hidden sense of the same act, a disparity something like allegory, whose dark side is a kind of aristocracy in the world of meaning.

But the recherché can become a formula too, and the effort to outwit habit produces new, more intricate customs of its own. It is very startling to hear the rumour that Fabrizio is kept in a cell twenty feet below ground, heavily guarded, denied this and that, when we know he is *high up* in a tower and wrapped in a cloud of sensuality. But the disparity conforms to a pattern: eventually we come to look for the mechanism known as *turning things upside down*.

Another means of evading habits is to rush on before anyone has time to be bored, as if weather on the lake was one's model, drenchings followed by bursts of sun, then more dark clouds, and so on. Preposterous as it may sound, boredom is a nineteenth-century discovery, and Stendhal is the most persuasive indicator of this. One only needs to put him next to Rousseau, with whose intelligence he shares so much. The earlier writer hasn't learned to give the name of boredom to the discontents without obvious cause, like a form of indigestion, to which he is subject.

In Stendhal there's been a further colonization of external reality by malaises of the ego. He pays closer attention to and tries more actively to quiet the wailing of the self. Yet all that tremulous subjectivity hides cleverly beneath the mask that society is the cause of the boredom, when the problem is really that one can't make contact with 'society'. Or, the habit of lumping all human reality other than one's own self in this idea 'society' is the clue to a tremendous imbalance. One is always perilously close to thinking that life *outside* society is possible.

The reader may be very sure that all the dreams of aristocratic independence, living up in a tower, belfry, or castle chamber (surrogates for the Parisian garret in which the book was written? from which Italy seemed far away below indeed), are all antidotes for some disappointment, signs of social ambition ungratified, or of frustration solved by promoting oneself over the heads of all rivals at a stroke, but the book seems blinded to such truths.

Here, however, is pretty certain to lie the secret of the novel's vitality, which is also a bewitching unreliability. More than most writers, Stendhal falls out of love with his inventions, and what seemed the quintessence of adventurousness will the next minute feel entirely tedious. Thus his habit of seeming to retract what he has just said – remember these are Italians and liable to foolish excess: I beg the reader's pardon for boring him with details of false passports etc. To this mind in its negative phases all details are false ones, all documents forged or fabricated. In fact Stendhal goes so far as to identify duplicity and intelligence – the interesting people are frequently occupied in hoodwinking others, and are at the same time spontaneous like the weather, a contradiction resolved in the supremacy of the ego and the impotence of any outside measure to stand up against it.

The book remains charming because it gives so many signs that it doesn't believe its claims of superiority. Somehow its fondest dream is to be taken seriously enough by anyone out there to be kept under police surveillance. If only it mattered to anyone else what papers one read, whom one consorted with, what dubious activities one engaged in. Even here we are in the presence of cerebral fantasy of course. For all its sophistication this is a mind which has next to no idea how the world actually works, and this insulating ignorance sets it free in the most outlandish dreaming.

Stendhal's irony is a kind of reality-insurance which allows him to take foolhardy risks, one element in a simultaneous affirmation and denial. For something nearer the standard idea of how irony works we might turn to Flaubert or to studies of provincial life like Leopoldo Alas' *La Regenta*. Alas was a professor of law in Oviedo in northern Spain, who wrote two novels, but was mainly known as an impatient, vitriolic critic. Not surprisingly his big novel raised a lot of patriotic and conservative opposition, was bundled out of sight, and had to wait seventy-five years after its publication in 1884–5 for resurrection in a different Spain, by which time it has become a chronicle rather than an attack.

Perhaps time has only completed the work Alas set out to do, for one of the tasks of his irony is to point up the irrelevance and backwardness of what he's writing about. Disparaging one's subject sounds self-defeating, yet resembles withholding a secret, or telling someone he won't be interested in x. What a ridiculous, unworthy place this is, Alas says of the sleeping town, where the only activity is vigorous gusting among the litter in the streets. But there is a sign of former grandeur, the cathedral spire, and in it ... two disgusting urchins like Murillo's beggars, who are joined by a pompous priest with a passion for climbing (ambitious and athletic), who gets out a spyglass and pries into the lives below, using the high perch as an auxiliary to the confessional.

It is a grotesque, emblematic portrayal. Vetusta, former capital, has-been among towns, is still dominated by priests. An outmoded little community of them infests the cathedral, disinterested piety long since fled (if it ever existed), its space filled by vanity, personal ambition, lewdness, and most vivid of all, greed. The great church is a sordid place and also the husk of something better than we can quite imagine. Perhaps the technique isn't utterly unlike parking a car by a redwood. One is far from that height oneself, but one guesses at true grandeur just by looking up from the meanness and backbiting of the current denizens of the sacristy.

Idealists are too late in Alas' world. Long venal habit has too much inertial force to be resisted by one or two romantic individuals. Yet although all is heavily stacked against them, and there is no ultimate hope of success, most of his sympathy is reserved for the quixotic holdouts who play by the rules of chivalry which any cold-headed person can see do not really apply. The novel presents the queer spectacle of an ironist whose favoured characters are haters of ironic scepticism, who would rather lose all than mistrust their ideals. Consequently one knows how every story must turn out here: irony gives the answer, but nothing can make one like it – trust is always misplaced.

Not that idealism isn't seen as a kind of pathology or weakness. We first meet Dona Ana alone and naked in her bedroom among fur and satin, luxuriating in plans for her penance before a handsome new confessor the next day. Religious experience has sexual roots which its partakers don't see. Likewise sexuality is clothed in metaphysical dress: Don Alvaro arriving on horseback offers the way out of a spiritual crisis to Ana suffocating in provincial existence. Such complexity entangles the romantic characters most of all. Materialists like Don Alvaro have an easier time, for there are no internal barriers to realization of one's desires. So the hypocritical relation with the priest is more interesting than the secular seduction: the priest will always be hamstrung by his vows and must find oblique correlatives of desire, though he sees more clearly than the judge's wife what his real aim would be if he could have it.

The book centres on this battle over the soul of a woman, between two bad angels, a perverted piety and a brazen sensuality. To his surprise the reader sides with Don Fermin, the priest who he knows is a robber and self-serving egotist. His superiority to the would-be Don Juan, Alvaro, is that passion masters and shames him and may be an instrument of reform (he will give up his fantasy of becoming Pope). Still, his talk of saving the woman from temptation is a filtered form of jealousy, and his 'love' is never self-forgetful, but in Alas those impeded in their gratifications are morally superior to those who succeed.

In both his novels, accordingly, cuckolds are sympathetic if absurd figures. *His Only Son* takes the spiritualization of cuckoldry to extravagant lengths. The pliable hero devotes himself to a 'son' in whom he finds occult likenesses, but who is biologically if not metaphysically the offspring of his enemy.

Like this 'father', Ana in *La Regenta* is victimized or inspired by literature, made ready for Don Alvaro by an intense poetic experience in the theatre, which he thinks silly but has the wit to take advantage of. What a strange avenue for heroism to traverse in making its entry into modern life. Stendhal's hero became one because of false stories in circulation concerning him. Simply from being *thought* by a girlish admirer, such illusions of real action came to inhabit his looks and gestures. In Alas the big dreams aren't even as solid as hearsay: they are tags taken from books or seen on stage.

Even while belittling such inspiration one recognizes that in a place where the whole achievement of civilization is to make one woman unhappy, stories may represent a way out, the only bolt-hole for the suppressed real self. In Alas the Sirens of literary artifice and those of the unconscious are saying essentially the same thing. All day Ana fights her inclination to sensual excess, and every night her dreams cause her to revel in it. Some force too powerful to withstand is pulling her back toward old motives; it is the revenge taken by whatever primitive impulse is also at work in myth.

If one knew more about Brazil, perhaps Machado de Assis would not continue to seem such a striking instance of the inversion of all conventional expectation. Certainly his career would still have an odd shape whatever one learned: voluminous sentimental production for decades until a bout of serious illness shocked him into the five economical, ironical, and more poignantly autobiographical novels for which he is now mainly remembered. This career is back-to-front, coming to childhood late in life as holding a key; seen, as one might expect, elegiacally, precious because so substantially lost. Which brings us back to the idea of the metropolis and the provinces, an analogue in the history of civilization for a distant past full of allure, set against the barren nearby present.

Brazil has a more convoluted cultural place than most colonies. For one thing the Portuguese court fled there in 1808 to remain thirteen years, confusing by that transfer of cultural memory the previous imbalance between tiny stagnant mother country and gigantic, fermentive colony.

This exile perhaps reinforced the frequently observed tendency of colonial places to cling extra-fervently to the mannerisms of the home society, thus one finds Anglo-Indians more English than anyone in England. Partly because colonials come after and there is a certain interval of transmission, partly because continuity or even inertia has more positive value in a place where civilization feels an insecurely attached veneer or a shallowly rooted plant – for such reasons, the colonial version of the mother-culture is often antiquated, a historical survival.

This by way of accounting for the wonderfully stagnant and effete society portrayed by Machado. For the most pious veneration of European civilization, one should go to Brazil, or so he makes us think. Machado himself is not a simple believer, but this backdrop of piety makes his scepticism possible: his subtlety flickers across the inert and encrusted spires of this frozen civilization.

The partial recluse or onlooker is a common figure in Machado, a sympathetic if elusive presence through whose eyes we gaze. At first the reader ascribes priestly withdrawal to Dom Casmurro of the novel by that name, or to Ayres of *Counsellor Ayres' Memorial*. But they are men over-full of experience, over-cultivated: they know too much to submit themselves to the primary turmoil of human emotions any more.

Yet there is a certain attempt to recapture former involvement vicariously, which these protagonists sense makes them a little ridiculous, because it is a prompting of incapacity. Counsellor Ayres looks on at an intricate drama, an old couple sponsoring a younger one, a happy marriage presiding over unformulated and already half-thwarted longings in younger people, who for various reasons can't acknowledge their mutual attraction. Such is Ayres' own fastidiousness that no one (including himself) is made obtrusively aware that he has fallen in love with the inhibited young woman, whose story retreats even further from the space directly in front of us. Ayres collects the later stages as hearsay from his sister. Finally he erects a memorial to these lives in which he's been a mute participant – an analogue, a shade more vivid, a shade more poignant, of our and the author's relation to these muted simulacra of human existences.

Casmurro's relation to events sounds simpler: the adolescence he surveys is his own. After introducing himself as a dull and comically grumpy fellow, he describes his efforts to join the two ends of his life to each other, leaving over the implication that there is a barren or painful middle, a tract he wants to excise. His first attempt at reconstruction was to erect an exact copy of his childhood home, complete down to the foolish medallions of Emperors painted on the dining room walls, in the suburb in which he lives now. But this failed, and he was led on to another device, the present book, which will re-erect the house and its lives in words.

It is too early to say if it has worked. This version of his past is drastically unbalanced, dominated by a single motif to an alarming degree. He picks out one afternoon in November as the beginning of his life, when he eavesdropped on a conversation about himself. One first imagines that the boy hiding behind the door is four or five years old. He leaves the house, stumbles around the yard in a delightful fog, and finds his way to a neighbour's, where he confronts a girl of his own age. He is in fact fifteen, and what he overhears reveals to him that he has been in love without knowing it. So the 'beginning' is the first stage of self-consciousness, and he is in some sense indeed five *and* fifteen, for his inexperience is childish, and his physical readiness adolescent. He has collected experience while remaining innocent, but now, as a writer, makes a thrilling recovery of intimacy which he didn't understand as it happened.

By a sly deflection, Machado causes the point at issue to appear somewhat different: the narrator's mother vowed at his birth to devote him to the priesthood. Now is the time to send him to seminary. Will he become an onlooker at life, or will he be able to carry on in his relation with the girl Capitu, a perverse and obscure character, more subtle than he, full of ideas for thwarting the grown-up plans?

From early in the book we know that things have gone wrong for the narrator. His position as he speaks is more like a priest's than Capitu's lover or husband's, yet he doesn't seem to *be* a priest. The part of his life he wants to forget is in fact missing, as it will remain until the novel's very last pages, at which point we will appreciate how carefully it was withheld. The book's final irony is that his mother's plan, which he seemed successfully to evade, dedication to a solitary, contemplative life, was the course he would eventually follow anyway, after a sustained trial of the opposite one.

At the beginning of the story the household consists of three widowed persons, a hanger-on of unknown provenance, and a child. As the hero says, it is a strange house, enshrining not completion or hopelessness, but a limbo-state, a life charmed or suspended. The way the story is told, youth is assimilated to this condition with untoward speed, as though the entanglement with Capitu were a detour, taking him outside the family and his proper milieu.

One of the narrative's distinctive features is its skittishness: it consists of short bursts, as if the author in spite of premature ageing and congenital melancholy is still deeply possessed by the impatience of youth. The story is told by the child of a stagnant, overprotective home, but takes a perverse, changeful form, antithetical to this establishment, like Capitu, the feminine nature whom the protected child Betinho finds outside the gate.

The mystery is that this profoundly widowed story should be related by such an un-widowable voice, resulting in opposing sets of signals: the lugubrious pattern of events (a boy breaks out of the burdened vision of his church mouse mother, is betrayed by the new attachments he forms, and returns after the early demise of the deceivers to a stasis like the one he started from, taking all widowhood, formerly spread over four of them, on himself).

Against this is played his irrepressible voice, that of the indecisive projector of a 'History of the Suburbs', an idea which suits him well, being all periphery and no core, staccato bits without lateral interconnection, which can be taken up and put down as the whim strikes. He is a failure who hasn't given up, who never finishes but who never definitively abandons his pursuits, the secret of whose continuing vitality is really this knack of slipping off the point, remaining a person to whom life doesn't quite happen, and in an odd way eternally young.

Henry James is well known for a perverse cultivation of the reader's uncertainty as to whether a certain event has occurred, even whether anything at all has. Testing his later stories too closely against day to day reality, one risks finding them hoaxes: they leave us hanging so completely, gasping for some real air or firm statement. His enterprise is deeply paradoxical, to reach the general through the particular, the ineffable through the material, the absent through the present. Pointing out the hopeless contradictions in his material is only to recognize what his purpose is.

The heroine, as he would call her, of *The Wings of the Dove*, for example, is more a vacated centre with reference to which other things are aligned than she is an actuality. Perhaps in an older version of the narrative she would have been the main pivot of the story, but here she has receded in the fog of memory to become a half-faded notion. Kate Croy, a secondary gear-wheel, but the motive element, in the main engine working on the heroine, is more vivid, more in evidence.

From the Preface written a few years later, rather than from the book itself, we gather that the heroine Milly Theale meant an unbearable, inexpressible lot to James. She is someone nearing the end when we meet her, the carrier of an unidentified fatal disease. And she is also someone just starting out, young and powerful (which is to say rich), who hasn't begun to live, all eagerness, innocence, and promise. She embodies an idea, which is, depending on where one seizes it, cruel, sad, or non-existent.

The plot's mainspring is the devilish plan of a spritely young couple for the man to seduce Milly, snag her money, wait for her death, expected momentarily, and then marry his present fiancée. To make an unconscionably long story shrink to nothing – this plot works, and doesn't work. The dying girl guesses their perfidy, or so we guess. The young man's final interview with her, in Venice, retreats from our gaze: marvellous and terrible exchanges take place from which we are excluded.

Only later we find we have jumped to conclusions: Milly still had not died when Densher left Venice, for news of her death has just arrived in London now. Was it heartlessness or delicacy which sent him away? Or the dashing of his hopes? Has the dove finally folded her wings? or spread them all the wider so that every character in the story can creep into their protective shadow? It is the beauty of the Jamesian deflected telling, that no one can say for sure. Milly has shrunk to a kernel or exploded to an aura; she is nowhere, or everywhere.

Certainly she invades Densher's consciousness more and more, but in the most trivially material form: she has written him a letter. It arrives late, and we deduce that it dates from the remote past, when she was strong enough for such efforts, and was saved for a moment when she knew the end was upon her, then sent. We deduce this from its existing at all, not from its contents. For no one ever reads it. Densher gets it, but cannot profane the seal – because reading the letter privately would be a betrayal of his fiancée Kate Croy? Or because his reverence for Milly has grown, until the relic thrills, frightens, and defeats him? In any case he hands it unopened to Kate, who pitches it into the fire.

This however is not the end of the matter. Densher is haunted more and more by the idea of the letter's lost contents. His solitary brooding on the unrecoverable message is a secret void dividing him from Kate. In the meantime a second letter has arrived from New York. It can be inferred that it comes from Milly's lawyers, but in another sense it comes from further back in her past, for she was a New Yorker. It can also be inferred that it duplicates in an official form the happy news of the first, telling Densher how far the dove's wings stretch, that is, how much money she has left him. Again he turns it over to Kate, again he trusts her not to open it, but this time she does. It was his plan that it should be returned unopened to New York, as a way of renouncing the fortune, and undoing the effect of not-opening its predecessor.

He refuses to learn what the letter contained, and on that disparity of knowledge his and Kate's relation founders. Kate correctly surmises that this renunciation means he has fallen in love with the idea of the dead girl and is therefore lost to her. The novel's famous last line, 'We shall never be again as we were,' sounds like a truism, yet expresses the grimmest disillusion: the voice of corruption recognizing and sentencing itself.

At the core of James' stories is a melodramatic death-struggle between angelic and demonic forces, in which the reward is ... money. These fights are attenuated, and the most effective weapons are charm, breeding, and refined intelligence. James has been censured for blurring moral distinctions: his villains are lively, his saints are smug, and their moral valency seems at times to ossify into an unthought constant. The more interesting issue is really the profound ambivalence in James' relation to worldliness. The World, which is to say the social hierarchy, the elaborate richness of invidious distinctions he came to Europe to sit in the middle of, continues to awe him. Is it fair to strip away from James' fictions their disguises of art and memory – gorgeous ceilings, ancient pedigrees, and the chain of lives stretching back? To strip all this away and reveal underneath dominance, cruelty, spiritual denseness?

The wings of the dove are her enormous financial resources. Money is a surprisingly easy subject to euphemize; most of us do it constantly, but James is in a different class. Many ways of being civilized come very nearly down to money, and its deployment is perhaps our principal means of extracting deference from others. Should we thank an imaginer, then, for mystifying an already mysterious subject still further? Thank him for confusing this disembodied yet material power with spiritual goodness? We have heard it said that the pivotal significance accorded to money in Henry James shows that it can't be literal money which is meant, that it is a metaphor for opportunity, for unrealized potential, for spiritual freedom, for the power to imagine, and so on.

One must grant that meanings are unusually liable to inversion in Henry James: a 'splendid' woman will seem a monster, a fortune hunter become a hermit. But these anomalies are signs of the struggle in him between the good and bad selves, between the snob and the lonely spiritualist. His endings are always the same, though perhaps *The Wings of the Dove* combines the strong and the indecisive more starkly than some others. The typical Jamesian resolution is a form of turning the world over to the dead, resolving all human choices by claiming nothing for oneself and the ones one admires. Complete renunciation is the only form of absolution available, but this is perhaps no more interesting or meaningful than choosing death. Perhaps someone as distracted by the world (in the sense above) as James has been, has a better reason for preferring death than most of us, but it seems a defeat nonetheless.

CHAPTER TWELVE

TRANSCENDENCE IN PROUST

If one stands a little way back from it or isn't attending closely, Proust's narrative seems a disordered flood of images or a delirium, which has drawn so many random sensations into its train that it reassembles the world out of order, attributing wrong causes, retaining vanished facts (inhabitants of memory alone now), hopping from Venice to a corner of Combray to a city in the East the author will never see. But close-up, or studied in detail, the fabric appears interconnected like a philosophical discourse. One could expatiate on these connections, yet perhaps one would need to say at last that they are more like poetry than prose, though it is a grand mental project of unification and not a sleepy fog which engenders them.

Like the book, the first page, a child waking, is steeped in colours of evening – though about youth, it is not young, but looks back on summer from winter, on day from dusk. Its most painful inclusion is passed off casually – for an instant the child's troubled waking has a point of contact with the neurasthenic's sleeplessness in his strange hotel. So the unhappy Proust of the present flits before our eyes in a lighthearted disguise, before returning us abruptly, not quite the same as we were, to the child's forecast of such a state.

Both ends of life are thrown together, and even more. This waking is a model of birth, and this sleep a model of death, one is newly carnate and loses an earlier body and life, one is spread over a landscape by the train's whistle, as if drawn forth to bridge the space the sound has crossed and to make an answering journey oneself. The fluidity of this mind plays havoc with the boundaries of narrative; they have had to change to accommodate it.

The scale of his work is different from all others. It is longer, and perhaps its difference really comes down to *how much* longer than other books it is. There are of course more telling measures of its difference. The easiest to perceive and most constantly felt is the length, or passage, of single sentences. The whole can appear endless; its smallest parts also in their way approach endlessness, which isn't to say they don't end, but cause us to wonder for a time if or when they are going to, marvelling at their continuance and far from wishing for their close, because like some Protean creature we have happened to get hold of, they keep changing for as long as we hang onto them.

Proust's sentences fall into recognizable patterns, it cannot be denied, but it was his main discovery to extend the basic unit of thought as if he had invented a new musical form. His preoccupation with music is no accident, as it is the art in which (and especially in the decades preceding his own book) sensations of barely differentiated expanses stretching away from one in every direction are most at home, in which progressions are more strongly felt and harder to grasp than they are in books.

Proust establishes archaic structural armatures which have almost the stiffness of religious dogma, like the two contrasting paths, the Méséglise and Guermantes Ways, the walks of different length and character, which therefore suit different kinds of day, are common and extraordinary, are bordered by their own species of plants, and stand for distinct realms of the author's mental life, as if they corresponded to the two sides of his brain or two human faculties.

He establishes them, then seems to lose them, starts down one of the paths, dawdles, forgets, resumes the thread without apology after digressions lasting pages, and finally when the other path is much more than forgotten, when it has been buried by ranges of fresh sensation, sets off on this second journey as if (which is evidently the case) he had always meant to return and to devote as much or more attention to the neglected member of the pair.

The reader now realizes that Proust's memory works in longer and more gradual curves than he has encountered before, that one of the pleasures of the book will prove to be how much time there is for things to be forgotten, to lie idle, before they need to be resumed. These resumptions are redemptive, and we do not even feel the oblivion from which the mislaid material is rescued to be a contrived one. We have not been conscious of their waiting outside the gate, wondering if they will be called, and we have a greater sense of the generosity of the mind which summons them, than if we had felt them waiting. The burden of suspense fell completely on the contriver, who carried a faint consciousness of the meaning delayed through the whole contrasting section, a labour we appreciate retrospectively, and therefore without pain.

The two ways are an old-fashioned kind of pattern, and not the only time Proust reminds one of Dante or Bunyan. He is a writer who would dearly love to find a cosmic order like Dante did in his experience, but gets for the most part only glimmers of it, which one trusts at one's peril, as one doesn't try to climb on stone walls reflected in water. There are moments, however – of extreme brevity it is true – when he produces all over again sensations we thought dependent on weird old structures of belief, and consequently separated from us by centuries. So in the narrator's first sight of Gilberte, divided from him by the stream, all his senses rush to the windows of the eyes, and his personified gaze dreams of carrying off this body, and with it the soul. Such is the intensity of the sensation that it slips imperceptibly into something like medieval allegory, in which faculties or portions of the self carry on independent negotiations with other persons, producing an effect not of creaking machinery but of rash or headlong directness.

When the narrator has just met the great writer Bergotte and is wondering if his own conversation seems absurd to the master, he pulls himself up with the reflection that he should have recalled, but did not at the time, that the same intelligence which admires Bergotte produces the reflections he supposes Bergotte despises, so that on the contrary the writer must have understood them, because the world is informed by a single intelligence toward which all individual minds turn as the members of an audience toward the stage. This is what I should have remembered and didn't, he repeats.

It is a frequent gesture in the book, to say that there was a way of resolving the difficulty the narrator was having, but it wasn't available, with the stress laid equally on the tranquil solution and the boy's ignorance, as if both are true and equally comforting. Or, an even more complicated allocation of forces: 'I didn't know then, *nor have I since learned* how to analyse a strong impression into its components,' which appears to say much time has passed, and I have not improved; I'm still back where I was. But this admission is uncandid to a degree, for the two states are subtly but greatly different, the second *understanding itself* as one which won't be improved on, and taking secret satisfaction in the fact. Some failures are badges of authenticity, or the natural offspring of enthusiasm, Proust's unconfessed god.

There are still other forms for bridging the difference between the past and present, one of them seen at its boldest in the mournful proclamation that the narrator will never be a writer. This goal is announced in the first volume, and has been nursed for some while when we first learn of it. Like many themes in the book it is one whose importance will grow and grow from this unpromising seed. At first the idea of being a writer produces only an alarming mental blank. The narrator is never more conscious of powerlessness than at these moments of trying to call up or test his powers, in front of a sight he abruptly decides he wants to record.

Yet we have a further perspective on this, of which we are blessedly not reminded by him. The would-be artist, accepting that this career is not to be, reaches us through the words of his later self. 'I returned, and there he was, gone!' (as a native functionary in British Malaya is reported to have said). The burden Proust places on Writing, as the validation of self and reality, is uniquely heavy, yet he only lets the pressure be felt indirectly. The possibility is always strongly present, though never with reference to the work we are now reading, that it is through art above all that we become fully real, giving the work and its creator awesome responsibility.

So one might single out all the artists, artists *manqués*, and artistic frauds the work contains, finding in the process that a large proportion of the whole cast fits here in one aspect or another. Many readers' favourite will be the musician Vinteuil, *composer* one would hardly dare to call him at first. Not because he wasn't a great artist, but because that was a later discovery of the disbelieving narrator, who knew Vinteuil first as a village organist and pathetically doting father, boring people with talk of his so-called compositions, which no one in that setting had the patience to hear or the originality to understand.

Swann, the great example in the book of one who should have been an artist and is not, finds himself in pursuit of Vinteuil's sonata, as of an elusive woman, but does not know what he is looking for, because no one else listened closely, because the composer's name is unknown to the guests where it was played, because Swann can describe but not hum the phrase when he meets real musicians who might recognize it. For it is only the smallest fragment which has transfixed him, a single phrase consisting of half a dozen notes, which flits by him and is gone, inspiring pages of emulative description which chase it persistently without hope of true recovery.

Though a hopeless task, it is one from which Proust refuses to shrink. Those unaware of the fact will not easily accommodate that Chopin, and not Wagner or Bruckner, is the musician Proust cares most about recovering or rendering in words. Chopin the miniaturist, as he is sometimes stupidly regarded, because his best works are short, not week-long operas with large beefy casts. Proust's depictions of Chopin's music are among the most original translations of this kind, and they reveal that Chopin does indeed have many points of contact with this writer's art, in balancing clear-headed and swooning impulses, almost running them together, and in the heavy reliance placed on the untoward or unexpected, which is not shocking by its loudness or intrinsic character, but solely by its placement, so that one has the impossible sensation of a stealthy bizarrie. It is as if, for those who know where to look, there are unplumbably vast depths, while for many there is only a bland surface to be skipped over. Not of course that Proust and Chopin are *alike* in this, Chopin's greatness being more imperceptible and mistakable, his success being (as Proust admits) more complete, in achieving the goal which matters more to the writer – of concealing great intellectual power, veritably philosophical clarity of vision, in seemingly effortless limpidity of surface, as if one were really letting the words *go*, in a long-drawn-out sigh or expulsion of breath.

Swann's artistic nature comes out, then, as does the narrator's, in a *response* to art; one can also be an artist in that. It is art which makes Swann recall and resolve to take up again his old project of creating something, it is art which makes him dissatisfied with society. The relation between Swann and the narrator is one of those uniquely Proustian subtleties so long drawn out, yet so inundating in those few moments when it is most felt, that it must have inspired other writers with the idea of writing equally long books in which meanings as important as this could be left undeclared as long as this one is left, so that at a relatively late moment the reader finds he's been collecting evidence unawares, of something which he is now ready to prove conclusively.

It is paradoxically as a labour-saving or labour-concealing device that Proust's obliquity achieves its most enthralling effects, and although it has sometimes been said that this obliquity and the bursting into consciousness of connections between seemingly remote bits of our experience, is like life, that learning often surprises us or unfurls already complete like illegitimate children we had forgotten, I think the opposite is the case, and that these miracles of comprehension are extremely far from what we can normally expect, corresponding only in an unimportant aspect to life as we find it. That is to say that we often experience the longing for things to knit themselves up, and the multiplicity of the world to consolidate itself into a more compact arrangement. So Proust contrives that one of the oldest dreams of art should seem to come true by a series of accidents, which feel more natural or spontaneous than the coincidences of melodrama, because he locates them in the characters' consciousness rather than in external events, and they become perspectival in appearance. Swann did not realize that the Vinteuil of the sonata was the Vinteuil of Combray, so we are able to overlook an incredible convergence in the realm of fact, because we are so much more interested in this supposed error of interpretation. Looking at it this way, one can see that

Proust has removed his melodramatic contrivance from scrutiny by veiling it in the dubieties of the mind's working.

Swann is the narrator's avatar in the previous generation, though Marcel is a long time realizing this. They are like each other and unlike almost everyone else in placing high value on intellectual pursuits, but also in having strayed from them or been too weak-willed to devote themselves to them. Perhaps the explanation is rather that passion overpowers this inclination in both, for the first point of contact between them (leaving aside that Swann has been better known to the narrator's family at some point in the past than he is now) is the narrator's senseless infatuation with a girl he does not yet know to be Swann's daughter.

Both Swann and the narrator are men who can be described or identified by their infatuations, who are ruled by love, which obliterates the refined aestheticism which would otherwise be the dominant strand in their characters. As Swann has foolishly loved the unintelligent courtesan Odette, the narrator loses countless hours in dreaming of her heartless, soulless daughter.

But the first story is told without cognizance of the second. Swann is not announced as the narrator's model. In fact some of his resemblances to Proust are suppressed in the book, but confirmed by what we know from outside it of its author. Swann's Jewishness is half erased, the first mention of it inserted after our notion of his character has formed and hardened, so that it never takes an influential part in it. In the story the narrator is not half Jewish, as Proust was, just as his persona in the book is not homosexual, though much more interested in the subject than a non-homosexual is likely to be.

One can hardly say that these subjects are avoided, or even disowned. The Dreyfus affair looms large in the later volumes, and the writer's sympathies are never in doubt. Instead of camouflaging his true feelings on these tricky subjects, Proust disguises his personal stake. And one cannot feel it was a cowardice, or even an insincerity, to do so. It is consistent with his desire to find less involving or parochial forms in which to cast the issues that interest him, that he should show an exhaustive panoply of perverse sexualities without depicting himself as a partaker.

Similarly many themes of his own character are announced first in Swann, and are in fact not repeated so extensively in the author's own experience. The affair with Odette which serves as a model for the narrator's with Albertine that follows, is not, as any reasonably witting reader is bound to consider the Albertine affair, a transposed homosexual passion. This priority inescapably suggests that heterosexual love provides the rules for homosexual, and the disguise suggests a further desire to be like it, to simulate. Consistently one finds this instinct for secrecy or disguise in Proust. Though passion is made to look more regular than it is, it is also shown on constant watch for deviations to which love is especially liable: Swann suspects Odette of straightforward deceptions, until someone puts in his head that she has had relations with girls, which opens the possibility that he has misread every sign, or missed much of what Odette feels and communicates in the time he spends with her. So he imagines glances he paid no attention to as the means of arranging furtive meetings with the other half of humanity from which he imagined no threat to emanate.

Vinteuil is something like an unconfessed invert in the world of art, his talent kept a secret simply because he is so used to incomprehension that he no longer displays it, so even the music lovers he has known all his life remain unaware he is a real composer. In a less dramatic but similar way, artistic sensitivity is like homosexual inclination, rare, unpopular, and highly prized in others by its possessors, who do not think that it does the owner himself any great good.

This isn't a view of art which Proust invented, but he gives it perhaps the most seductively ramifying expression ever. In a way it is only half the story: Françoise, the narrator's servant inherited from his family, can be taken as the exemplar of a contrary aspect of his view – in which the French peasant, without giving it a thought, lives nearer the heart of reality than we can ever come. For us, our learning and the comprehension granted by art are of central value, but in the scale of ultimate truth they count for little, next to the unconscious wisdom of simple folk. Proust tries very hard to profess this heresy sincerely, but it usually has a flavour of Franciscan poverty about it, stemming from well-meant choice made late in life.

The contrary kind of moment seems less complicated by defects of conviction – self-communion in rhapsodies made of memories, while one's present companions sit around waiting for one's soul to return to one's body, if they've even noticed the absence. Such intense solitudes are the highest spiritual states, activated by physical signs like the change in pressure, strange sky-colours, and gusts of an approaching storm – but quickly retreating to wander in imagination along a far distant stream inhaling forgotten odours. If a sensuous experience, it is sensuous in an even more preserved or candied way than paintings are. Such reverie, Proust realized afresh, belonged in the realm of art even before it left the mind. But one cannot stop there. As usual in this writer a double motion carries us first away from and then toward society. The rhapsodic moment is the capstone of a piece of architecture, built in isolation, of private materials, but capable in the end of dispassionate communicable analysis.

Experiences which perform these crowning or ruling functions are usually obscure, like the two ways, obscurities appended to or trailed by a prior obscurity, a village deep in the country, from which depart two paths leading nowhere much, or leading back to their start, leading to certain flowers, via certain odours or heat-effects. At the end of the whole Combray section, when he circles back to the paths, they become obscurely tangled with his mother's bedtime visits to his room, as if they are a deflected, less obvious version of her. Even the epiphany of her nightly appearance is already somewhat apparitional – an anomalous messenger from the other realm, from which one is oneself barred.

Repeatedly the moments containing the most precious suggestions are only semi-palpable, are brief or seasonal, and though founded on objects, like the distance between the church steeples of the villages seen from afar, elusive and in some way just phantasms.

The pretentious hostess Madame Verdurin appears ludicrous when claiming that she is so affected by her favourite pieces of music that she cannot bear to hear them played, or that she feels full after inspecting the grapes on a chair back, and finds that they work like an intestinal purge. She invites Swann to finger the bronze mounts on her furniture, and he is too polite to stop when he has had enough. So she mistakes his behaviour for enthusiasm and decides to encourage this abandonment.

But she is not entirely remote from the author's own physical relation to art or sense experience, for what in Mme Verdurin is hollow pretence verges in Proust on painful fact, that one is killed by what gives one pleasure, that the intensest sensations are incapacitating, and that receptiveness having crossed a certain threshold is pathological. So the narrator finds that the hawthorns he loves make him ill, in asthmatic attacks connected above all with the invisible and indefinable odours arising from the crown of nature, the blooms of a small number of plants.

So, as is well known, Proust in later life became a strange kind of invalid, protected from light, sounds, and pollen, shielded from the most pleasing and exciting features of the natural world as if shut in a vacuum flask. In fact it is the precise reverse of Mme Verdurin's fate, who overwhelmed reality, professing to be overwhelmed by it. Proust erected analgesic screens of art around his darkened bed to filter or moderate the primary force of sense experience, while the hostess gave herself away by inverting the true apportionment of crudity and refinement, loud and soft, importunate and tactful in art and life outside it.

But her dream of powerlessness in the presence of art, of a response so strong that one fears for the physical safety of the organism which undergoes it, remains an alluring fantasy to one like Proust so committed (for reasons forever inexplicable) to the central significance of art, who knows at the same time that for the greater part of mankind the disappearance of all *true* artistic accomplishment would not be lamented or even perceived. Such disparities as that – one's own overmastering need for art, the general indifference – will occasionally drive one to make unreasonable claims – that art is another, higher range of existence, that it grants something like immortality in its presence, that it dwarfs everything outside the magic circle of its influence.

Devoting himself to love, Swann prefers life to art, and such is the mental setting provided by the narrator that this seems a very bold and original decision. The narrator himself claims that he is spurred to the finest perceptual discriminations, between pearly and dull tones in Parisian skies, by the question of whether Gilberte will go outside on a given day, and hence whether he will see her.

At first we take this as a reversal of the world's values, a way of saying that personal things count most, and that delicate skills are properly slaves of the ego's desires. But the contest between art and its rival is protracted over the whole length of the work, and the force which appears to be winning at the start suffers mounting reverses in the later volumes.

Even in the early stages, where sexual desire is proclaimed stronger than anything else, there is a certain air of trampling on truths one can't permanently deny, which one always knew would find a way of reasserting themselves. Besides, as it is one of the book's philosophical functions to show, longing is an aesthetic phenomenon, too, as it were a trick on us played by our imagination, which appears to take the part of the other, as if it sought new ways to oppress us.

But that great triumph, to claim for the shaping power of imagination the manufacture of the most awful sensation of insufficiency one ever feels, to say it is oneself who engineers this after all, is long deferred. In the meantime, we can see that Proust's mind is spoken to most powerfully by art-effects, or by nature when it resembles art. So that from an early stage in the narrative, whatever he may say to the contrary, we feel that the god presiding over this whole temple-complex is the deified Art, seen detached from its conditions of manufacture and its maker. There are artists in the book and there is art, but the connection between them is broken or in some way unfathomable, the explanation being that there is really no way the men we know as Vinteuil, Elstir, and Bergotte could produce these enthralling notes, canvases, and pages. There remains an essential discontinuity between ordinary human nature and the deathless transfigurations of art.

Even Odette's clothes partake of the miracle which occurs when material things become expressive, and creases, flounces, rows of buttons, or piping in a different fabric convey moods and subtleties of approach which are beyond human faces and limbs by themselves. When she changes to lighter weaves and colours in recognition of spring's approach, letting a small bird or some flowers appear on her hat, the narrator is more overcome than by actual flowers and fields, because though awkward to a degree, and clearly simulacra of another reality, these signs are all painstakingly *meant*, so whatever their inadequacy (and they are not exactly what they are saying) they leave room for, in fact demand, interpretive response as the streams and skies of even the loveliest countryside do not.

The narrator voices early in his long, unconsummated love affair with the old Italian towns the perverse theory that countries for which we yearn occupy us far more than those in which we happen to live. Gradually the meaning of Florence, Pisa, and Venice becomes clear: they are places of which he will so persistently dream that going there will become increasingly impossible. The first time such a journey is mooted various stages of anticipation are traversed until we come to vivid imaginings of what clothes he will pack, prompted by his father's warnings of cold weather. This leads the boy to change the air of his room in imagination for Venetian air, from which he apparently takes a chill, for the next day he has a sore throat and fever which cause him to be forbidden travel for at least a year.

In some part of himself the reader rejoices at this, the Italian cities already standing, against their gold backgrounds, for inviolable sanctities, which preserve their purity better if we go on endlessly revising our ideas of them. Not that they can be preserved as ideal bodies simply by being placed beyond the range of visits, for there must continue to be this delicate seesaw by which they always run the risk of assuming a disappointing gross reality.

Translated into social terms, such idealism takes the dispiriting form of snobbery. From the earliest times the narrator has shown himself susceptible to the magic of aristocratic titles. The first inkling of this is connected with the windows in the church at Combray, full of richly coloured heraldry and naive pictures of quasi-mythical forebears of the Guermantes. That family appears to him first in this phantasmagoric, semi-molten form linked to religion, though if his concentration on the glass is an expression of residual piety, it is equally a violation of it, the conversion of spirit to sensuality.

In any case the Guermantes begin as an idea – though the owners and Platonic essence of Combray, they have apparently never, or at least rarely, paid it a visit. They begin as pure Name, which the author loads with astonishing wealths and depths of significance.

When he comes to meet them in theatres and drawing rooms they continue to express entirely different meanings through actions which only look like those of ordinary mortals. When a Princesse passes a Duc a sweetmeat, saying much what any ordinary person would say, and if divergent, *less* expressive than average, this is a tremendous condescension or playing at life, a means of protecting her real life (consisting of truly unimaginable gestures and murmurings) from profane gaze while wishing at the same time to give pleasure by doing something understandable to the mass of mankind.

Similarly when ordinary artisans and respectable bourgeois persons like the narrator's family rent quarters in the Parisian hotel of the Guermantes, it does not bring them closer to the condition of aristocrats, but is like the funny little shops formerly clustered against the sides of cathedrals. If anything, physical contiguity makes the spiritual abyss more vividly evident.

There is a character who is said to have devoted ten years to the dream of being visited by the Duchesse and Princesse de Guermantes, to have made steady if slow progress, and to hope that five more years will prove sufficient, except that the project is now threatened by a fatal illness which may or may not grant her that many years of life. In Proust we meet over again the claim (which we found in Stendhal) that certain of his characters cause every head to turn and every eye to follow them as they pass.

In the low view, this motif is a vision of exclusiveness and superiority. Or one can see it as pseudo-Dantesque, a sad translation of the celestial hierarchy, of a world which has true pinnacles or centres. And finally, one must concede that the book chronicles the narrator's disillusion with these and other ideas, that the history of his mental life is the progressive depopulation of the realm of the Absolute, as various hoped vehicles of perfection are discarded in turn, sexual passion, high society, even art in some of its disguises.

However impatient we become from time to time with the narrator's credulity, each retraction produces a sense of loss. Proust's snobbery was, among other things, the dream of a rich and passionate life, in which every glance held momentous meanings. When they are over, such ideas of concealment seem little more than a wish that there should be a great deal beneath an unremarkable surface. But who has not longed, when telling friends goodbye and finding himself at a loss for real feeling, for richer relations than we ever have, for the uninhibited congress with other people which life is too bare of, sending us into books like Proust's to seek.

The great event of the narrator's maturity, the love affair with Albertine, is a protracted failure: his possession of her feels more and more like a form of loss as time goes on. Living with a prisoner becomes a way of being one. Among the most powerful figures and sensations through-out the book have been various renderings of being shut up in rooms – the sun on a carpet or breaking in at the window, like the comparison of opening the curtains to removing the linen wrappings from a gold sarcophagus within. Beneath much of the mental extravagance so continual in this writer is a strong sense of the self held prisoner, of a field in some way pitifully limited, above which the mind constructs its fictitious flights.

For a long time Albertine was shut in; after she disappears the narrator becomes more reclusive, his existence a living death or a dangerous illness. Paradoxically this virtual cessation has been accompanied by an opening out, and he is granted an answer to the aimlessness of an existence hitherto devoted to holding onto or capturing experiences or human subjects which attempt to escape by some deep principle of their being.

He understands his grandmother's love only when she begins to be taken away. On the telephone without her face to help him, he sees the utter unselfishness of her voice, which raises him to a kind of exaltation he has never felt in her presence, as if it needed the clinical isolation of a single factor for the real nature of the whole to come through, or as if only the threatened disappearance of what one values would ever cause one to register it correctly.

Hers is a death which stands for something else, a premonition of the end of all human ties, and his nearest approach to his own mother's end. As his relation with *her* mother was purer, so his relation to that earlier death is less troubled, more exemplary. The witty description of how reality is enhanced for the deaf man, because a sense subtracted leaves more room and peace for the rest of one's faculties to play in, is a cheerful version of the same theme. Loss is seriously brought forward as one of the world's principal beauties or meanings.

The narrator's own death is elaborately foreshadowed in two others, which come not very near the end of the whole. As before, there are at the same time brief, infrequent, but drastic comments on the narrator's health. He has little life left in him, and is capable of almost no exertion, claims which are contradicted – like many of the suggestions about his age – by almost every other word of the text.

Proust's death is imaged in the ends of Swann and Bergotte, from both of which we feel strangely detached. We have lost sight of Swann and are caught off guard by mention of his illness, already far advanced. It has effected a convulsion in his attitudes and habits which only makes him more like himself. Like the well-mannered person he is, Swann avoids all reference to his pain and fear, until one day he decides to tell his great friend the Duchesse de Guermantes. This lands her in a difficult spot. She is torn between the important intelligence that Swann is dying, and the wish to be on time for dinner. So she chooses to disbelieve the frankest truth the ironist has ever uttered, and rushes off to change her black shoes for red ones.

Bergotte endures his final illness characteristically, deciding near the end that he must see a certain painting of Vermeer's again, and dragging himself half-dead to Holland, where a small patch of yellow wall makes him revise his ideas about art, and dream of writing in a wholly different way. But the journey has hastened his death, and his plans for further work remain intimations only.

Both these deaths are martyrdoms, the first of a number. It is a persistent pattern in the latter half of the work, Charlus the most lurid, the narrator the most discreet, like a sentence half-uttered. Swann's world has not kept faith with him. Odette's surprising social climb is founded on anti-Semitism, and their daughter (rumours now undermine Swann's paternity) becomes a snob and forbids mention of his name. By this time the narrator is seeing her again, his oldest passion, now grown cold and abstract, so she contributes to Swann's oblivion in his mind too.

The narrator is haunted by a sense of his own disloyalties and betrayals, which seems strange to us in view of his devotion to his mother, his grandmother, and the places he has known longest. But, as he apparently denies (while remaining in some way true to) his Jewishness and homosexuality, he lets Albertine and Venice usurp the places of the older women, if not permanently, long enough to see that he can perform great wickedness indeed. He is guilty of another betrayal, in some way greater still, the denial of his vocation. Throughout the years of idleness the saving truth is withheld from him that one may need to waste one's life to retrieve it completely. When this illumination comes, it is almost too late. But that is another story and must be deferred.

The sense of waste overtakes the book in the middle. If Swann is the author's good angel, the Baron de Charlus is his bad, a bogey raised among other things to warn him of the dangers of indulging one's desires without restraint. As one would expect, theirs is a tangled relation. In this character who looms so large over the later sections of the book, so much more vivid than Swann, Proust expresses repulsion and pity, equally mixed, for the parts of himself he found most alien and hardest to broach.

Charlus first appears all-powerful – haughty, witty, profoundly intelligent – better than others and the object of their envy and desire. His unmasking is the most striking of many on the same pattern. Things and people are not what they seem; reality practices ludicrous deception after deception on us, most commonly in the form of mistakes about sexual identity. This particular focus isn't accidental of course, and has a secret tendentious aim, but it also stands for others, and is the instance we happen to hit on of the metamorphic nature of perception.

From time to time Proust tries to lend this unmasking an appearance of relativism. His characters are each of the incompatible qualities which we have successively believed to be the whole truth about them. Although the consequences for our view of knowing are indeed profound, these episodes are not so undermining as to make us think there is no truth except in the beholder.

No, for there is a corollary to 'Things aren't what they seem,' which is 'Things aren't what they were,' and the moral tendency of both processes is similar. We continually uncover not secret goodness, or even neutral difference, but secret flaws and failings. Likewise historical development and the march of generations is a sad tale of decline. By the end of the book the Princesse and Duchesse de Guermantes have been replaced or are scheduled for replacement by usurpers whose unfitness makes one gasp, though causing as well the perverse satisfaction of seeing anything turned upside down.

The Duchesse's title will be taken by the offspring of a Jew and a whore, whom she refused for years even to meet, the Princesse's by the vulgar poseuse Verdurin. So the pattern is far from a random flicker of mistakes and half truths appearing and disappearing. It is a heavily accented picture of decay and dissolution. A new generation rises to take the place of those who have fallen, but bogus, vapid, colourless to the point of non-existence. Earlier selves of the older characters are purer, earlier holders of shifting titles, realer.

Charlus provides the key signature for the whole section, a bitter comedy of social cruelty. He is a gigantic figure but monstrous, and Proust wreaks on him and hence on part of himself a horrible vengeance which culminates in the visit to a homosexual brothel in wartime Paris, where, with bombs dropping outside, a collection of social wreckage indulges passions like pointless parodies of the sufferings of war. Charlus is chained and beaten, a saint whose only fear is that his tormentors aren't sincere, but simply actors, or *half*-serious/*part*-vicious.

Such is the strange phosphorescent glare of Proust's last volumes that these dark dungeons are only a step removed from the drawing rooms where other kinds of murders are planned. It is a side of him we hardly guessed, the wit wilder, more annihilating, and makes us think of his searching pages on Dostoevsky's fascination with crime.

But he leads us through society as through a barren wilderness not to abandon us there but to deepen our desire for the way out, intermittently announced. Death has been his introduction to life, a life without illusion. The cruelties met in its gathering places have helped cure him of his attraction to society. Deaths or the spectacle of aging make him turn from persons to the impersonal, work; and there the moralist he has become rejoins the aesthete, and both the main divisions of his nature find their use.

Much time has passed. The narrator has forgotten Albertine, has returned to Combray and repeated the old walks in the other direction with much less emotion. Then he withdraws to a sanatorium, and on returning to Paris finds an invitation which calls him back to the world. The old name Guermantes scrawled at the bottom still has the power to summon him forth. But he sets out in a strange, excited state, leaves his carriage in the streets near the Champs Elysées, the Guermantes having moved to a less venerable part of Paris, and meets another traveller, like one of his Guermantes memories. It is Charlus, who is in no condition to attend a party. He has suffered a stroke and become a kingly baby whose wit and snobbery are reduced to a gentle imbecility.

The narrator rides some more, then walks again, and coming into the courtyard of the Guermantes' replacement-palace, full of memories and apprehensions, not looking where he steps, stumbles on the uneven stones of incomplete paving. The chance mis-step sets off one of those illuminations like the madeleine steeped in tea. Searching for the source of the radiance, Proust realizes it is the floor of a church in Venice. He mounts the stair in ecstasy and is kept waiting in a little vestibule because his hostess won't allow a piece of music which has begun to be disturbed by the entrance of new guests.

In the tiny room lined with books it happens again. A servant trying to be quiet causes a silver spoon to ring against a saucer, and Marcel has a hallucination of pine trees outside the window of a halted train. To occupy him while he waits they bring him petits fours and orangeade and when he picks up the starched napkin to wipe his mouth, he smells the sea at Balbec.

Now his greatest fear is that he will be called before he manages to extract the lesson from these enigmatic impressions. For it feels to him that he is being told something, and given direction about what to do with his life. The intensity of these conjunctions shows him a way of triumphing over time, through materials which already exist within him.

He is carrying his work at this moment, and need only shut himself up to find it. In the time left to him he is able to sketch out the respective parts of his mother, Swann, Albertine, and Charlus, their part, that is, in the formation of himself.

And then with everything settled and the future mapped out before him, he is called back to the world and admitted to the party, a summons which appears to form a discord with this great summons to solitary effort among the figures of the past. He turns from books to life absolutely incandescent with new knowledge. His lonely ecstasy has equipped him as never before to interpret the passing show of the world, and there follow fifty of the most glittering, exuberant, disillusioned pages in all of literature.

Proust brings his great work to a close in the distracting hubbub of a large party, as viewed by one returning after many years who finds everyone so altered he thinks they've assumed disguises for a masked ball. It is a spectacle whose infinite sadness takes grotesque form. Beautiful women from the past appear as cumbersome jewel-laden sacred fishes. Familiar voices issue from deep within unrecognizable masses of wrinkles. And the narrator learns that he is himself old: the old ones greet him as their oldest friend.

His consolation is that these cruel discoveries can only enrich his work, as we have seen even Swann's failure to recognize him in their last meeting do. The final determining impression is the sight of Gilberte's daughter moving toward him, like a crossroads in the forest where all paths meet, where different parts of his past lead off in their several directions, Swann and the Guermantes, seriousness and beauty, at a momentary point of contact.

On his way out he suffers giddiness (a symptom Proust in these years knew very well). Three times, like a creature in a fairy tale or in the Arabian Nights, which become towards the end his model for the power of stories to outwit death, three times he is on the point of falling. The illumination which began in stumbling backward ends in pitching forward, and in the strange figure of the rememberer perched on his memories as on living stilts, tall as the church towers which lit Proust's youth, a giant steeped in the ocean of time.

So the greatest of books is fulfilled among books with the decision to write, a less embracing experience than the ageing and dying which envelop it. But that is only the decision's local form, its covering of accident because its undergoer is studious in spite of everything. For his prompting is really the resolve to dedicate himself, and to assume the burden of manhood. It is one of the wonders of this particular life that such discovery of purpose should abut so closely an imminent death.

Proust has refurbished an old pattern of spiritual election, or the voice from the cloud which summons the prophet. The final elevation of art is more than that, an invitation to immortality which comes from the blue and knits up the whole, which changes the meaning of the work, and leaves the author standing at its entrance. From such an end and a beginning we cannot easily tear ourselves away, for the sensation that the book stops here is a kind of illusion. It ends because at this point his life ended and his work began.

INDEX